JACK THE RIPPER

JACK THE RIPPER

QUEST FOR A KILLER

M J TROW

True Crime

Published in conjunction with 'Jack the Ripper: Killer Revealed', an Atlantic Productions film in association with Discovery Channel, Science Channel and FremantleMedia Enterprises

First published in Great Britain in 2009 by
Wharncliffe True Crime
an imprint of
Pen & Sword Books Ltd
47 Church Street
Barnsley
South Yorkshire
S70 2AS

Printed and bound in England by
MPG Books

Pen & Sword Books Ltd incorporates the imprints of Pen & Sword Aviation, Pen & Sword Maritime, Pen & Sword Military, Wharncliffe Local History, Pen and Sword Select, Pen and Sword Military Classics, Leo Cooper, Remember When, Seaforth Publishing and Frontline Publishing.

For a complete list of Pen & Sword titles please contact
PEN & SWORD BOOKS LIMITED
47 Church Street, Barnsley, South Yorkshire, S70 2AS, England
E-mail: enquiries@pen-and-sword.co.uk
Website: www.pen-and-sword.co.uk

Contents

'The identity of the elusive killer is an abiding mystery which has engaged the minds and imaginations of every generation and ... make no mistake about it – the field is still wide open.'

James Tully – *The Secret of Prisoner 1167:*
Was this man Jack the Ripper? 1997

'Most sensible writers accept that Jack was a local man, of the same class as those he murdered and was someone the victims would readily have accepted as one of their own.'

John H Eddleston – *Jack the Ripper; An Encyclopaedia,* 2002

List of Maps

List of Plates

Acknowledgements

My thanks for help in writing this book must go first and foremost to my wife, Carol, whose photographs, copy-editing and all-round enthusiasm are, as always, invaluable. To Rupert Harding and his team at Pen and Sword, for meeting impossible deadlines. To Elliot McCaffrey and his team at Atlantic Productions for their faith in me. To Professor Laurence Alison, Director of the Centre for Critical and Major Incident Research, University of Liverpool; Spencer Chainey of the Jill Dando Institute, University College London; Alan Humphries, Librarian of the Thackray Museum, Leeds and Dr Peter Dean, Coroner for Suffolk and South East Essex, for their professionalism and insight; and to Ripper expert John Bennett for his profound knowledge of Jack's killing fields.

Chapter 1

The Problem:
The House That Jack Built

The bare facts are these. In the Autumn of 1888 a disputed number of women, all of them prostitutes, were murdered in the East End of London, by person or persons unknown. Because the killer was never caught, in itself the result of extraordinary luck on his part and ineptitude on the part of the police force of the time, a whole industry has grown up around the case, taking us further and further away from the truth.

The myth of the man who was Jack the Ripper began on 24 September 1888 when an anonymous letter was sent to Sir Charles Warren, Commissioner of the Metropolitan Police at Scotland Yard. Intriguingly, bearing in mind what we now know about the psychology of serial killers, its opening sentence is darkly real – 'I do wish to give myself up I am in misery with nightmare ...'[1]

It smacks of another serial offender, William Heirens, who, having stabbed and shot Frances Brown in Chicago in December 1945 scrawled with her lipstick on the wall above her body, 'For heaven's sake catch me before I kill more. I cannot control myself.'[2]

But in fact, the letter to Charles Warren was a hoax, as were nearly all the other 220 letters and postcards sent to the police and the Press in the months surrounding the Whitechapel murders.

It was the second letter, sent to the Central News Agency in New Bridge Street three days later that captured the public's imagination and launched the phenomenon that shows no sign of abating today. 'Dear Boss,' it began, and gloated over the 'grand job', the 'funny little games' and apologized for having to write in red ink because 'the proper *red* stuff' had congealed. It gave a deadly motive for the crimes

– 'I am down on whores' – but most importantly, it gave the 'trade name', 'Yours truly, Jack the Ripper'.

Today, informed opinion follows senior police officers' views at the time that this was a piece of journalistic mischief, posted to his own office by Thomas J Bulling of the Central News Agency. If this is so, then the 'Dear Boss' was a very 'in' joke, because the editor-in-chief who would have received it was John Moore, quite possibly in on the whole thing. Another possibility is that the author was John Best, a freelance who wrote for the *Star*, working with the connivance of its editor, T P O'Connor. In a sense, it does not matter who wrote the 'Dear Boss' letter. What is important is that as soon as it was published, a rash of 'copy-cats' followed and the infamous name stuck for ever. Right through to October 1896, missives in all sorts of handwriting and styles created the kernel of the myth.

One came from George of the High Rip Gang, one of the dozens of armed and dangerous low-life who terrorized the East End. Another was written by Jack the Cunquerer [sic]; a third by 'Yours when caught, the Whore Killer'. They were not confined to London postmarks, proving how quickly the Ripper phenomenon became national and eventually international. One Jack was hiding in a quarry in Plymouth on 10 October 1888. Another one was enjoying a holiday in Leicester on the same day. 'Mr Englishman', rather annoyed that his work had been hijacked by the Ripper, wrote indignantly to complain from Colchester. 'JR' was busy by the middle of the month at the Leylands in Leeds and 'HTB', though writing from Portsmouth, threatened not only to murder several rich women in Clerkenwell, but Lady Warren, wife of the Police Commissioner.

A Frenchman, giving himself the gloriously exotic name 'Isidore Vasyvair' wrote to 'Monsieur le Chef de la Police' early in October, and on the same day the Ripper wrote from Dublin, but claimed to live in Calcutta. In an obvious pastiche of Bulling/Best, 'Jack, o estripador' wrote from Lisbon on 24 October. A scholarly letter from Philadelphia arrived later that month, taunting the 'Scotland Yard boys' and promising, once the writer has the 'lay of the locality' to rip and cull between twenty and forty more victims.

The hoaxers who began the Ripper industry throw a spotlight on the bizarre mindset of 1888. To my knowledge, no one has analyzed these letters in terms of psychology. Most of them exhibit gallows humour with bad drawings of knives, skulls, guns, coffins and dripping blood. They abound with 'ha has' and endless criticism of the police, for being unable to catch them. Some are barely literate – 'Dear Sir, I drop a line to say hav sniped enother and send ...so I'll do me job furst he gon on catle bote or with muckers Yours truly JR. Rite gain in a weak.' Some are highly literate – 'I am writing to you this while in bed with a sore throat, but as soon as it is better I will set to work again' – this one purported to be a policeman. One was in verse form:

The Miller's Court murder a disgusting affair
Done by a Polish Knacker[3] rather fair
The morn (of the murder) I went to the place –
Had a shine but left in haste.
I spoke to a policeman who saw the sight
And informed me it was done by a Knacker in the night ...

Some letters were intensely personal – 'old Charles Warren shall die' Jack wrote on 4 October. And on the 15th, Mr Smith (possibly Major Henry Smith, acting commissioner of the City of London Police) read in his post, 'A few line to you to let you know that you will soon meet your death. I have been watching you lately...' By December, there was clearly a feud going on when Mrs Shirley of Upper Holloway was informed that her husband – 'the carroty looking cur', 'the ginger looking swine' was a target of Jack the Ripper. Mr Shirley's crime? 'If he is clever at nothing else, he is a pretty good hand at getting children.'

Individuals are mentioned who have no known links with the Whitechapel murders – Polly Wright was one; Luisa Whitring another; Mary Bateman a third. Some have odd political references. On 3 November an untidy hand scrawled a resolution passed by the council of midnight wanderers of Belfast, offering 'hearty fraternal congratulations to "Jack the Ripper" on the grand success he has recently scored'. The 1880s was a dangerous decade for Anglo-Irish relations, with the Irish secretary murdered in Phoenix Park, Dublin and a Fenian bomb demolishing part of Scotland Yard.

There was also a fanatical, religious mania theme that crops up frequently – 'Dear friend,' began one forwarded by the News Agency to Chief Constable Adolphus Williamson at the Yard, '...If she [a corpse found in Whitehall and not Ripper-related] was an honest woman I will hunt down and destroy her murderer. If she was a whore God will bless the hand that slew her, for the women of Moab and Midian shall die and their blood mingle with the dust... Do as I do and the light of glory shall shine upon you.'

The most disturbing letters prove that if the Whitechapel murderer was one of the first of his kind, there was no shortage of psychopaths in Victorian England – 'No animal like a nice woman – the fat are the best'; 'I have been offered double money for her womb and lower part of the body... I do like to find them nice parts'; 'you had better be careful! How you send those Bloodhounds about the streets because of the single females wearing stained napkins – women smell very strong when they are unwell.'[4]

Behind the bewildering variety of letters – which also offered the clearly helpless police equally useless advice on how to catch the killer – stalked the Victorian Press. The 1880s was perhaps the first decade that saw the convergence of two major improvements in society. One was the increase in literacy created by compulsory education for the first time (Mundella's Act of 1881) and the other was the cheap manufacture of paper from wood pulp and the improvement of the speed of printing presses. This led to a new proliferation of newspapers and a readership hungry for news. What sold newspapers, then as now, were sex and ''orrible murder' and since sex was a taboo subject for polite society, vicious crime naturally stole the headlines. George Newnes, one of the advocates of the 'New Journalism' summed it all up admirably when he wrote to W T Stead of the *Pall Mall Gazette*:

> There is one kind of journalism which makes and unmakes Cabinets, upsets Governments, builds navies and does many other great things. That is your journalism. There is another kind which has no such ambitions. That is my journalism. A journalism that pays.[5]

Today, police forces work closely with the Press, especially in major investigations like multiple murder. In 1888 the policy of the police – more so the Met than the City Force perhaps[6] – was to give no information to journalists at all. They were even excluded where possible from murder sites and discouraged from attending coroners' inquests. Consequently, reporters felt edged out and took out their spleen on police performance. It was not good, but a bitter Press made it seem worse, from national magazines like *Punch* to local papers such as the *East London Advertiser*. The more determined newshounds skulked around police stations like the one in Leman Street, Whitechapel to collar witnesses as they left. Israel Schwartz, a Hungarian Jew who saw Elizabeth Stride shortly before she was murdered was one of these; so was George Hutchinson who gave an extraordinarily detailed description of a man he saw talking to Mary Kelly on the night she died in Miller's Court.

People who might be reticent about talking to the police[7] could be persuaded for the price of a pint (three farthings in 1888) to chat for hours to a newspaperman and, as with Chinese whispers, the stories grew out of all proportion and created a whole forest of mythological trees which modern researchers have to chop down. When stories were not detailed or interesting enough, there was always pressure on harassed, deadline-haunted journalists to make them up. This is almost certainly where the legend of Fairy Fay began – the Ripper's supposed first victim who never actually existed. The *Daily Telegraph* and *Reynold's News* between them whipped up this tale from a mish-mash of other assault cases in an effort to keep the Ripper story alive in relatively quiet periods (there was, for example, no attack for the month of October 1888).

But if the *Telegraph*, *Reynold's News*, *The Times*, the *East London Observer*, the *Star* and the *Daily News* got it wrong (which they all did from time to time)[8] they are all models of journalistic rectitude by comparison with the *Illustrated Police News*. Founded in 1864, in clear imitation of the *Illustrated London News*, this paper had no links with the police whatsoever and its lurid tabloid drawings are what most people conjure up when discussing the Whitechapel murders today. For example, in reporting the 'double event' killing of Liz Stride and Kate Eddowes on 30 September, the cover showed a completely invented face purporting to be the 'Berner St Victim' (Stride) in life, a truly awful profile of Inspector Edmund Reid who was the investigating officer and a series of re-creations of the scene. In no sensible order: Liz Stride is shown 'going to her doom' talking with her killer; Constable Watkins summoning assistance with his whistle in Mitre Square (although he did not carry one); Louis Diemschutz (with no sign of the horse and cart we know he had on this occasion) finding the Berner Street victim; a mortuary scene at St George's-in-the-East with the fifth victim under a shroud; her sister in profile; the crowd in Berner Street once news had got out; and Louis Diemschutz again (now with horse and cart) finding the body and a policeman throwing the light of his bulls-eye lantern on Kate Eddowes' mutilated remains. 'Two More Whitechapel Horrors', the paper trumpeted. 'When will the murderer be captured?' The answer, we now know, was never.

As the years passed – the Ripper case was officially closed in 1892 – retired policemen, very aware of the huge furore the case had caused and perhaps to whitewash themselves or exaggerate their importance, added cryptic comments which are usually far from helpful. Sir Robert Anderson was appointed Head of the CID on 31 August 1888 – by coincidence the date of Mary Ann (Polly) Nichols' murder – and did little more than place the competent Chief Inspector Donald Swanson in charge of the case before going to Switzerland (again, by coincidence on the day of Annie Chapman's murder) on the advice of his doctor who believed the man to be overworked! Not until 6 October, by which time Stride and Eddowes had been added to Jack's tally, did he actually take up his post. In 1907 he wrote *Criminals and Crime* and three years later *The Lighter Side of My Official Life.* This was first serialized in *Blackwood's Magazine* and contains two statements which are not only unbelievably smug and complacent (he had, after all, failed to catch Jack) but have fuelled endless speculation and contributed to the Ripper legend:

> I am almost tempted to disclose the identity of the murderer and of the pressman who wrote the ['Dear Boss'] letter... But *no public benefit would result from such a course* [my italics] and the traditions of my old department would suffer. I will merely add that the only person who ever had a good view of the murderer unhesitatingly identified the suspect the instant he was confronted with him; but he refused to give evidence against him. In saying he was a Polish Jew I am merely stating a definitely ascertained fact.[9]

This is of course an appalling example of journalese and how easy it is to claim knowledge where there can be no comeback. The 'he' in the penultimate line could be either the witness or the killer and it is to the credit of modern researchers Paul Begg and Martin Fido that they were able to identify a possible 'face' that fits – Aaron Kosminski.

Melville Macnaghten became Assistant Chief Constable in June 1889. His memoirs *Days of My Years* appeared in 1914 and was not helpful but he did leave the tantalizing Memoranda, written in 1894 and given to researcher Daniel Farson by his daughter, Christabel, Lady Aberconway, seventy years later. Even more so than Anderson's suspect and Anderson's witness, Macnaghten's Memoranda are minefields of dubious information. To begin with, there are three versions, which make them suspect in themselves. The Scotland Yard file version, discovered by researcher Donald Rumbelow in 1975, begins with the mantra we have heard so often now that it is difficult to think outside that particular box – 'Now the Whitechapel Murderer had 5 victims – & 5 victims only' – and he itemizes them; Mary Ann Nichols, Annie Chapman, Elizabeth Stride, Catherine Eddowes and Mary Jane Kelly. 'No one ever saw the Whitechapel Murderer,' he says in flat contradiction of Anderson, but he makes the reasonable point that the mentally ill Thomas Cutbush, put forward as a suspect by the *Sun* in February 1894, is less likely to be the killer than three others whom he lists. Thomas Hayne Cutbush was the nephew of a police superintendent and was admitted to the Lambeth Workhouse Infirmary as a lunatic on 5 March 1891. Having escaped from there, he stabbed two women, Florence Johnson and Isabelle Anderson, in the buttocks on 9 March. As Macnaghten says:

> It seems highly improbable that the murderer would have suddenly stopped in November '88 and been content to recommence operations by prodding a girl behind some 2 years & 4 months afterwards.

His three more likely suspects however – M J Druitt 'said to be a doctor [sic] and of good family'; Kosminski, 'a Polish Jew & resident of Whitechapel'; and Michael Ostrog, 'a Russian doctor [sic] and a convict' – have turned out to be three more red herrings, effectively cleared by modern research. We shall discuss them in more detail in a later chapter.

The problem with senior policemen's memoirs, apart from the passage of time involved in all such works, is the frustrating awareness that they may have known more than we do by virtue of being on the spot. A great deal of hard evidence on the Ripper case has vanished, more by accident than design and who knows what gems the missing files might have contained? Anderson and Macnaghten may have been in possession of these lost facts.

Middle-ranking policemen like Inspector Frederick Abberline are equally guilty of muddying the waters. Originally from Dorset, Abberline had worked as an inspector in Whitechapel's H Division of the Met for several years before his transfer to the Yard in 1887. Beloved of film-makers in our own time, Abberline was once believed to have written diaries claiming a royal and Masonic connection with the killer. These are known to be forgeries, but some of his attributed comments have started various hares among Ripperologists. When Severin Klosowski aka George Chapman was arrested for the murder of his wife in 1903, Abberline said to his old colleague, the arresting officer Inspector George Godley, 'I see you've got the Ripper at last.' In a subsequent article for the *Pall Mall Gazette*, Abberline admitted that Chapman's behaviour and antecedents fitted well with 'the man we struggled so hard to capture fifteen years ago'. He sailed into dangerous waters when he claimed that it was not inconsistent for a man to change his method of operations (Chapman was a poisoner) and indeed his motive (in Chapman's case, greed) over time. Abberline was wrong on both counts.

Walter Dew was a detective constable who had been with H Division for a year when Jack struck. 'Blue Serge' as he was known for his famous (and probably, bearing in mind police pay, only) suit, he achieved a kind of immortality in 1910 when he chased H H Crippen and his mistress across the Atlantic with the aid of a fast ship and – a first – wireless communication. His 1935 book *I Caught Crippen* reminds us of the fact that he was one of the first policemen on the ghastly scene of Mary Kelly's murder in Miller's Court. Even police apologists however admit that the book is riddled with mistakes. Police memoirs are usually written years after the event, without access to original notes or official files and inevitably, errors creep in. Recently, researcher Andrew Rose has effectively demolished the case against Crippen by revealing that the supposed body of Belle Elmore (Mrs Crippen) found by police was, in fact, male. It remains to be seen what this does to the reputation of Walter Dew.

After a number of articles and pamphlets appeared in various papers as the century turned, the first full-blown book offering a solution to the murders was *Hvem Var Jack the Ripper?* (Who Was Jack the Ripper?) written by Carl Muusmann in 1908.[10] Since this was a Danish author and work it is good evidence of the international interest in the Whitechapel murders simmering under the surface. Muusmann's Jack was Alois Szemeredy, first mooted as a suspect in 1892 by the *Daily Graphic*. Born in 1844, Szemeredy claimed to be an American surgeon and later a sausage-maker. He almost certainly served in the Austrian army from which he deserted and fled to Buenos Aires before commitment to an asylum in 1885. In August 1889, he was at large in Vienna and possibly emigrated to America. On his return to Austria in 1892, he was arrested on suspicion of murder and committed suicide in prison before coming to trial. There is no reason to suppose he was ever in London, let alone during the 'Autumn of Terror' and he appears as merely the first in a long list of highly unlikely suspects. What is interesting is that the book also set the scene on the foreigner as perpetrator, a myth that has never gone away.

Tom Robinson's *The Whitechapel Horrors, Being an Authentic Account of the Jack the Ripper Murders* failed to impress in 1924 but Leonard Matters' *The Mystery of Jack the Ripper* four years later was regarded as a seminal work. Matters was a widely travelled and well-regarded journalist who was a boy in Australia when Jack struck. He was relying on largely second-hand sources and made mistakes, but the book is workmanlike, with useful and rational observations (especially the updated version of 1948).

By the time Matters wrote, 'worse' examples of serial killers had come out of Weimar Germany – the homosexual cannibal Fritz Haarmann and the indiscriminate sadist Peter Kurten, the 'Monster of Dusseldorf' – and a real attempt to explore motive was the order of the day. Matters' suspect was the elusive 'Dr Stanley' and the plot involved the fact that Stanley's son Herbert met Ripper victim Mary Kelly on Boat Race night 1886 and that she infected him with syphilis from which he died two years later. Heartbroken, Stanley took his knife first to Kelly's friends then, most spectacularly, to Kelly herself before sailing to Buenos Aires where he died in 1918. All this hinged on death-bed confessions, a lurid revenge theory and preposterous plotting. 'Stanley' was clearly a cover for someone else, allegedly an aristocratic surgeon practising at the Charing Cross Hospital and living in Portman Square. As researcher John Eddlestone says, 'The story has more holes than Swiss cheese'[11] and crime writer Edmund Pearson claimed that the theory bore 'about the same relation to the facts of criminology as the exploits of Peter Rabbit and Jerry Muskrat do to zoology'.[12] What Matters' book did was to establish the famous red herring of a murderous doctor, driven mad by whatever pressure, which continues to run through the Ripper story even today.

But if Leonard Matters was writing fiction in 1928, Mrs Belloc Lowndes did it better. Her book, *The Lodger*, written as a short story in 1913, is important because it is the first novel in English on the Whitechapel murders. Within forty years, despite the fact that some of those working on the case, as policemen and journalists, were still alive, Jack's handiwork was now legitimately regarded as entertainment. The book also created the myth – rather like Muusmann's foreigner and Matters' doctor – that the killer was not 'one of us'. He could not be a local, but a mysterious visitor to the area – a lodger with no past, no future and only a terrifying present. The book became a film tie-in and it took the story of the Whitechapel murders even further into la-la land.

The first movie about Jack appeared as early as 1915 when a country reeling from the effects of the First World War was invited to watch *Farmer Spudd and His Missus Take a Trip to Town* directed by J V L Leigh. No copies of this single-reeler survive, but the Spudds' visit to London included Jack in the Chamber of Horrors at Madame Tussauds. The waxwork theme was taken up enthusiastically by Paul Leni in the brilliant tradition of Weimar expressionist film-making in the 1920s. *Das Wachsfigurenkabinett* (The Waxworks) appeared in 1924 and starred Werner Kraus[13] as Jack. Interestingly, Jack is referred to as 'Spring-heeled Jack', a semi-fictitious 'monster' who terrified young women in London in the 1850s. The fictional Jack looked the epitome of a 1920s' German 'toff' with long black coat, black homburg and flying white silk scarf.

Belloc Lowndes' lodger would be played by singer/actor heart-throb Ivor Novello and the subtitle retained on Alfred Hitchcock's film posters was 'A Story of the London Fog'. What *that* did was to create the myth of the notorious London smogs or pea-soupers – 'London particulars' as they were called then – as an explanation of how the Ripper was able to pounce, kill and escape so silently and eerily. In fact, of course, there was no fog on any of the actual murder nights and this book contends that it was this very phenomenon – bad fogs – that helped prevent any killings in October 1888. Novello's wide eyes were by no means as terrifying as those of Laird Cregar in the film's far better remake.

Because Novello was a matinee idol, it was unthinkable that he could be a serial killer, so Mrs Lowndes' original story, which had already been altered for her 1926 book, now underwent further changes for the silent film and still more for the 'talkies' remake of 1932 and the Cregar version of 1944. As Denis Meickle says in *Jack the Ripper: The Murders and the Movies* – 'by this point, the story has moved a very long way from Jack the Ripper'. If Mrs Lowndes loosely based her original anti-hero on one of the East End's oddities of 1888, G Wentworth Bell Smith, a Canadian lodging in Finsbury Square and who kept odd hours, creeping about in crepe-soled shoes, many of the elements now associated with Jack came from her written version and the film. Again, the elegantly dressed man and the shiny black bag are the most obvious examples.

The 1930s saw a proliferation of supposedly factual books on the Whitechapel murders with theories that went in any number of directions. Bearing in mind that no *man* was charged with the killings and perhaps because of the arrival of political equality for women (the vote for twenty-one-year-olds was achieved in 1928) ex-policeman Edwin Woodhall reasoned that the real killer was in fact 'Jill the Ripper'. His 1938 *When London Walked in Terror* managed to conflate the female theory with yet another foreigner. His suspect was a Russian immigrant, Olga Tchkersoff, whose sister Vera had been inveigled into prostitution by Mary Kelly and who died from sepsis after an abortion. The whole thing was lurid in the extreme and it is unlikely that the Tchkersoffs ever existed.

The following year William Stewart went one better with *Jack the Ripper, a New Theory* and again dealt with abortion and focused on Kelly. He made the assumption that the Miller's Court victim was pregnant and that the slaughterhouse was merely a diversion to disguise a bungled termination. Abortion was illegal in Britain in Jack's day and there were certainly midwives who made a little cash on the side by performing the service. A bloodstained *woman* walking the Whitechapel streets would not attract the attention of the police. The ramification of this theory is that at least four other women were also pregnant and used the same midwife, who bungled four more times. Since all four women were probably menopausal at the time, the theory falls apart. The rediscovery in 1987 of Dr Thomas Bond's post-mortem report on Kelly proves categorically that she was not pregnant.

In terms of veering from the truth however, one of the most unfortunate combinations in Ripper research was William Le Queux and Donald McCormick. Both men were involved in espionage and neither could be trusted not to embellish for the sake of a rattling good yarn. Le Queux was a journalist who covered the Ripper murders as they happened for *The Globe* and openly admitted that he and his colleagues vied with each other to produce ever more preposterous theories. His suspect was Dr Alexander Pedachenko, a member of the Russian Ochrana, the secret police, whose brief from the Tsarist government was to embarrass the Metropolitan police by committing crimes they could not solve. The reason? Because Britain willingly accepted Jewish Russian émigrés, some of whom at least were wanted by the Russian government. As if that were not farcical enough, Le Queux claimed to have discovered this from the papers of Grigori Rasputin, murdered by boyars in 1916 for his perceived pernicious hold over the government of Nicholas II. With phrases like 'the greatest and boldest of all Russian criminal lunatics' to describe Pedachenko, Le Queux's rubbish should have died with him in 1927.

Unfortunately, in the 1930s the torch of silly theories was taken up by McCormick. A prolific writer on espionage, (he was a friend of James Bond's creator, Ian Fleming), witchcraft and the occult, McCormick was a dazzling conversationalist and bon viveur. As the authors of the *Jack the Ripper A-Z* put it, 'All the conventions of his generation led [him] to invent dialogue and eschew sources for many of his interesting discoveries and revelations.' His *The identity of Jack the Ripper* in 1959 returned to Le Queux's Pedachenko by way of another dubious theorist, Dr Thomas Dutton. Dutton died in 1935 but not before McCormick had taken notes from the doctor's unpublished thesis *Chronicles of Crime* which has subsequently disappeared.

What emerges from both Le Queux and McCormick is the obsession with conspiracy that has haunted the Ripper case for far too long. Both writers pandered to the reading public's enormous appetite for lurid, complicated and above all neat theories, each of which seems more implausible than the last.

The 1950s was the last complete decade in which the murder sites of Whitechapel were still standing. It was also the decade which saw the advent of television and the rise of the Hammer Studios at Bray, some of whose writers cornered the market in Ripper films. The Lodger theme was revisited in *Room to Let* (1950) and by a deeply psychotic Jack Palance three years later (*The Man in the Attic*). In this 'Mr Slade' is actually a matricide, reliving the experience by slaughtering street women. This is the stuff of modern research into serial-killer motivation so it comes across as authentic. Horror actor Boris Karloff played Jack twice – in *The Grip of the Strangler* and *Corridors of Blood*.

Perhaps one of the earliest attempts to recreate a genuine account was one episode of *The Veil* which Karloff hosted by a crackling log fire. Clifford Evans played Inspector James McWilliam, head of the City Force investigating the murder of Kate Eddowes. One line from him sums up the historicity of the piece – 'Two women, murdered within an hour. One in a yard at the back of Berner Street; the other in an archway off Mitre Square. Both of them... hacked to pieces... every man available was on duty in the East End last night... And yet it happened...'

Allowing for the pardonable error over the mutilations – Stride in Berner Street was not 'hacked to pieces', this is really pretty accurate. The result? The series could not find a sponsor and it was never shown.

In the meantime, journalist Daniel Farson was off on a wild goose chase of his own, even though at the time, his research was deemed immaculate. While working on a series for television called *Farson's Guide to the British* which featured a programme on the Ripper, the investigator was given a privately published pamphlet called *The East End Murderer: I Knew Him* written by a Lionel Druitt. His researcher also uncovered the Macnaghten Memoranda naming Montague Druitt as a possible suspect and for several years the barrister-cricketer-suicide led the field as the most likely Jack.

American journalist Tom Cullen also plumped for Druitt in *Autumn of Terror* (1963) but three years later Mid Century films working out of Shepperton Studios hit upon the clever idea of pitting the genius of Sherlock Holmes against the Whitechapel killer; they were, after all, contemporaries. In this version, the 'toff' has come of age. The Ripper is revealed as Lord Carfax (the name clearly stolen from the Abbey in the Bram Stoker *Dracula* story) and of course the fictional overlay of Holmes, Watson and Scotland Yard's Inspector Lestrade add a new and totally unhelpful direction of their own. To illustrate how wrong the film-makers got it, twenty-nine-year-old Barbara Windsor, all blonde curls and big bust, played Annie Chapman, Jack's Hanbury Street victim. Her red velvet dress and feathered hat would have represented over a year's takings for the real Chapman.

Seven years earlier, Joseph E Levine's *Jack the Ripper* had presented a similar 'updated' view. The film's poster showed a voluptuous blonde, all of twenty years old lying semi-naked at the feet of a dark figure with cape and knife. 'This lady of the night,' said the poster, 'has taken her last walk... The swinging purse... the painted lips... the languid pose against the lamppost...' – all of it is light years away from reality. In most of these cinematic romps of the '60s, dry ice would creep along the 'streets' of the studio set. A buxom tart would flaunt a feather boa at the camera, her cheeky smile turning to a mask of horror as she realizes that her next client will be her last. There is a shadow on the wall behind her – huge, top-hatted, caped. The shadow's arm is raised. A knife flashes in the darkness and the credits – usually blood-red – roll. Every single thing about this scenario is wrong.

Does it matter? Emphatically, yes. Because today, in a time of decreasing literacy, the photographic image, the moving picture especially, is what creates our experience of the past. It is all part of the industry that is Jack the Ripper and it does historians and genuine researchers no good at all.

But it was the 1970s that saw a huge impetus in the Jack business. Ask anyone today who Jack the Ripper was and they will all tell you that he has some connection with the royal family – the toff writ large, the highest in the land. We shall look at these theories in detail later, but journalist Stephen Knight's *Jack the Ripper: The Final Solution* not only bent history to fit his own preconceived pattern, it spawned a host of imitations which led researcher Philip Sugden to call the first chapter of his book[14] 'A Century of Final Solutions' and the last twenty years have seen an escalation of tempo in theory-production and in nonsensical plot lines. Sugden dismisses Knight's as a 'cock-and-bull' story and pours equal scorn on Ripperologist Melvyn Fairclough who relied on the highly dubious Abberline diaries.

A turning point was reached in the house that Jack built with the publication in 1993 of the Ripper diaries. These will be discussed elsewhere, but they essentially turned the Ripper industry nasty with accusations of fraud and counter-accusations flying backwards and forwards. Two armed camps had emerged by the 1990s. On the one hand were the genuine researchers and historians, among whom I would number Martin Fido, Paul Begg, Keith Skinner, Stewart Evans, Donald Rumbelow, Paul Gainey, John Eddlestone and Philip Sugden. These men – and it is perhaps odd that they *are* all men – have worked tirelessly over the years to drag Ripper studies back from the brink of lunacy and outright fiction to a level where accurate research, primary evidence and the historical method are paramount. As fictional cop Joe Friday used to say in American television's *Dragnet* series in the 1950s, 'Just the facts, Ma'am.' On the other hand we have the Ripperologists – Melvyn Fairclough, Melvyn Harris, Shirley Harrison, Tony Williams, James Tully, Bruce Paley, Paul Feldman and Patricia Cornwell – who have got carried away with a particular pet theory. They are at least the acceptable face of Ripper studies; beyond them are bad writers and a whole army of the misinformed who believe the latest hype, buy the latest book and swallow any nonsense as long as it has the name 'Jack' in it somewhere.

The film world continued to play fast and loose with history. *Murder by Decree* (1979) combined the Holmes/Watson duo with Stephen Knight's theory, throwing in the royal family en masse, authentically-named constables Long and Watkins and a distinctly *un*-Victorian anarchist detective played by David Hemmings. In the same year, Nicholas Meyer directed an even more bizarre piece called *Time After Time* in which Malcolm McDowell's H G Wells hunts David Warner's Jack across the time/space continuum by means of the scientist's machine. The nonsense is certainly fun, but it bears no relation to reality. The one line that bears repetition because it is a sad commentary on crime today comes from a jaded David Warner who says 'The world has caught up with me and surpassed me. Ninety years ago, I was a freak. Today, I'm an amateur.'[15]

Today, Google provides 187,000 sites on Jack the Ripper. Many of them advertize books and Ripper walks around Whitechapel. From time to time scientists, psychologists and criminologists around the world posit a new theory (which usually turns out to be an old one) and the vast army of Ripperologists out there surfing the super-highway howl their derision; there is no theory but theirs – theirs is the only true Jack.

One beacon shines in a naughty world. Where the Ripper's name has been hijacked by film-makers, playwrights, rock artists and video gamers, only a tiny handful of historians struggle to keep the flame of genuine research alight. Central to this is the Jack the Ripper Casebook founded in 1996 to provide accurate, detailed information in a search for the truth. It carries articles, photographs, transcripts of official documents, maps and a blog and chat room which allows aficionados to discuss the most minute details. Some 5,451 newspaper articles from 298 countries are listed as I write, proving what an extraordinary job Tom Bulling did back in September 1888 in coining the name Jack the Ripper.

But in doing so he had help. Help from the one man that all this hype is really all about – the Whitechapel murderer. No one could catch him at the time. How can we hope to catch him now?

Chapter 2

The Solution:
The Murder Map of Whitechapel

Among hundreds of letters offering advice to the City Police on how to catch the Whitechapel murderer is one, dated 16 October 1888, from Major R D O Stephenson, c/o the London Hospital. This is the time-wasting busybody and one-time suspect Robert Donston Stephenson who believed that the infamous 'Juwes' written in chalk in Goulston Street on the night of the 'double event' (29/30 September) was actually 'Juives' and therefore the killer was French. Since Stephenson went on to denounce Dr Morgan of the London Hospital, he was clearly throwing unhelpful barbs in any number of directions.

As a self-confessed Satanist, Stephenson had some bizarre comments on the Whitechapel murders, seeing in them a ritualistic necromancy involved in Haute Magic. Various body parts are required for the spells to work, including 'a preparation made from a certain portion of the body of a harlot'. How Stephenson's magician was supposed to obtain the other ingredients – the skin of a suicide, nails from a murderer's gallows, candles made from human fat, the head of a black cat which has been fed on human flesh and the horns of a goat used as murder weapons – is unclear; but presumably acquiring the genitalia of a prostitute was simple by comparison!

What is more interesting – and relevant – to reality is Stephenson's take on the pattern created by the murder sites. Because the Kelly murder was committed indoors, Stephenson believed that she was not a victim of the Whitechapel murderer (which is a theme more rational people have also taken up). The remaining six – like most contemporaries, Stephenson adds Emma Smith and Martha Tabram to Macnaghten's 'canonical five' – form, he said, a perfect cross. By drawing a line between Mitre Square (the Eddowes murder) and Buck's Row (Polly Nichols) we have one arm of the cross. By joining Hanbury Street (Annie Chapman) with Berner Street (Liz Stride) we have the other. Martha Tabram, Emma Smith and the Goulston Street graffito all lay along the longer arm of the cross. Kelly of course had to be discounted because Dorset Street lay outside the cruciform pattern. 'Did the murderer, then ... deliberately pick out beforehand on a map the places he would offer [the sacrificial victims] to his infernal deity of murder? If not, surely those six coincidences are the most marvellous of our time.'

As Paul Roland says[1], 'Once you start playing "join the dots" you can make any series of random events and locations assume an unintentional significance provided you are selective in choosing the pattern you wish them to conform to.'

Supporters of this 'hidden pattern' hypothesis have also discovered a satanic pentagram, a uterus-shaped *vesica piscis* (the womb being the killer's target in the eyes of many theorists) and even an arrowhead which points to the West End, specifically the Houses of Parliament.

But ironically, the peculiar Major Stephenson is *nearly* right; serial murder does create patterns of a different kind and it is these which we must understand to find our killer. The term that covers this hypothesis is geographical profiling, coined in the late 1980s by Canadian police officer Kim Rossno in describing an aid to psychological profiling which we shall discuss in the final chapter.

Just as we might scoff at 'Roslyn D'Onston's' black magician murderer stalking the East End, so some police forces and even sections of the media still dismiss profiling as nonsense. 'Criminal profilers,' wrote the *Washington Post*, 'may be the logical outgrowths of a society that believes all of human reality can be quantified ... a touching faith in the truth revealing ability of statistical analysis.'[2] Benjamin Disraeli once dismissed statistics as 'lies, damned lies' as though statistics were worse still; and quantitative history as taught by universities today does tend to deny the human element. But that said, there is a sure reality in the concept of geographical profiling – murder-mapping – that cannot be denied.

All seven of the women murdered by the man the media dubbed Jack the Ripper were flesh-and-blood people, with families, friends, hopes and fears, but that is not why Jack killed them. Follow that path, that the victims were interconnected and/or known to their killer and you arrive at the conspiratorial nonsense we mentioned in Chapter One.

Although several people are recognized today as geographical profilers of eminence, I have chosen Dr David Canter as the man most in step with Jack, even though I believe he eventually misses him by several hundred yards. In connection with the Washington sniper killings in 2002, Canter asked himself what was it about the victims that made them victims? His answer was 'not who they are, but where they are'. In working this out, we have to take into account two features. The first is the home or base of the killer, which is a fundamental focus for his operations; and the other is how far he is prepared to travel in search of prey. Psychological profilers often use the hunting analogy because we can all recognize the image readily. The hunting area of a big cat in the wild is huge and any number of hapless victims cross its path. It selects them as a human murderer does. They are random, but they are not random. The cat will pick on the old, the lame, the young because they cannot run or fight back. It has no concept of honour or fair play or sport; it simply wants to obtain its next meal as quickly and with the expenditure of as little energy as possible.

In the case of Jack the Ripper, the original media nickname – the Whitechapel murderer – says it all and anchors us in reality. His victims were found in his killing zone, which for him meant Whitechapel and Spitalfields. Only once, through necessity, did he kill elsewhere – as we shall see in the case of Kate Eddowes. It is important to remember that the murderer killed *on foot*; all his victims were within easy walking distance of his base of operations. This is why some suspects do not work. Foreign sailors, like the Portuguese four – José Laurenco, Manuel Xavier, Joao Machado and Joachim de Rocha – do not fit the bill because they arrived in the Port of London by merchant ship and left in the same way. They had no working knowledge of the killing ground and would have had to have been magical, not merely lucky, to get away with the crimes.

Likewise, the notion of a carriage being involved – various aspects of the 'highest in the land' theory depend on one – falls apart for the same reason. All the victims, we know, were killed where they were found – there is no forensic evidence of body-dumping – and no tracks of wheeled vehicles near any of the murder sites. Modern serial killers use motorized transport, often in connection with their jobs and this means that their geographical range is huge. The Yorkshire Ripper, Peter Sutcliffe, struck on both sides of the Pennines. He was a long-distance lorry-driver and acquired knowledge of places far afield. And he cruised red light districts in his car. Even so, most of his murders happened on his own patch, within the 'circle' of Yorkshire. Child-killer Robert Black was a highly unusual killer in that his crimes were not only committed as far apart as Oxford and Edinburgh, but there were also huge distances between the murder/abduction sites and the places where he dumped his victims' bodies.

Because of the nature of the area, the type of victim and the man I believe the Whitechapel murderer to have been, we know that he travelled over small distances in search of prey and was able to return just as quickly. As behavioural investigative adviser Professor Laurence Alison says:

> Today's geoprofilers would break down the sub-tasks the offender needed to accomplish in order to escape and examine the exit points from the scene of each attack. They would systematically consider the most likely route home, including temporal (time) and topographical (detailed lay of the land) patterns that may influence the choice the offender makes in targeting crime scenes.[3]

The seven murder sites form dots on a map and, as David Canter says, each dot 'encapsulates layers of meaning, the explosive mix of a criminal's and a victim's habits'.[4] What is it about each of the locations that was important? In investigating the brutal sex killings committed by Robert Napper in the 1990s, Laurence Alison found the pattern which I believe closely mirrors Jack:

> 'First by committing the first offence in one direction ... then moving the next offence in a different direction, then the third in [yet another] only returning [to the first direction] after a further offence. In other words [serial killers] use in sequence all points of the compass.[5]

Martha Tabram was killed on Tuesday 7 August 1888 in George Yard Buildings to the south of Wentworth Street. George Yard itself, narrow, dark, infested with a criminal underclass, linked Wentworth Street to Whitechapel High Street and is today called Gunthorpe Street. The White Swan pub still stands and it was from here that Martha Tabram vanished into the darkness with a soldier client. George Yard itself was demolished in 1972, although sections of Victorian walls still survive. The best known image, taken from William Stewart's 1938 book, shows the original archway through which Martha walked. The precise murder spot was on a first floor landing. The space here, hemmed in by stairs and walls, is important to our killer as we shall see later.

Polly Nichols died in Buck's Row in the early hours of 30 August. The street had already been renamed Durward Street when Leonard Matters visited it in 1928, but the actual buildings had changed little:

> It is a narrow, cobbled, mean street, having on one side the same houses – possibly tenanted by the same people – which stood there in 1888. They are shabby, dirty little houses of two storeys and only a three foot pavement separates them from the road, which is no more than twenty feet from wall to wall. On the opposite sides are the high walls of warehouses which at night would shadow the dirty street in a far deeper gloom.

As we shall see, the cramped, confined space was important as a crime scene, but the fact that Polly was killed at the entrance to an even more enclosed space, the stables known as Brown's Yard, is more claustrophobic still. William Stewart's 1938 photograph shows Emma Green's New Cottage still standing and the original stable doors now fronting a garage.

'Dark Annie' Chapman met her end on Saturday 8 September behind No 29 Hanbury Street, one of a terraced row of once-smart houses built for the Huguenot weavers who moved into the area in the eighteenth century because it was outside the trading restrictions of the City itself. Photographs taken in 1961 by Margaret Whitby-Green show the narrow passageway that led from the front of the building to the yard at the back. Ahead of Annie and her killer as they walked was a set of wooden stairs rising to the upper floors. The corridor itself kinked to the right and the back door to the yard, hinged on the left, opened outwards. Here, three stone steps led down to the yard itself, with its privy (lavatory) and rickety wooden fencing all round; it was another confined space, better for the killer's purposes than Buck's Row. Another of Margaret Whitby-Green's photographs shows the view from the back door, with the stairs to the right this time. This was the view seen by Annie's murderer as he left. It was already dawn and he had places to be.

Berner Street was formed on 1 May 1868 out of a combination of Upper and Lower Berner Street and Batty Buildings. It was a dingy area twenty years later, with two-storey terraced houses facing each other, but it was considered respectable at the time and was dotted with shops, like Matthew Packer's grocers, two doors down from the killing ground of Dutfield's Yard.

> 'The scene of [Liz Stride's] murder,' wrote the *Star* on 1 October 1888, 'was within the gateway at No 40, which is occupied by a Jewish working men's club... It is a building of two storeys. A passage wide enough to admit a cart separates it from the next house... The court is very small... At night, this courtyard is dark except for the light from the house windows.'

Again, a dark area. Again, a confined space. On the night of 29/30 September, it was almost perfect.

But not quite. The second murder site on that night of the dreadful 'double event' was Mitre Square, near Aldgate in the jurisdiction of the City Police. The basic outline of the square still exists, but new buildings have given the place a sense of light and space that it did not possess in the Autumn of Terror. There were three gas lamps in the square which gave very little light and the only major way in was via Mitre Street. The other two passages were very narrow, probably only allowing access for one person at a time. The square was dwarfed by tall warehouses and only one of the two private houses there was occupied – No 3 was the home of City policeman Richard Pearse. William Stewart's photograph of 'Ripper's Corner' where the body of Kate Eddowes was found on the broad slab of the pavement shows what is probably leaking rainwater from a downpipe, but it looks eerily like blood.

Of all the sites of the Whitechapel murders, it is most difficult today to imagine that of Mary Kelly, killed on 8/9 November 1888. Leonard Matters, writing in 1929, was aware of the new developments:

> What Dorset Street was like sixty years ago can only be imagined... it is undergoing a rapid change [by then it had been renamed Duval Street] and the buildings on the left hand side going east have nearly all been torn down to make room for extensions of Spitalfields Market... The house in which Kelly was murdered was closed, save for one front room still occupied by a dreadful-looking slattern who... swore at me and shuffled away down the passage.

Matters took what was probably the last photograph of the place because three days later a wrecking crew moved in. The passageway that led to No 13 Miller's Court was three feet wide and twenty feet long; the yard itself almost fifteen square feet. Kelly's room was 'a dirty, damp and dismal hovel, with boarded-up windows and a padlocked door as though the place had not been occupied since the crime was committed'.[6] That was only twelve feet square.

Many writers on the Whitechapel murders have found something different or even special about the murder of Mary Kelly and I agree. But it has nothing to do with her age, her alleged attractiveness or her personal history. It has everything to do with the room in which she died.

The crime scene of the last victim, 'Clay Pipe' Alice McKenzie, on Wednesday 17 July 1889, was described by the *East London Observer*:

> The scene of the murder is probably one of the lowest quarters in the whole of East London and a spot more suitable for the terrible crime could hardly be found on account of the evil reputation borne by this particular place... The thoroughfare itself [Castle Alley] is blocked up, both day and night, with tradesmen's carts and wagons and costermongers' barrows. This alley, which is entered by a passage, not more than a yard in width... is entirely shut off from view of the main road and would hardly be observed by the ordinary passer-by... Although the houses... are densely populated, the people generally enter them from the Spitalfields end, especially at night time on account of the dark and lonely nature of Castle Alley.

As the paper says, the clutter of vehicles rendered the gas lamps almost useless and Alice's body was found between two wagons chained together. It was not ideal, but it would have to do.

> 'The murderer,' continued the *Observer*, 'on account of the narrowness and intricacy of the surrounding thoroughfares, would have no difficulty in getting away unobserved; and if, as is believed, he is residing in one of the dozen common lodging houses or small houses within a stone's throw of the spot where the deed was committed, he would have no trouble in concealing his identity after making his escape.'[7]

Any Ripperologist with a conspiratorial bent should have read these words before embarking on the theme of Masonic ritual, foreign sailor, arrogant artist or unpleasant Liverpool cotton merchant. As if to underscore this point and to back up the correctness of the *Observer*'s journalist 120 years ago, a study conducted in 1994 found that the average distance travelled by one sub-group of stranger murderers was just 525 yards.[8]

One problem for any researcher trying to identify the man who was Jack is what profiler David Canter calls the 'plague of coincidence'. I believe that seven women were killed by the same man in the space of eleven months (six of them within four months) in one relatively small area of London's East End. One of the myths of the Ripper case, which has been used pivotally in more than one silly theory, is that all the victims (the 'canonical five' as the core) knew each other. If we plot their early lives: Polly Nichols came from central London (Fetter Lane); Annie Chapman from Paddington; Liz Stride was Swedish; Kate Eddowes came from Wolverhampton; and Mary Kelly was almost certainly Irish. In the context of the dosshouses where they spent their final weeks: Annie Chapman stayed at Crossingham's at 35 Dorset Street; Polly Nichols at 18 Thrawl Street and the White House, 56 Flower and Dean; Liz Stride lodged at 32 Flower and Dean and 35 Devonshire Street; Kate Eddowes stayed at 55 Flower and Dean. Mary Kelly of course, had her room in Miller's Court, off Dorset Street. As far as we are able to plot the pubs in which the victims drank: Polly Nichols frequented the Frying Pan; Annie Chapman, the Britannia; Liz Stride the Queen's Head and the Bricklayers' Arms; and Mary

Kelly the Britannia, the Horn of Plenty and the Ten Bells. Only the Britannia is common ground – to Chapman and Kelly, not the others and the only vague concentration of doss is Flower and Dean Street, not Dorset Street as many Ripperologists contend. In other words, all that connects the victims is that they followed the same (highly dangerous) occupation (as did several hundred like them) and lived in the same area, along with half a million others.

Given the similarity of names, it is not surprising that coincidences occur and they do confuse. There are Annies, Sarahs, Elizabeths, Kates and Marys all over the Ripper story. The fact that Kate Eddowes used the name Kelly when she pawned items on the day of her death has fuelled all sorts of speculation, but before the Jews moved in, Whitechapel was a strongly Irish community and most street girls used aliases to keep one step ahead of the law.

Certainly, all the Ripper's victims were prostitutes and this is important in establishing motive – we shall examine it further in the last chapter – but the plague of coincidence is continued even in descriptions of the clothes the dead women wore and those worn by their clients, according to eyewitness accounts.

David Canter is writing about modern serial killers when he says:

> As the anonymity of cities grows and the mobility of even established rural communities is overlaid with the cosmopolitan values of the Internet and mass media, we all know each other less and less.[9]

But even by 1888, London was the largest city in the world. Whitechapel and Spitalfields, known as the Abyss or the Ghetto, was home, as we have seen, to half a million people. In part, it was that very anonymity that sheltered Jack the Ripper and it was partly the reason he was never caught.

To understand who the man was, we have to visualize the 'mental map' of his crimes. This is the 'bundle of knowledge, feelings, familiarity, habitual paths and half-forgotten experiences...'[10] which fill a murderer's mind. Put simply, a serial killer will follow a certain geographical pattern. The Whitechapel murderer is what is known by some profilers as a 'marauder' – he killed within a circle of comfort, the first full-blown crime the nearest to his home, the others radiating outwards as he got bolder and more experienced and also because of the need to avoid a return to his former crime scenes. Some eyewitnesses certainly saw him talking to his victims before he struck, but no one saw him leave because he knew the area so well. Every court, every alleyway, the position of every lamp, the beat of every policeman – all of this formed a vital part of his mental map.

David Canter fits the circle hypothesis to the Ripper murders but is led astray by the Maybrick Diary. He finds the psychological tone of the diary disturbing, believing that it could well have been written by someone with a deep psychosis. This may be true (although dozens of crime fiction writers produce similar stuff for their readership as a matter of course!) but it does not give us Jack. The diaries have Middlesex Street as the killer's lodgings, so that becomes the home or lair or centre of operations and all the murders radiate out from that to form a distinctive pattern.

We know that the Maybrick Diary is a fake, so that Middlesex Street is yet another red herring in a long list of red herrings.

That said, Dr Canter's thesis still holds good. There *is* a pattern to the Whitechapel murderer's crimes. Each location *does* have deep significance for him. Geographical profiler Spencer Chainey of University College London's Jill Dando Institute has plotted a profile map of Jack's killings. If we place the canonical five in a computer programme, we get a focus of activity centred on Wentworth Street. If we factor in the murders of Martha Tabram and Alice McKenzie we get a slightly different pattern which, intriguingly, shifts the emphasis further east. The main centre of activity, which includes the doss-houses frequented by all of Jack's victims, represents his hunting ground. The other, less pronounced, may be his home or a similar focus – the Ripper's lair. As ever, the secrets lie in the Abyss.

Chapter 3

Looking into the Abyss

'So one is forced to conclude that the Abyss is literally a huge man-killing machine and when I pass along the little out-of-the-way streets with the full-bellied artisans at the doors, I am aware of a greater sorrow for them than for the 450,000 lost and hopeless wretches dying at the bottom of the pit... Four hundred and fifty thousand is a whole lot of people. I should not like to hear them talk all at once. I wonder if God hears them?'

Jack London – *The People of the Abyss*, 1903

Some of the lost souls spoke to the police in the Autumn of Terror. Many more did not.[1] We have a handful of names from the record of the day, from the newspapers vying with each other for the grisliest morsel, the hottest news, to the solemn, yet frustrated, coroner's inquests. We see a few of the 'hopeless wretches' caught on camera where an enterprising journalist of The *Star* or the *East London Observer* captured them, posed in their street-clothes outside the doss that was their home. Many of them were Jewish, recent refugees from Russia and Poland and they regarded the police with hatred and dread, victims as they were of pogroms and refugees from the tsarist-imposed violence that rippled through all the Russias after a dissident bomb eviscerated Alexander II.

The best way to study the killing grounds is on foot, as Jack was in his trawling phase, his blood up, wandering the night in his search for prey.

It is night – any night, for they are much the same – in the Autumn of 1888, the Autumn of Terror. We have caught the Metropolitan District Railway's extension line to the station at Aldgate. This was a new building when Jack struck, twenty-four years old and standing 200 feet to the west of the present one. Its platform was too short for a full length train, belching steam and smoke, clanking through the gas-lit station, rattling east. It is a reminder that we are already living in a modern age, an age of steam and electricity, telephones and trams and typewriters. We need reminders of these tangible, everyday things if we are to keep our grip on reality on this journey. For we have entered a long-vanished netherworld, where life is cheap and nothing is quite as it seems.

'At the best,' wrote the American journalist Jack London fourteen years after Jack the Ripper struck:

> 'City life is an unnatural life for the human; but the city life of London is so utterly unnatural that the average workman or workwoman cannot stand it... [they] are well on their way to the shambles at the bottom of the Abyss.'

So are we.

John Griffith London was known as Jack too, that most common of English Christian names made chill forever by its hijacking by person or persons unknown, the perfect murderer from Whitechapel. London was on his way to cover the Anglo-Boer War in 1902, but never got further than Spitalfields, Whitechapel and Wapping. In the seven weeks it took him to write *The People of the Abyss*, he lodged with Sergeant William Thick, of the Metropolitan Police, known to the criminal underworld as 'Johnny Upright'. 'No other book of mine,' London wrote later, 'took so much of my young heart and tears as that study of economic degradation of the poor.'

His friend, Upton Sinclair, remembered that:

> '...for years afterwards the memories of this stunted and depraved population haunted him beyond all peace.'

Punch or *The London Charivari* painted this word picture at the end of September 1888:

> Where hags called women, ghouls in the guise of men,
> Live on death-dealing, feed a loathly life,
> On the chance profits of the furtive knife.
> ....Whither comes

The haggard hag of the pavement, she,
The victim's victim, whose delirious glee
Makes with a cackling horror; hither shrink
The waifs of passion and the wrecks of drink...
... Look at these walls; they reek with dirt and damp,
But in their shadows crouched the homeless tramp
May huddle undisturbed the black night through.
Those narrow winding courts – in thought – pursue.
No light there breaks upon the bludgeon'd wife,
No flash of day arrests the lifted knife,
There shrieks arouse not, nor do groans affright.
These are but normal noises of the night ...
... Must it be
That the black slum shall furnish sanctuary
To all light-shunning creatures of the slime,
Vermin of vice, carnivora of crime?

By that time Jack had struck three times and the *Charivari* accompanied the poem with its odd, faltering metre with one of its most haunting engravings. John Tenniel's *The Nemesis of Neglect* is shown as a hideous ghoul with shroud and upraised knife, floating through the rotting, black street furniture of Whitechapel.

To our right is the Minories, on the edge of the Abyss. Dr Thomas Thynne had a surgery in 1879 at Number 140 and his sometime assistant was Dr Lionel Druitt, cousin of Montague of the Macnaghten Memoranda.

In the Minories, in the early morning of 18 September 1888, City Constable 866 John Johnson was patrolling his beat at the regulation two and a half miles an hour. He heard a scream of 'murder' coming from Three King's Court and went to investigate, truncheon at the ready, heart pounding. Here he found eighteen-year-old prostitute Elizabeth Burns wrestling (as best she could with only one arm) with a client, Charles Ludwig. 'One-Armed Liz' was a well-known character in the Abyss, a friend of the Ripper's fourth victim, Elizabeth Stride. As for Ludwig, he had pulled a knife on Liz, but the arrival of Johnson saw him take to his heels. The man was dangerous and a drunk. He had recently arrived in the Abyss from Hamburg, where he had carried on a barber's trade. He worked briefly for C A Partridge in the Minories and lodged with a German tailor, Johannes, in nearby Church Street.

But we turn left into Middlesex Street, its iron-framed street stalls empty now and their canvases hanging in the lengthening shadows. This is Petticoat Lane, but it lives only on Sunday, the Jews' working day and tonight is not Sunday.

> 'On Sunday,' wrote the journalist S Gelberg, '"the Lane" and its adjoining thoroughfares are a howling pandemonium of cosmopolitan costerism, a curious tangle of humanity... Round its stalls the coster humour reaches its finest fancies, the coster philosophy its profoundest depths, the coster oratory its highest flights.'

Constable Daniel Halse walked this way on the trail of the man who had just slaughtered Kate Eddowes, shortly after two o'clock on the morning of Sunday 30 September. He was moving back into the Abyss, stopping men on the way, jumping at shadows. Had he but known it, he was following Jack to his lair.

And this was the beat, too, of Constable 272H Walter Andrews, on his way to find the mutilated body of 'Clay Pipe' Alice McKenzie in Castle Alley on 17 July 1889. In Middlesex Street the forged diary of the Liverpool cotton merchant James Maybrick will claim, years ahead, that the Ripper took lodgings, walking those grease-cobbled streets night after night until he knew them and had the killing grounds by heart.

James Maybrick never lodged in Middlesex Street, but others did. George Bolam was a cowkeeper; Mrs Polly Nathan ran a fish and chip shop. Solran Berlinski followed the calling of many of the Chosen People in the Abyss and sold rags. Isaac Woolf, more enterprising and up-market, made playing cards. As a fading memory of the street's more prosperous past, Samuel Barnett still ran coffee rooms there.

For Whitechapel and Spitalfields had not always been the Abyss. The Huguenot weavers who arrived here, fleeing from religious persecution in France and the Netherlands, brought the skills of their calling and built fashionable houses large enough to house their impressive *jacquard* looms. Their houses still stand along Wilkes Street, gentrified once more, their 'long light' windows a reminder of their workshop origins. Their wares were much in demand and they left their imprint on local names like Fournier Street (Church Street in Jack's day). A Huguenot chapel was built there in 1742.

But we have already turned right into Goulston Street. Sarah Smith was the manageress of Whitechapel Baths and Washhouses here, the building with its back to Castle Alley. Mrs Smith's own rooms overlooked the spot where Clay Pipe Alice would be found. Mrs Smith had gone to bed that night between a quarter and half past twelve and had sat up reading for some time. Her windows were closed, but she was certain she would have heard a scream in the darkness. All she heard was the shrill screech of Constable Andrews' whistle.

It is the spot past the Wentworth Model Buildings and the standpipe near their entranceway that has gained a certain notoriety in the Ripper case. At a little before three o'clock on the morning of Sunday 30 September, Constable 254A Alfred Long was walking his beat here when he came upon a piece of bloody cloth dropped by the drain and only a yard or so away, scribbled on the wall in chalk, the words 'The Juwes are the men that will not be blamed for nothing.' The cloth carried the blood and faecal matter of Kate Eddowes, the second of Jack's victims on the terrible night of the 'double event'. The graffito raised issues in the Whitechapel murder case that have never gone away.

For this is the Abyss, the Ghetto, with its 90 per cent Jewish population of Eastern European immigrants – 'A hundred thousand men, women and children,' wrote Gelberg, 'some of them fugitives still suffering the punishment of Cain', crowded into an area barely a mile square. They were, he admitted:

> ...a complicated piece of human patchwork, with the ringletted Pole at one point, the Dutch Jew at another, the English Hebrew in his own corner and the Gentile coster running like a strange thin thread through the design... If you would understand the immortal agony of Jewry, go into its East-End colony.

To Gelberg, and many others, Jew and non-Jew, the Ghetto was 'a fragment of Poland torn off from Central Europe' and in the Ripper case, the language barrier remained a problem.

'You are in a city of endless toil,' wrote Gelberg, years after Jack
was dead and his legend was forming. 'All day long and far into
the night the factories make dismal music in the Ghetto...
"Weiber! Weiber! Leimische Beigel!" sing out the women... and
long after the shadows have lengthened... they are still
vouching by their own lives or the kindness of Shem Yisboroch
(God) to Israel for the quality of their wares. So spins the
toiling Ghetto round its daily orbit.'

Gelberg was at pains, where less sympathetic 'Gentile' journalists were
not, to point out that the abject poverty of the Abyss was not universal:

It is really homespun lined with ermine, Dives cheek by jowl
with Lazarus.

Kosher restaurants and butcher shops were everywhere – there were
seven of them at the junction of Middlesex and Wentworth Streets –
and even the poorest would be able to dress up in hired finery on
Chometz Battel night (the night before Passover).

We walk ahead into Whitechapel High Street, where the journalist
George Sims (himself once taken for Jack the Ripper) noticed:

...there are kerbstone auctioneers, knockers-down of old
clothes and patched-up umbrellas, who will patter the whole
night... 'I ask no more; I take no less'. That is the ultimatum.

The White Hart stood here, one of the scores of drinking-kens in the
district, immune to Mr Gladstone's licensing laws, open all hours.
Prostitutes Martha Tabram and 'Pearly Poll' Connolly drank with two
soldiers here the night that Martha died. Emma Smith, a forty-five-
year-old widowed prostitute with two children spent the day along
Whitechapel High Street, on 2 April 1888, soliciting, looking for
custom among the down and outs – 'Are you good natured, dearie?'
Three men who were not good natured attacked her in the early hours
of the next morning, grabbing her near St Mary's Church, smashing
her in the face with their knuckles, ripping her right ear almost off and
raping her. One of them, perhaps the nineteen-year-old she mentioned
at the London Hospital later, rammed a stick into her vagina.

It was along this street that Constable 221H John Gallagher arrested
Charles Ludwig on the morning of 18 September 1889 for his attack

on One-Armed Liz. Another of Ludwig's victims was Alexander Freinberg, known as Alexander Findlay. He lived in Leman Street, the centre of German London, but ran a coffee stall on Whitechapel High Street. Freinberg committed the unforgivable sin of looking at his customer when Ludwig went berserk and pulled a knife. The coffee-stall holder threw a dish at him and was no doubt delighted at the timely arrival of Gallagher.

Right into Wentworth Street:

> ...a street of ugly, featureless houses... Each ground floor is a shop and the kerb on either side of the road is encumbered with stalls... Your companions are mostly women, Jewesses, the majority wearing the black wigs of the matron over their own scanty locks. There are blowsy and haggard mothers of clinging families; and full-blooded girls with dark eyes, languorously bold, ripe red lips and ebon tresses. The men are of two kinds, the frowsy and the flash. Fish and poultry are the articles of commerce in which trade is most brisk...

– but journalist Edwin Pugh, writing a few years after Jack struck, was talking of the daytime. At night, Wentworth Street is very different:

> 'Although it is only a little after eight,' observed Gelberg, 'the last stall has been spirited away and the "Lane" is so utterly deserted that the few children playing at leapfrog over its littered stones look lost in it.'

The engraver Gustave Doré had been drawn to it twenty-one years before the Whitechapel murders, when the man who was Jack was already living in the area, descending slowly into madness. Doré drew children in outsize adult clothes squatting in the gutter. They sold old shoes to passers-by. Here the hanging pipe smoke and the stale beer smell of the Princess Alice lured John Pizer, the weird anti-social cobbler called Leather Apron, to its sawdust floors and its grease-scummed tables. He drank here with Mickeldy Joe, his only friend in the world. Frances Coles drank here too. She was Frances Hawkins and Frances Coleman and had packed goods for a wholesale chemist until 1884, when she suddenly, unaccountably, took to the streets to make her living in a different way altogether. She was a good-looking girl, outgoing and vivacious. The artist who drew her from descriptions of those who knew her well caught the sparkle and the beauty. But she looked very different in the mortuary photograph taken soon after Valentine's Day 1891. Her left earring had been torn out and her throat had been cut. The photographer who captured her that day showed the full lips slightly parted, the hair, unkempt and greasy, swept back and just the hint of the jagged rip that killed her below her right ear.

Go out, out of the Princess Alice with its noise and its smoke, along Commercial Street with its carts and clutter, its tramlines and its penny-gaffes. The intention was to make this a major highway that ran from Nicholas Hawksmoor's Christ's Church to Shoreditch and to demolish the slums that lay on either side of it. Somehow this never happened and it lies at the heart of the Ripper's stalking grounds. Here stood the Britannia, licensed to Walter Ringer and his wife. It was not actually a pub, merely a beershop; but that did not stop hundreds of locals nipping into 'The Ringers' at all hours of the day and night. It was outside this pub that dosshouse deputy Caroline Maxwell claimed she saw Mary Kelly, Jack's penultimate victim, talking to a plump man in a plaid coat hours after the Irish girl was dead. And it was outside the George, a few yards away, that Alice Graves last saw prostitute Rose Mylett, a little under the influence and talking to two sailors. Constable Robert Goulding found her body in Clarke's Yard, Poplar, at a quarter past four in the morning of 20 December 1888. She had been strangled – 'Murder' as too many coroners' inquests decided in those days, 'by some person or persons unknown'.

And in Commercial Street stood the Victoria Working Men's Home, one of dozens of common lodging or dosshouses that littered the area. Except that this one, Victoria Home No. 2, had delusions of grandeur. The building was divided into two blocks separated by a central corridor with a staircase 'leading to subterranean depths'. Here, a door was marked 'Shaving Saloon'. A second flight of stairs led to a kitchen and coffee shop. Its tariff explained to journalist T W Wilkinson 'how some of the dejected specimens of humanity scattered over the kitchen can live on a shilling a day, lodgings included'. Hot roast beef cost 3d; pudding was 1d; half a pint of tea cost ¼d. The food, Wilkinson believed, was 'good and wholesome'. Upstairs, the bedrooms were light and airy and surprisingly clean. The sixpenny beds were placed in small cubicles made of hollow tiles, each space having the luxury of a mirror and a picture – something Biblical and uplifting, no doubt. The fivepenny beds were partitioned with zinc and the fourpennies had four beds to a room...

Downstairs, the recreation rooms boasted a piano, a billiard table and three bagatelle tables. When Wilkinson visited the place in 1902, he took in the 'human wreckage' who loitered in the kitchen:

> ...some clustered near the huge coke fire, some eating at the tables, some sitting aloof from their congeners, apathetic, dull-eyed, temporarily oblivious of their surroundings.

One of these, in the Autumn of 1888, was George Hutchinson, a friend of Jack's penultimate victim, Mary Kelly, a tall man with an upright bearing who gave a suspiciously over-detailed description of a foreign-looking 'toff' with Mary on the night she died.

On the East side of Commercial Street is the graveyard of Christ Church – 'Itchy Park' – where the desperately poor slept rough. Jack London remembered it years later:

> The shadow of Christ Church falls across Spitalfields Garden and in the shadow of Christ's Church, at three o'clock in the afternoon, I saw a sight I never wish to see again. There are no flowers in this garden...

There was a police station in Commercial Street, one of those beacons in a naughty world outside of which the blue light shone and moustachioed constables with watch chains and 'bull's eye' lanterns and hardwood truncheons would march out in pairs into the Whitechapel night. In the Autumn of Terror, they wore rubber strips on their hobnailed soles in the faint hope of catching Jack red-handed.

We are already in Thrawl Street, littered with dosshouses like Cooley's where Mary Kelly stayed. The Victoria Homes were palaces by comparison with these.

> 'The little private doss-houses,' Jack London wrote, 'are unmitigated horrors. I have slept in them and I know... From the kitchen came the sounds of more genial life... But the smell... was stronger and a rising nausea drove me into the street for fresh air.' But it was no better here – 'The colour of

life is grey and drab. Everything is helpless, hopeless, unrelieved and dirty. Bath tubs are a thing totally unknown, as mythical as the ambrosia of the gods. The people themselves are dirty, while any attempt at cleanliness becomes howling farce, when it is not pitiful and tragic. Strange, vagrant odours come drifting along the greasy wind and the rain, when it falls, is more like grease than water from heaven. The very cobblestones are scummed with grease.'

Wilkinson was there too. 'There is no need to knock: the door is open' and at four in the morning, the hour when Jack was on the prowl, it swung back to let out the market porters on their way to work. The smell of bloater stayed with Wilkinson, drifting out from the kitchen 'the loafing place of the idle and the workshop of the industrious'. The fire burned continuously because it was the dosshouse's only means of cooking. There was to be no washing [of clothes] on a Sunday and other grimy notices reminded inmates of the house rules. Where the deputy was a man – as in Cooley's – such people were chosen for their bulk, acting as 'chuckers' should the conversation turn to fisticuffs of an evening.

Wilkinson took in the typical dossers draped before him – 'a seedy, frock-coated failure' dipping bread into his tea, itself the sweepings of the tea-shop's floor. An old man with a snowy beard gnawed a hambone. A 'pallid youth' ate his supper of bread, tea, margarine and the inevitable bloater with his fingers; his tablecloth was an old newspaper:

> All have that haunting expression – that dull, despairing look in the eyes – which hunger and buffeting engender.

They are living, at least for tonight, in the fourpenny hotel. Tomorrow? Who knows?

Jack London knew:

> But the girl of fourteen or fifteen, forced [by circumstance] to leave the one room called home… can have but one end. And the bitter end of that one end is such as that of the woman whose body the police found this morning in a doorway in Dorset Street… Homeless, shelterless, sick, with no-one with her in her last hour, she had died in the night of exposure… She

died as a wild animal died.

Elizabeth Mahoney went out to buy supper at a chandler's shop in Thrawl Street in the early hours of Tuesday 7 August. She would walk past the landing where Martha Tabram would be found at George Yard Buildings later that morning. Rumour had it that another dead woman lived at a dosshouse at 18 Thrawl Street and her fellow inmate, Ellen Holland, told the police her name had been Polly. That was her street name; in reality she was Mary Ann Nichols, Jack's second victim. At Number 6 lived Eliza Gold, the sister of another of Jack's victims, Kate Eddowes.

We are walking north into Flower and Dean Street.

> 'Over no other part of the kingdom,' wrote D L Woolmer, 'do the two angels of life and death hover more continually; and nowhere… is the fight between good and evil more fierce and stubborn.'

James Greenwood in *Strange Company* described the place as 'perhaps the foulest and most dangerous street in the whole metropolis', although five years before Jack struck, the philanthropist Nathan Rothschild had bought up part of it to provide good 'affordable' housing for the poor.

Here stood Cooney's dosshouse at Number 55 where Kate Eddowes and her sometime lover, John Kelly, shared a bed in one of those houses where couples were afforded a modicum of privacy. Frederick Wilkinson was the lodging-house deputy and he would testify that the pair ate breakfast there on the morning of Saturday 29 September. Kate would not live to eat another breakfast.

Next door stood the White House, the doss at Number 56. An anonymous photographer took a picture of street life here, with a huddled group of women and their children outside the front door. It looks natural, but was probably posed – there is a girl in a clean white apron and a woman wrapped in a shawl. Only her face is partially covered, as if, at the last moment, she did not want our world to capture too closely an image of hers.

> 'I stood yesterday,' wrote Jack London, 'in a room in one of the "Municipal dwellings" not far from Leman Street. I looked into a dreary future and saw that if I would have to live in such

a room until I died, I should immediately go down, plump into the Thames and cut the tenancy short.'

Perhaps the woman in the photograph felt the same.

We have walked along Brick Lane that runs parallel with busy Commercial Street. The Lane was home to a brick and tile workshop but the Black Eagle Brewery dominated the site. In Jack's time, the Frying Pan public house stood at the corner of the intersection with Thrawl Street. The Ripper's second victim, Polly Nichols, staggered out of its doors at half past twelve on the morning of Friday 31 August, the last morning of her life.

Dr Timothy Killeen, who performed the post mortem on prostitute Martha Tabram, Jack's first victim, lived at Number 68. Jack's penultimate victim, Mary Kelly, lived for a while with her lover Joseph Barnett along the Lane. Dr William Dukes lived at Number 75 and was the first medical man on the ghastly scene at Miller's Court to view her body. Sitting on the step of a barber shop nearby, Margaret Franklin saw her friend 'Clay Pipe' Alice McKenzie pass by at twenty to midnight on 16 July 1889. She was on her way to her death.

Let us go north into Fashion Street, made famous for years after Jack by Israel Zangwill in his *Children of the Ghetto*. Of the houses there, he wrote:

> It was not a room... It was a den, a lair. Seven feet by eight were its dimensions and the ceiling was so low as not to give the cubic airspace required by a British soldier to live in barracks... Five dollars would have purchased everything in sight. The floor was bare, while walls and ceilings were literally covered with blood marks and splotches. Each mark represented a violent death – of an insect, for the place swarmed with vermin, a plague with which no person could cope single-handed.

It was in Fashion Street that Kate Eddowes, Jack's fifth victim lived. That at least was the address she gave, the common lodging house at No 6. But since she also gave her name as Mary Anne Kelly we cannot be sure of that. Those responses, about her name and address, were given to Constable George Hutt at Bishopsgate Police Station in the early hours of Sunday 30 September. He asked her to close the door on her way out. Approximately fifteen minutes later she died in Mitre Square.

The Queen's Head stood on the corner of Fashion Street and Commercial Street. Elizabeth Stride was drinking in this pub hours before she died and it was outside the Queen's Head that George Hutchinson saw Mary Kelly on her last day on earth, talking to a man.

If we stand, as Jack probably did hundreds of times at the end of Fashion Street, we are facing the parallel alleyways of White's Row and Dorset Street. White's Row does not figure centrally in the complex story of the Whitechapel murders, but one lodger in the dosshouse at No 8 was Annie Millwood who was actually the trigger for the whole series. Dorset Street, however, has assumed a huge importance with many Ripperologists and historians accepting the tenet that, in the Ripper case, 'all roads lead to Dorset Street'. By Jack's time, it had so many common lodging houses that locals called it Dosset Street and it was equally full of pubs. At the corner of Commercial Street stood the Ringers' Britannia and, at the far end where it met Crispin Street, the Horn of Plenty. Mary Kelly drank there with her prostitute friend Julia Venturney and 'Danny', who was probably Joseph Barnett. The Blue Coat Boy stood in the centre, not far from the narrow entrance to Miller's Court in whose shadows the most appalling ritual of a serial killer was carried out. Along Crispin Street, Isaac Mendoza sold furniture and Meyers Markos tin-plate toys. The Street Directories of the time list saddlers and sack-makers, beer-retailers and farriers, largely Jews all trying to prove the Chief Rabbi wrong when he warned that emigration to England was a sort of descent.

T W Wilkinson was writing of the Farm House doss in Southwark, but his description of female dossers could equally well apply to Crossingham's or any of the dozen more along Dorset Street:

> How many of the women bear marks of brutality – swollen lips, cut cheeks, black eyes! ... a young woman with dishevelled hair and open bodice... is frying steak and onions. By her side a companion equally untidy... drops her 'halfpenny tea and sugar mixed' into a pot, cautiously lets two eggs sink on the heap and pours boiling water on the lot.

Wilkinson knew all too well what a grim round there was for the people of the Abyss:

> Look back long, long ago – twenty years, thirty, forty in some

cases – numbers of these women came here or to a neighbouring house as girls. And now look forward. You can see them all going to the workhouse or the hospital gate. That is their well-nigh inevitable end, unless they meet a worse fate.

Seven of them did.

Annie Chapman lodged at Crossingham's for four months prior to her death – the deputy there, Timothy Donovan, confirmed it at her inquest. Two years earlier, she was living across the road at No 30 with John Siffey or Sievey who may or may not have been a sievemaker. Another resident at Crossingham's was 'Clay Pipe' Alice and she often shared a bed there with her lover John McCormack, also known as John Bryant. T W Wilkinson commented on dosshouses like Crossingham's:

> The difference between a place of this class and one for men or women only lies solely in the sleeping accommodation. There is more privacy… though not much in some cases, for the cubicles are like stable stalls. In general, they are similar, only smaller, to those boxed-off spaces which the coffee-shop keeper dignifies with the name of bedrooms.

Wilkinson noted that single men might keep the same 'kip' for five or ten years or longer, but couples rarely stayed anywhere for more than a few days together:

> So that some phases of life in cubicle houses are not so exceptional as the circumstances surrounding certain murders which have been committed in them have led many to suggest.

On one point however, Wilkinson's comments seem demonstrably wrong:

> In these places… no questions are asked and no names taken. A man or a woman may live in a fourpenny hotel for years and yet be known to the 'deputy' by the number of his or her bed. The majority of lodgers in hotels for the poor, too, are casuals, not regulars.

Yet, without exception, the deputies, like Timothy Donovan of

Crossingham's, who gave evidence at Ripper inquests, seem to have known their charges well and to have been very aware of their movements.

John McCarthy owned a chandler's shop at No 27 and the adjacent 26, which included Miller's Court. That made him Mary Kelly's landlord and it was McCarthy's gofer Thomas 'Indian Harry' Bowyer who went to fetch overdue rent from Mary and found her mutilated corpse instead.

'Governor, I knocked at the door and could not make anyone answer. I looked through the window and saw a lot of blood.'

We have left depressing Dorset Street behind and are walking due north along Commercial Street. The Ten Bells stood here, where Mary Kelly drank under the shadow of Christ Church. And if we turn right into Hanbury Street, we are at the northern extent of the Ripper's hunting grounds.

At No 29 stood a house occupied in the year of the Ripper by seventeen people, none of whom ever saw or heard anything in the early hours of Saturday 8 September when 'Dark Annie' Chapman was butchered in their backyard. Amelia Richardson lived there with her fourteen-year-old grandson, Thomas. A Mr Walker lived in a back room with Alfred, his retarded son. Walker senior made tennis boots, somewhat incongruous in the Abyss. Mr and Mrs Copsey made cigars; Mr Thompson and Mr Davis were carmen, those luckless souls up by four in the morning and trudging through the scum-cobbled streets to work at Spitalfields or other markets in the area. Another resident was Harriet Hardiman who lived with her sixteen-year-old son and ran the cat's-meat shop at the front of the building.

It was Albert Cadoche, who lived at No 27, who may have heard what was Annie Chapman's last word on earth. It was shortly after quarter past five that morning that he heard the cry 'No!' and a thud, as though something heavy was hitting the fence that divided Nos 27 and 29. At 23A stood the premises of packing-case manufacturers Messrs Joseph and Thomas Bayley, the company that employed several men who were the first on the scene of the murder. Little Laura Sickings lived at No 25 and was only trying to be helpful when she told the police she had found bloodstains in her backyard. They turned out to be urine. Somewhere along Hanbury's dingy frontage, H Smith was the undertaker who supplied the hearse that carried Annie Chapman to her final resting place.

At the end of Hanbury Street, we are walking towards the site of the second of Jack's killings, that of Polly Nichols in Buck's Row. But we have two stops to make first. Hanbury and Old Montague Street converge on Baker's Row that intersects the Whitechapel Road to the south. Here stood the great, grey edifice of the Whitechapel Union Workhouse and its casual ward, known as the Spike. Between them, Jack London and T W Wilkinson summed up the horror of the place:

'I have been to the spike,' London wrote, 'and slept in the spike and eaten in the spike; also I have run away from the spike.'

Wilkinson took in the flotsam that found itself at the Spike's front door, 'the doorway of sighs'. He saw a man tired of the unending struggle with poverty, his steps slow and unwilling, his eyes dead and old. He saw a wastrel, who called himself an artist, but was actually an 'in and out' man, of the casual ward, discharging himself at dawn and back again by nightfall. And Wilkinson saw another type:

...a man for whom the poor house has no secrets and no terrors. He was born in the workhouse – he has lived in the workhouse; and he will die in the workhouse.

The workhouse was an object of horror to most people because that was what it was designed to be. The Whigs, in their zeal to save money in 1834, had introduced the concept of 'less eligibility', that a man would take *any* work, no matter how poorly paid, rather than enter the 'Bastille' as the various houses of industry were called by the poor. A contemporary wrote:

The Bastille stretched further than the eye could see and seemed a standing rebuke to its poverty-stricken surroundings, for it was clean, not a spot on it, not a stain, nothing to show a trace of sympathy with the misery and sin of the people who lived in this neighbourhood.

The 'grubber' or kitchen was at the heart of the workhouse. It was lined with white-glazed bricks and boasted twenty steam-jacketed coppers, roasting ovens and tea coppers. The 1881 census shows that

695 souls lived in this building and they all had to be fed. The equipment could cook sixty-gallon milk puddings, 240 gallons of tea, a quarter of a ton of bacon and a ton of cabbage at one sitting. The mincing machine was vital in chewing up the meat for toothless and senile paupers unable to manage on their own. Tuesday was roast mutton and potatoes with bread, four and a half ounces of meat and bread for the able-bodied, twelve of potatoes. Breakfast was bread, a pint and a half of porridge or a pint of cocoa. Supper was six ounces of bread and one and a half pints of broth – hell-broth as it was often called.

In the dormitories and the segregated wards, men sat huddled in groups, playing dominoes, sleeping, talking. They made their own bread and ground their own coffee, 'fulfilling the primeval curse' of work to the grinding, squealing crank of the machines. They chopped their own wood in the lumber yard and cranked the machine that drove the circular saw screeching through the timber. In the French polishing shop, the stench of methylated spirits filled the nostrils and an endless collection of hand-me-down boots filled whole piles for gardening work, being adjusted by the hand-stitching of the cobbler, the leather-aprons down on their luck.

In the women's wards, many of the inmates were octogenarians, their white-capped heads nodding in conversation over their afternoon tea. They seemed happy enough on the days when Wilkinson visited, but 'most of them will gradually rust out and die at last of the workhouse complaint, old age'. The apartments for the Darbies and Joans were as pleasant as the institution could make them – the odd knick-knack on the bedside table, the photograph hanging on the wall.

In the nurseries, where the orphans and the abandoned lived, milk and bread and butter were available all day. Wilkinson noticed 'a chubby-cheeked girl who never takes her eyes off your face' and wondered where her parents were and what had happened to them.

At six o'clock, as dark descended in the Autumn of Terror, the doors of the casual ward opened. In trooped the out of work artisans – 'too old at fifty', families with sobbing babies, prostitutes too battered and exhausted to offer their services that night. The answers to the night porter's questions are always the same:

'Where did you sleep last night?' 'Nowhere.' The key to the

street; dropping asleep on a doorstep or, worse still, while still walking… dodging about in the cold, grey dawn to get a wash at a street fountain when a policeman is not looking.

Beyond the gate, the 'casuals' peeled off into male and female queues, the men searched for pipes, tobacco or matches. Any money above 4d was taken from them, to be returned when they left – often the next morning. But we are left wondering why, if they could afford a doss, they didn't spend their 4d more profitably. It may be because here, they got a bed and a room of their own. 'This is the life of those who by the vicissitudes of things, are undermost …'

Among the undermost in the census of 1881, Eliza Adams was a needlewoman from the City; Harriet Ashley was a carman's widow (a reminder of the fragile fortunes of the working class dependent on a breadwinner now gone); Jane Bernardin was a silk weaver, listed as 'imbecile'; Michael Callaghan was a coal whipper; Mary Chaplin was a domestic servant and blind; Adelaide Cowlan was a prostitute (a lucky one who escaped Jack's knife); Margaret Foxley was an orphan, one year old; William Hayward was a cattle drover. Robert Holme was a ship's steward, referred to as 'lunatic' and hailed from Denmark; Robert Mann was a dock labourer; Mary Over was a hatter; Thomas Pike a walking-stick maker – and so it went on. Six hundred and ninety-five of the flotsam of the Ghetto, the people at the very bottom of the Abyss.

At the end of Baker's Row, we can see, as darkness falls in the Abyss, the looming front of the London Hospital. Seamstress/prostitute Ada Wilson was brought here on Wednesday 28 March 1888, having been attacked in her own home in Maidman Street, Mile End. She survived. Dr Thomas Openshaw worked here and on 18 October he received a visit from Mr F S Reed, assistant to Dr Frederick Wiles of the Mile End Road. He brought him a human kidney preserved in spirits of wine and asked him for his medical opinion. And when he published his findings on the kidney he received one of the 122 known letters or postcards attributed to Jack the Ripper.

A far better known colleague was Thomas Barnardo, an Irishman who, appalled by the squalor he trudged through on his way to work every day, took particular pity on the ragged waifs dogging his footsteps and begging for food. In the year of the Ripper, he wrote in his *Three Truths*:

> In cellar, in garret, in alley and court,
> They weep and they suffer and pine,
> And the wolves of the city are prowling near.
> Back wolves. For the children are mine.

And it was Thomas Barnardo who had visited the doss at 32 Flower and Dean Street and talked to Liz Stride there. He went to see her butchered body in the mortuary in St-George's-in-the-East.

On 26 July, the occultist and fantastist Robert Donston Stephenson booked himself into the London Hospital for treatment for neurasthenia. He was there until 7 December, covering the whole period of Jack's spree.

But it was not all murder and mayhem. In the summer months, weather permitting, convalescent patients were stretchered out into the grounds for open-air concerts. Standing at the entrance to the place, journalist R Austin Freeman noted the 'pale consumptive' jostling with the sturdy labourer with a bandaged head. There were the rasping coughs of those destined to roam the streets so near to the river; patients on crutches; patients swathed in bandages. An enterprising coster sold bottles at a stall near to the main gate because the hospital did not provide them and most people brought their own containers – 'the jovial whisky bottle is degraded into a mere receptacle for cod liver oil'.

All human life was here, as it was everywhere in the Abyss. Visitors were only allowed on certain days, creaking in polished shoes along the corridors and 'Nightingale' wards past rows of starched nurses with white caps and aprons, silverware gleaming at their waists. Bed No 23 had his leg amputated above the knee yesterday, but he was cheered by the visit of his wife and little son – 'for he cannot see her blinding tears or hear her sobs as she hurries away through the echoing corridor'.

But this side of the hospital, the dingy thoroughfare called Buck's Row was the site of the second of Jack's killings, that of Polly Nichols. The street converged with Winthrop Street halfway along its length and was very broad for an East End road. There were residential, terraced houses along the narrow part and warehouses, known as wharves because they edged a canal. A huge Board School dominated the site from 1870 and it was near the stable doors opposite the fancy-fronted manager's house of Essex Wharf that Polly Nichols' body was found, lying on the pavement with her head to the east and dark blood oozing from the gash in her throat.

What lies behind a high wall along Brady Street has brought us to the end of our journey across the Abyss – the Jews' burial ground. Properly the Brady Street Ashkenazi Cemetery, it was opened in 1761 and by 1840 was close to being full. Most of London's graveyards were in the same state, with coffins and bones jutting out from the ground and 'miasma' floating in a green and sulphurous gas across residential areas. In 1839 there had been between eight and ten burials a day, which kept four full-time gravediggers pretty busy.

The overcrowding problem was solved by creating a new layer of earth four feet deep over the top of existing graves and placing the tombstones back to back, one for the upper level, one for the lower. Various trade symbols were carved into the stone – hammers, fish, shuttles, knives. The hereditary priests (kohanin) had hands and water pitchers ready for the blessing sculpted above their names and many of these residents had their addresses written on them, if only to prove that they had now moved on to a better one! Thirty years before the Ripper, the gates were locked forever.

We have walked where Jack walked. We have glimpsed, if only for moments, the world into which he was born, in which he died and in which he killed.

An East End expert, Bill Fishman, wrote:

> Even now, in the still hours, as the moon strikes the steeple of old Christ Church and casts a long shadow over the rickety tenements of Spitalfields, a sudden catch of movement, crouched silhouette in a desolate alleyway, all senses alert, as Old Jack poised momentarily en route, continues on his way to a rendezvous with murder in the City of Dreadful Night.

Jack was just one of the 450,000 lost souls who inhabited the Abyss. Our only problem now is to find him.

Chapter 4

The Unusual Suspects

No self-respecting book on Jack the Ripper would be complete without a discussion of the various theories, some nonsensical, some ingenious, all of them fascinating, which have emerged in the long trail on the search for the most elusive killer of them all.

In the process of any criminal investigation, part of the work of the police is to eliminate suspects as quickly as possible and that is what we must do here. Unfortunately, such is the grip of the Ripper that the number of suspects has risen dramatically in recent years and shows no sign of diminishing, however far-fetched and preposterous the idea. As I write, a book is about to emerge naming the anonymous (of course!) pornographer 'Walter' as Jack. Another alleges that the whole thing was a media enterprise born of the need to win a newspaper circulation war.

The police, under outrageous and mounting pressure at the time, arrested nearly 200 men in the weeks over which Jack struck, only to have to release all their suspects for lack of evidence. Most of the men discussed in this chapter were not arrested. Many of them did not come to the attention of the police at all and come under the category of 'non-contemporaneously alleged'. This is the silly season of the Ripperologists, the far-fetched theories which cause such delight.

I must admit to being slightly schizoid. As a writer of true crime, I know that murder is grim and that no one exposed to it emerges quite intact; not the victim, obviously, nor his/her family. But neither do the police who investigate it, the journalists who cover it; nor, controversially, the murderer himself. Crime *fiction* however, is one great romp, in which the reader curls up with a good book in order to be entertained.

The same schizophrenia is apparent in Rosemary Herbert's

definition of murder in her seminal work on Crime and Mystery Writing:

> From the time of its origin as an Old English word until today, the term 'murder' has meant the most heinous kind of taking of life, the killing of one or more than one human being by another, also known as homicide. The term often denoted secret homicide and it carried the sense of great wickedness, deadly injury and great torment. In the laws of England, Scotland and the United States, murder is defined as the criminal killing of a human being with malice aforethought or wilful murder. In the law courts of these nations, conviction on a charge of wilful murder rests upon establishing that the perpetrator was of sound mind when the act occurred.[1]

So far, so factual, but the definition in the context of fiction immediately widens to an unbelievable degree. We are presented with detective novels, police procedurals, private eye novels, the quest for means, opportunity, motive and much more. It is in this context that many Ripper theories lie. When I wrote my essay for Maxim Jakubowski's *Mammoth Book of Jack the Ripper* I pointed the finger at Frederick Nicholas Charrington, the heir to a brewing fortune who, outraged by the violence instanced by the consumption of his own family's beer, turned his back on the Charrington fortune and spent years in the East End battling the demon drink on behalf of others and fighting prostitution. What better way to throw a spotlight on the social evils of the East End than to kill and mutilate unfortunates and start an outcry? At the end of my essay I formally apologized to the shade of Frederick Charrington, a good man in a troubled time, but what I was doing was showing how easy it was to put almost any contemporary in the frame.

This is where William Ewart Gladstone steps into the picture. 'The People's William' had become the 'Grand Old Man' by 1888. He had already served three times as Prime Minister and still had one term left. He was a fierce Christian, seventy-nine years old and in the year of the Whitechapel murders was leader of the Liberal opposition. He had no known links with Whitechapel. It is certainly true that the GOM's moral fervour had led him as an undergraduate at Oxford to fight the social evil of prostitution. He did visit prostitutes, but notably the rather more fashionable streetwalkers of the West End whom he would invite politely back to tea with Mrs Gladstone.

As we saw in Chapter One, the public image, despite years of mythbusting and excellent Ripper research, is still effectively the suave monster in the top hat and cape. The mythology of the doctor runs like a blood-trickle through the case and so the bag carries the deadly surgeon's blade. The bag had no actual link with the politician in that Gladstone never carried one, but the context can be traced to 1876. In that year, the Turks massacred an estimated 12,000 Christian Armenians in Bulgaria. Gladstone, all the textbooks assure us, came 'thundering' out of retirement to demand that Disraeli, his nemesis at No 10, kick the Turks out of Europe 'bag and baggage'. The Gladstone libel is patent nonsense.

Algernon Charles Swinburne must be among the silliest candidates ever for Jack the Ripper. He is a classic example of the non-contemporaneous alleged suspect; nothing about him fits. He was born in 1837, which certainly does not rule him out as the Whitechapel murderer, but certainly no fifty-one-year-old stranger was seen in the company of any of the victims on the various nights in question. A slim, effeminate, narrow-shouldered boy, he was mercilessly bullied at Eton and failed to obtain a degree from Balliol College, Oxford. He became a friend, in the 1860s, of the great and good among the literati, had a nervous breakdown and was 'rescued' by the minor poet and critic Theodore Watts-Dunton with whom he lived in semi-retirement until his death in 1909. He has no known links with Whitechapel and was known to have masochistic tendencies. Whatever else motivated the crimes of Jack the Ripper, masochism was not among them.

Charles Lutwidge Dodgson was, like Swinburne, an oddity and underneath the outward trappings of Victorian respectability, quite possibly a little bit sordid. He took holy orders in 1861 and burst onto the literary scene under his pen name Lewis Carroll four years later with *Alice's Adventures in Wonderland*. The focus of the book, and the vicar's attention, was the eleven-year-old Alice Liddell, the daughter of the dean of Christ Church. It was Ripperologist Richard Wallace who suggested the man in *Jack the Ripper: 'Light-Hearted Fiend'*, in 1997. Wallace believed that various entries deleted from Dodgson's diaries, now at the British Library, held clues to the killings. There is in fact absolutely nothing to connect Lewis Carroll with Jack the Ripper.

Dr Thomas Barnardo is of a different calibre altogether. For the first time in this chapter, we have a man with contemporary links with Whitechapel who actually talked to Liz Stride shortly before she died and viewed her corpse in the mortuary. Barnardo underwent some sort of Christian conversion in 1862 and began preaching in the Dublin slums before coming to London to study medicine as a preliminary to missionary work. He never got further south-east than Stepney, where he founded his East End Mission for destitute boys. Ripperologist Gary Rowlands has read something sinister into Barnardo's lonely, repressed childhood and the sudden religious fervour, which became a way of life by his young manhood. Religious mania has often been cited as a motive for murder and such characters litter crime fiction. In fact, it is extremely rare and there is absolutely no sign of it in the Whitechapel killings. Rowlands took the commonly held medical theme of the murders and added into the mix an alleged diary of Barnardo's in which the murder dates were left curiously blank. Barnardo was a well-known figure in the Whitechapel/Spitalfields area and he was surely too familiar a face for no one to have commented on his being seen at at least one murder site, for example. To explain the sudden end to the killings, Rowlands postulates that this was brought on by a swimming pool accident shortly after the death of Mary Kelly, which left him deaf!

But the medical theme refuses to go away. We have already dismissed Barnardo, but other medical men have been suggested. The first is Dr William Wynn Westcott. Serious books on the Whitechapel murders do not even include the man as a footnote, but this chapter, devoted as it is to the lunatic fringe, will be more generous. Westcott was educated at University College, London and practised medicine in the West Country before moving to Camden and became coroner for Central London. In the year before the Ripper killings he co-founded, with MacGregor Mathers and William Woodman, the Order of the Golden Dawn, a sub-Masonic society given to Rosicrucian and occult rituals. Ripper theorists Andrew Holloway, Ron Maber and Christopher Smith put Westcott forward in a series of newspaper articles in the 1980s, based largely on the assumption that the

Whitechapel killings had a ritualistic element to them beyond that of the disorganized serial killer. There is no actual evidence against Westcott at all.

The second medical murderer is Dr Thomas Neill Cream who committed his first killing in Chicago in 1881 and was lucky to get a mere ten years. An inveterate womanizer, Cream's target was his mistress's husband and his method was poison, specifically strychnine. He came to England early in 1891 and settled in Lambeth where he used the same corrosive MO on local prostitutes. An extraordinary exhibitionist, Cream wrote taunting letters to the police under a variety of assumed names and tripped himself up. He was executed by the hangman James Billington in the autumn of 1892 and, under the muffling hood and with the rope around his neck, muttered the infuriating half sentence, 'I am Jack the ...' before Billington's pulling of the gallows lever cut him short. Despite the efforts of devotees who have tried to claim otherwise, Cream was still in Joliet prison, Illinois, serving time for the Chicago murder, when the real Jack struck. Lambeth is not Whitechapel and although the victims were all prostitutes, serial killers do not change their modus operandi. Strychnine, not the knife, was Cream's weapon.

What are other possibilities? Frederick Bailey Deeming horrified both Britain and Australia in the years shortly after Jack's work by committing mass murder. His first victims were his wife and four children, killed at Rainhill near Liverpool. As a plumber and fitter, Deeming had the tools and the expertise to bury them in concrete under the kitchen floor before leaving for Melbourne in 1892. Here he used the alias of Drewen or Druin, well aware that he was a wanted man. Having killed his second wife in Melbourne, Deeming was caught, tried and found guilty. He supposedly confessed to the last two canonical murders in Whitechapel, that is Kate Eddowes and Mary Kelly, although this seems to have been a fiction invented by the Australian newspapers. The 'evidence' is non-existent. Deeming's crimes were domestic – his victims were all family members, not random strangers of the night and we have incontrovertible proof that he was in South Africa in the autumn of 1888 taking him out of the frame altogether.

Dr Roslyn D'Onston was another fantasist whose macabre

fascination with the Whitechapel killings has led to an assumption that he was the murderer. We have discussed his puerile map theories already. His name was fictitious – Robert Donston Stephenson was born the son of a Yorkshire seed-oil mill owner in 1841 and at twenty-two was working in the Customs office in Hull. An insufferable snob who grated on his workmates, he was fired and moved to London to become a freelance journalist, writing mostly for William Stead's *Pall Mall Gazette*. It is likely that he was addicted to both alcohol and drugs and may have been charged with assault in June 1887 and indecent assault in the October of the Autumn of Terror. He booked himself into the London Hospital in November and was visited by Dr Morgan Davies, Resident Accoucheur at the hospital who described the Whitechapel murders so graphically that Stephenson believed Davies to be the killer. Stephenson's biographer, Melvin Harris, claims that Davies was a red herring and that Stephenson himself was the killer. This is odd in that the Stephenson/Davies take on the Ripper's *modus operandi* involved sodomizing his victims, which did not happen. Stephenson owned a number of ties which were apparently bloodstained and which were used to carry away the grisly body parts from several of the Whitechapel victims. That Stephenson was a liar, a drunk and made a nuisance of himself (as did several others), pestering the police with ever wilder theories, is not in doubt. As for his being the Whitechapel killer, there is no evidence against him whatsoever.

At least George Chapman was a genuine murderer. Born Severin Klosowski, in Nagornak, Poland in 1865, he seems to have obtained genuine medical qualifications in Warsaw before moving to England in June 1887. Here he worked as a hairdresser, first in the West India Dock Road, then in a basement shop below the White Hart on the corner of Whitechapel High Street and George Yard. He was thirty-seven when William Billington hanged him at Wandsworth for the murders of Isabella Spink, Elizabeth Taylor and Maud Marsh. All three were Klosowski's mistresses and they all three died by antimony poisoning.

Why should anyone link him with the Ripper? He was in the area, had violent tendencies, surgical knowledge and access to sharp blades. The murders stopped because Klosowski emigrated to the United

States relatively soon after Mary Kelly's death. Retired Chief Inspector Abberline believed Chapman might be Jack and when asked to explain the different MO. involved said, rather limply, that Klosowski's mistresses, were 'of different classes and obviously call for different methods of dispatch'.

The theory which blew Ripperology apart in the 1990s was that of the Liverpool cotton merchant, James Maybrick. Whereas many of the suspects in this chapter are born of little more than wishful thinking, Maybrick at least has two tangible pieces of evidence linked to his name. Unfortunately, there is a very high chance that neither of them is genuine. Maybrick holds a rare distinction; he is at once an alleged murderer and an incontrovertible victim. On 11 May 1889, seven months after the death of Mary Kelly, he was given arsenic by his wife Florence and subsequently died. Sentenced to death for murder, she was reprieved and released from prison in 1904.

Ninety years later, the 'Diary of Jack the Ripper' – allegedly written by Maybrick in 1888 – was published. Some Ripperologists rejoiced – we knew who Jack was at last. Others were sceptical. The so-called Hitler diaries had been authorized by the eminent historian Hugh Trevor-Roper, bought by *The Times* for £1 million and were subsequently found to be forgeries. We do not have time in this brief survey to trace the provenance of the Maybrick diaries, except to note that at one point the owner of the book claimed he had forged it himself – a confession immediately retracted by his lawyer.

Exhaustive tests were carried out on the diary, checking ink and paper, not to mention graphology expertise, which was brought to bear on the handwriting (it may be worthy of note that this does not match the only known example of Maybrick's hand, his signature). Such tests were inconclusive – the paper is old, the ink is old. What cannot be ascertained by science is exactly when the two were put together. The narrative, interspersed with family details and confused, bad poetry, is certainly gripping and reads like the work of a seriously disturbed mind:

> I thought it a joke when I cut her breasts off, kissed them for a while. The taste of blood was sweet, the pleasure overwhelming, will have to do it again, it thrilled me so. Left them on the table with some of the other stuff...

'Maybrick' is referring to the murder of Mary Kelly, but Kelly's breasts were not on the table next to her bed – one of them was on the bed itself, underneath her body. These facts were not common knowledge until 1987 when the long-lost medical report of Dr Thomas Bond was rediscovered. Whoever the writer was, he was working without this evidence and he was not the Whitechapel murderer.

The diary claims that the killer took rooms in Middlesex Street – and the sense of the text implies that this was in July 1888 – which places him at the heart of the Ripper's killing grounds and gives him time to learn the street pattern and the habits of the nightwalkers. From that point on the errors multiply – there was clearly no actual attempt to decapitate Polly Nichols as the diary states; there were no rings or coins near Annie Chapman's body, although the diary says there were; the timing of the deaths of Liz Stride and Kate Eddowes is impossible, with the diary's fifteen minutes between the murders. In short, the Maybrick diary is a forgery, an example of fiction which has been better written by a number of authors who are perfectly happy to put their names to the work.

In June 1993, a gold half-hunter watch came to light which had scratched on the interior of the case 'J.Maybrick', 'I am Jack' and a series of initials which are those of the canonical five. We have the same problem here as with the diary – the watch is old, but when were the scratches made and by whom? The diary and the watch were supported in 1997 by Ripperologist Paul Feldman who used various 'clues' from the murders to bolster the case. Feldman claimed that the police were checking the torn envelope found near Annie Chapman's body in Hanbury Street to match the 'M', 'J' and 'Sp' handwritten on it. In fact, from Inspector Chandler's reports of September 1888, the 'J' (for James in Feldman's contention) is clearly a figure 2. 'Sp' is obviously Spitalfields and 'M' is the first letter of any number of addresses in the area, e.g. Miller's Court, Montague Street, the Minories and so on. The inverted 'v's carved into the cheeks of Kate Eddowes, Feldman contended, formed the Maybrick 'M' if placed side by side. If not placed side by side of course, they form two inverted 'v's!

Well-known Ripper experts have placed the Maybrick theory firmly in context. Philip Sugden wrote[2]:

A reading of the diary still leaves me baffled as to how any intelligent and reasonably informed student of the Ripper case could possibly have taken it seriously.

And Melvyn Harris went one better, noting that the diary's 'time-wasting stupidities will linger on to dog historians for years to come'.

But of all the theories which have captured the public imagination, none has struck a chord like that delicious old chestnut, the 'highest in the land'. The British are obsessed with their 'toffs'. We are a lord-loving country and if it can be proved that our lords are also serial killers, then so much the better. There is undoubtedly an element of envy in this. We love our lords, but we also hate them for their wealth and power – to prove that one of them was a sexual deviant and lustmurderer would be wonderful! Theorists have reasoned, over the last century, that the reason that Jack was not caught is that there was a conspiracy and cover-up of monumental proportions that could only be orchestrated by the highest echelons in their corridors of power.

Although the 'highest in the land' is not one theory but several interwoven, I will deal with the elements separately for sanity's sake. The highest of the highest involved was Prince Albert Victor, the Duke of Clarence and Avondale who was the eldest son of Edward, Prince of Wales. 'Eddie' as he was known in the family, had inherited his mother's deafness and his father's well-known aversion to study. He died from influenza early in 1892 (which some Ripperologists believe was yet another lie by the establishment to mask something altogether more sinister) so we will never know what kind of monarch he would have made; his younger brother, in turn, became George V.

Eddie was taught privately at home and went through the sham of attending Trinity College Cambridge where his deafness made real study an impossibility. In the year of the Ripper, in accordance with the sycophancy of the time, he was given an honorary Doctorate of Law by the university and was gazetted to his father's elite cavalry regiment, the 10th Hussars. He was twenty-four.

The concept that Clarence was the Ripper appeared as early as 1970 when Dr Thomas Stowell put the notion forward in *The Criminologist*. However, he also wrote to *The Times*:

I have at no time associated His Royal Highness, the late Duke of Clarence, with the Whitechapel murderer or suggested that the murderer was of royal blood...

– so perhaps he had had second thoughts or was misrepresented in the first place. By the 1960s, an awareness of the psychological compulsion found among sociopaths was already known, so Stowell (actually an expert in industrial medicine, not psychiatry) assumed that Eddie had become sadistically aroused watching the skinning and dressing of deer on innumerable hunting parties at Balmoral. By 1888, with his mind going because of the ravages of tertiary syphilis, he turned his attention to random killings – and subsequent mutilations – in the East End.

Jack Spiering developed these theories into *Prince Jack*, but the evidence against Eddie is non-existent. Despite the elaborate contrivance of journalist Stephen Knight (see below) there is nothing to link him with the East End and physically he was too tall to fit any one of the eyewitness accounts of those seen with the victims shortly before they died. The weakest element of the story is the syphilis contention – and it is extraordinary that Dr Stowell should think this possible. For Eddie to have been syphilitic to the extent that his brain was affected, he would have had to have suffered from the disease by inheriting it from his parents. Bearing in mind that his father was a notorious womanizer, this is entirely possible, but syphilitic children *always* exhibit Hutchinson's triad, that is congenital eye problems, badly disfigured teeth and jaw and deafness. Only the last fits Eddie. He also has fairly watertight alibis for the nights in question. On 31 August 1888, when Polly Nichols died, Clarence was the guest of Viscount Donne at his country home, Derby Lodge, in Yorkshire, where he stayed until 7 September. From there, he went straight to the cavalry barracks at York on the day before Annie Chapman was killed and stayed there until 10 September. When Liz Stride and Kate Eddowes died on the night of the 'double event', Clarence was with his grandmother, the Queen, at Abergeldie, in Scotland. Victoria was a diligent diary keeper and recorded that Eddie had lunched with her – this was ten hours after Jack butchered Kate Eddowes in Mitre Square. At the time of Mary Kelly's death on the morning of the Lord Mayor's Show, Clarence was staying at Sandringham, the family home in Norfolk.

Conspiracy theorists who have the heir presumptive in the frame contend that such alibis are meaningless because the entire family, plus their huge entourage of servants, would have colluded to concoct them.

For those who find the Duke of Clarence too high profile to be Jack, the focus has shifted sideways and down a little to his tutor, J K Stephen. The son of the judge in the Florence Maybrick murder trial and a cousin of the darling of the literati, Virginia Woolf, Stephen was a Cambridge-educated scholar who wrote poetry and was a regular contributor to various journals. He may have been a misogynist (one theory runs that he and Clarence were lovers) and he was certainly a manic-depressive – his father became insane and Virginia Woolf committed suicide – and it may be that an accident on holiday in Felixstowe in 1886–7 in which he was hit on the head by a windmill's sails, made matters worse. There is nothing to link Stephen with Whitechapel, unless we implicate Clarence in some way. In short, the evidence against him is nil. He died at the end of February 1892, at St Andrew's Hospital, Northampton, of 'mania, refusal of food, exhaustion'.

The best known of the 'highest in the land' variety is that concocted by Stephen Knight and Joseph Sickert in 1976. It has spawned its own spin-offs and at least two films – *Murder by Decree* and, more recently, *From Hell*. So well-established has this hokum become that even the most ill-informed on the Ripper case will tell you – 'It was the Queen's doctor, wasn't it?' Knight's *Jack the Ripper: The Final Solution* begins as many potentially good books do with speculation and scepticism and ends up with 'proven fact'. Knight's confidante, Joseph Sickert, claimed to be the son of the influential Victorian artist Walter Sickert, but he was, in Knight's own words, 'vague' and 'disordered'.

Knight's story goes like this. Walter Sickert worked from a studio in Cleveland Street (for which there is no evidence) and the Duke of Clarence occasionally visited it on his way to and from the homosexual brothel in the same street, which became a hotbed of scandal in 1889. There is, of course, no evidence for this either, although certain members of the aristocracy were certainly on the visitors' list. The bi-sexual Clarence, it is alleged, fell in love with and subsequently married a Catholic shopgirl who worked in Cleveland Street, one Annie Crook. Apart from there being no evidence that any such marriage took place, Knight's assumption is that the whole mess had to be covered up because the royals were unpopular and that the country was on the brink of an Anarchist revolution as evidenced by the 'bloody Sunday' riot in Trafalgar Square in 1887. Since Clarence was the heir presumptive, he could not have remained married to a Catholic anyway, as the events of Edward VIII and Mrs Simpson were to prove in 1936.

In the tortuous plot of the Knight-Sickert conspiracy, the witness to the wedding was Mary Kelly who saw a wonderful opportunity to blackmail the government. The Marquess of Salisbury, then Prime Minister, turned to his fellow Lodge member in the Masons, the queen's physician-in-ordinary, Sir William Gull.

The royal doctor set out to find everyone connected with the case. Annie Crook was illegally kidnapped and placed into Gull's own lunatic asylum where various operations were carried out on her brain. Gull's coachman, John Netley, spent the next four years trying to find and run over little Alice, the child of the Clarence-Crook marriage. Since all five of Jack's victims were friends and shared their deadly secret, they all had to die. Netley obligingly drove the increasingly deranged Gull to the murder sites in his coach and the look-out, who made sure the surgeon's work was not interrupted, was Walter Sickert, who knew Mary Kelly well.

It is difficult to know where to start unravelling this farrago of nonsense. Knight's times and dates do not add up. His motivation is weak in the extreme. More recent writers, who should know better, have accepted the coach theory to explain why no one was apprehended covered in blood. A coach of Gull's calibre would have been *very* unusual in Whitechapel and no eyewitness mentions one. The police at the time may have had little scientific knowledge of a forensic nature to help them, but they could recognize wheel-tracks and found none.

Most bizarre of all is the Masonic connection. Stephen Knight's second book, *The Brotherhood*, threatened to blow the lid off the supposedly sinister cult and he died only two years later. There were rumblings at the time that he had crossed the wrong people, still 'the highest in the land'. In fact he died of a cerebral tumour despite surgery, having developed epilepsy in 1977. Much has been made of the Masonic clues left at the murder sites. A neat row of coins was placed between the feet of Annie Chapman in the yard at Hanbury Street, a Masonic symbol. The cutting of the throat and the placing of entrails over shoulders follows the pattern of the method of execution meted out to the murderers of the great mason, Hiram Abiff, who built Solomon's Temple in Jerusalem. Even the inverted 'v' on Kate Eddowes' cheeks is the Masonic triangle created by the architect's divider, Knight claimed. Most significantly of all is the tortuous and perplexing red herring of the Goulston Street graffito – 'The Juwes are the Men who will not be blamed for nothing' – scrawled in chalk above the bloody, torn apron of the Mitre Square victim. This is not a mere misspelling of 'Jews' but a dark hint at the names of Abiff's murderers – Jubela, Jubelo and Jubelum.

It is ludicrous in the extreme. There was no need for panic in the royal household or government even if the marriage did take place. Merely buy off Kelly and the tiny handful in the know and the problem was solved. The Marquess of Salisbury was not a Mason, so his link with Gull is implausible. According to the records available, Annie Crook was Anglican, not Catholic. There is no record of a marriage having taken place ('Well, there wouldn't be, would there?' conspiracy theorists rejoin). The address at which Knight claims Annie Crook lived was a hole in the ground in 1886. An Elizabeth *Cook* lived in the new apartments built on the site, but she lived there until 1893 rather than being whisked away at dead of night to an asylum. The Juwes are purely fictitious characters who have no links with Masonry and there was no neat row of coins between Annie Chapman's feet, merely the random scattering of items from her pocket.

Most potently of all, John Netley, whose apparently murderous attempts on Alice Crook ended with his being chased by a mob into the Thames, where he drowned, actually died in a fall from his coach near Baker Street in 1903. And Sir William Gull, master Mason and butcher *par excellence*, had had two strokes by the autumn of 1888 which left him seriously paralyzed and totally incapable of the ferocious attacks on the Whitechapel victims.

Ripperologist Melvyn Fairclough, a friend of Joseph Sickert, took up the torch after Stephen Knight's death, leaning heavily on the diaries allegedly written by Inspector Frederick Abberline of H Division, one of the detectives leading the hunt for the Whitechapel murderer. Again, the Masons are cast as the villains, but this time the net is wider. The instigators of the killings are members of the most exalted level of Freemasonry, Royal Alpha Lodge No 16. Cover-ups aplenty took place because Sir Charles Warren, the hapless Commissioner of the Metropolitan Police, ensured that the incriminating 'Juwes' wall-writing was obliterated, not to prevent anti-Semitic rioting, but to protect his fellow Mason, William Gull. In Fairclough's version, fed to him by Joseph Sickert, the actual mastermind is, to use Abberline's diary phrase 'the Candlestick Maker', Lord Randolph Churchill. By 1888, the cavalier Churchill had destroyed his own career by quarrelling with both the Prince of Wales and Lord Salisbury and his own life by contracting the syphilis that would kill him in 1895. The inconsistency of Caroline Maxwell, who knew Mary Kelly and who gave evidence at her inquest that she talked to her some hours after she was in fact dead, led Fairclough to speculate that the real corpse in Miller's Court was actually Winifred Collins, another friend involved in the Cleveland Street clandestine marriage.

By the time Fairclough's book *The Ripper and the Royals* was published in 1991, he had already acknowledged that the Abberline diaries were almost certainly forgeries. There are errors throughout, not least the reversal of the inspector's own initials, G F, rather than F G. We have already effectively dismissed both the clandestine marriage and the trumped-up Masonic connection; grafting on Churchill would seem gratuitous in the extreme, although oddly, the extraordinarily detailed description given by George Hutchinson of a man he saw in the company of Mary Kelly shortly before she died, *could* just about be the man.

The remaining survivor of the 'highest in the land' theory is Walter Sickert and crime writer Patricia Cornwell put her reputation and a vast amount of money into making grand claims with her 2002 book, *Portrait of a Killer: Jack the Ripper – Case Closed*. Cornwell's case rests on the fact that Sickert suffered a fistula, a malformation of the penis which made sex impossible and that this led to an abnormal and sadistic impulse to kill women in Whitechapel. Ms Cornwell also claims that Sickert's stationery was of a similar type to that used in the infamous letter to Dr Openshaw at the London Hospital and that traces of Sickert's DNA can be found on the stamp of that letter's envelope. The stationery evidence is weak in the extreme – the Scottish firm of Alexander Pirie and Sons was a very common brand, but no examples of this company's paper came from Sickert's correspondence in 1888, when he was using exclusively Johnson Superfine. The DNA evidence, which ought to be relatively conclusive, is anything but. The condition of the Openshaw stamp is too poor for nuclear DNA testing to be accurate, so the less convincing mitochondrial DNA (by no means unique) was used by Cornwell's researchers. Admittedly this gives us only 1% of the community who carried this particular DNA configuration, but all it proves is that Walter Sickert *may* have written one or more of the hoax letters sent to the police or newspapers; it certainly does not prove that he was the Whitechapel murderer.

As for the fistula, the evidence suggests that this was an anal condition, corrected by surgery and that the artist had a perfectly natural sex life which resulted in several illegitimate children.

Now that we have eliminated the fictional and the fanciful, we can look at the plausible. Although there are different versions of the Macnaghten Memoranda and the biographical details in it are confused, the names written there are at least flesh and blood characters who were clearly at one time considered likely suspects.

The first 'possible' is M J Druitt. Macnaghten gets the man's age and occupation wrong and tantalizingly drops in the line – 'From private information I have little doubt that his own family suspected this man of being the Whitechapel murderer.' Montague Druitt was a graduate of New College Oxford, a keen cricketer and a teacher at a boys' boarding school in Blackheath. He was called to the Bar in 1885. In July of that year his mother was admitted to an asylum in Clapton and, soon after that, Druitt lost his job at the school for reasons that were never made clear. His body was fished out of the Thames on 31 December, seven weeks after Mary Kelly's murder. The inquest returned a verdict of suicide as a note was found in his chambers which read 'Since Friday I felt I was going to be like mother and the best thing for me was to die.' Druitt's dark hair and moustache certainly ties in with various eyewitness accounts of men seen talking to various victims on the nights they died, but other than that, as Inspector Abberline admitted to the *Pall Mall Gazette* in 1903, there is 'absolutely nothing... to incriminate him'. Rather like the Duke of

Clarence, whom Druitt superficially resembles, he had alibis for most of the nights in question – his cricketing fixtures with the MCC and other clubs rule him out.

Next, Macnaghten cites 'Kosminski, a Polish Jew'. This is much more realistic, because the man was a Whitechapel resident and clearly deranged. Along with 95% of Victorian society, Macnaghten believed that Kosminski's insanity was 'owing to many years indulgence in solitary vices' [masturbation]. Further research by Ripper experts found that Aaron Kosminski was committed, via the Mile End Workhouse, first to Colney Hatch asylum (1891 to 1894), then to Leavesden, near Watford, where he remained until his death in 1919. He was one of those tragic victims of what Karl Marx called 'alienation', one of the countless wanderers of Jack London's Abyss who litter the Ripper story. He never washed, heard voices, refused to work and only ate scraps from the gutters in the belief that fresher food might be poisoned. Macnaghten says Kosminski had a hatred of women and showed homicidal tendencies; certainly he attacked an attendant (albeit a male) with a chair while in the asylum. Notes on the man by Robert Anderson and Chief Inspector Swanson are very confused, however. Anderson arrogantly says he knew who the Whitechapel murderer was but could not name him. He also states that Kosminski was recognized by an eyewitness 'the instant he was confronted with him'. Macnaghten claims the man was seen by a City PC near Mitre Square, which is untrue and Swanson claims that Kosminski was identified at the Police Convalescent Home in Brighton. Apart from the peculiarities of this venue as a place for identification, the witness – by deduction, probably the civilian Joseph Lawende – was now apparently, sixteen months after Kate Eddowes' murder, positive in his identification of a man he claimed even at the time he would not know again. All in all, it looks as though policemen even as senior as Macnaghten, Anderson and Swanson were easily swayed by the stereotypical image of a raving lunatic.

Macnaghten's third suspect is Michael Ostrog, 'a mad Russian doctor and a convict and unquestionably a homicidal maniac'. Some of the silly theories I have *not* included in this chapter (for lack of space) include deranged Russians, so perhaps Ostrog should not surprise us. Macnaghten believed him to be a knife-carrying misogynist, whereas he was actually a conman with a tally of fourteen known aliases, fraudster and thief. Convict he certainly was, having been imprisoned first in Oxford in 1863. He did time in Cambridge and Burton upon Trent too and was released from the Surrey Pauper Lunatic Asylum on 10 March 1888. This in itself may have been a con trick, because he was transferred there from Wandsworth Prison, which may have had a harsher regime. The most recent research has revealed that Ostrog was incarcerated in a Paris asylum at the time of the Whitechapel murders, which effectively takes him out of the frame. Although he once pulled a gun on a policeman trying to arrest him, there is no hard evidence that he carried knives or had any antipathy towards women. He is last heard of in the St Giles Christian Mission, Holborn, in 1904.

There are many other suspects, real and imaginary, who could be placed in this chapter, but space prevents it. Most criminologists today concur that the Whitechapel murderer lived in the area where he killed – we saw this in Chapter Two. Of the 103 suspects named by John J Eddleston in his excellent *Jack the Ripper, an Encyclopaedia*[3] only nineteen have established Whitechapel links. All of those can be excluded on a variety of logical grounds. As Eddleston himself says:

> Though few writers will readily admit it, there is a good chance that the real Ripper has never come to public attention. Most sensible writers accept that Jack was a local man, of the same class as those he murdered and was someone the victims would readily have accepted as one of their own. The suggestion that after claiming his victims he vanished back into obscurity, for whatever reason, and has never been traced is much more likely than claiming a Royal, Masonic or similar connection.

It is time we looked for such a man.

Chapter 5

The Trigger
– Annie Millwood

Annie Millwood met Jack the Ripper on Saturday 25 February 1888. On that day, the satirical mirror of society, *Punch*, carried an imaginary courtroom scene in which a prisoner is trying to confess to a crime. The magistrate will have none of it – 'It is the aim of Justice to give everyone in England the chance of getting off, whether guilty or not guilty.' When the prisoner confesses, the magistrate screams 'Confess! The man must be mad! Let him be removed.'

The man who was Jack never confessed. Neither was he mad in the conventional sense. What finally removed him was death.

Annie Millwood was thirty-eight and the widow of a soldier, Richard Millwood. In the freezing February of the Ripper's year, she was living in a doss at Spitalfield's Chambers, 8 White's Row, a narrow, dingy thoroughfare that ran parallel to Dorset Street. At five o'clock that afternoon, as dusk settled on Whitechapel, Annie was attacked by a complete stranger who whipped a clasp knife from his pocket and stabbed her.

The attack on Annie Millwood was part of the endemic violence of the East End. Her case would have been regarded by the authorities as an everyday event. Over the whole of London in the 1880s, there were four murders per 100,000 of the population. Robert Anderson, Head of the CID, considered this 'normal'. On the face of it, the assault was inexplicable. Annie did not know her attacker and the records of the infirmary to which she was admitted merely refer to stabs to the legs and lower torso. The *Eastern Post* gave more detail –

It appears [Millwood] was admitted to the Whitechapel

Infirmary suffering from numerous stabs to the legs and lower part of the body. She stated that she had been attacked by a man she did not know and who stabbed her with a clasp knife which he took from his pocket. No one appears to have seen the attack and as far as at present ascertained there is only the woman's statement to bear out the allegations of an attack, though she had been stabbed cannot be denied.

We must remember that this article appeared seven months before the Ripper killings began, so at this stage the media are very low key. There is no slaughterhouse, no rising panic; but even so the implication that the wounds may be self-inflicted is odd. Why should the journalist even hint at this? The reason lies in the whole alien world of the workhouse, the casual ward and its infirmary.

The first house of industry for the benefit of the poor in the area was set up as early as 1724 in Ayliffe Street near Goodman's Fields. This was part of the parish of St Mary Matfelon – the white chapel – and was a response to the problem of poverty here as it was elsewhere in the country. The Poor Law of 1601 provided a system of outdoor parish relief in which the wealthy paid an annual sum – the poor rate – which was distributed amongst the destitute. Even by the 1720s the gathering speed of the Industrial Revolution meant that the workforce became ever more mobile and parishes were unable to cope with the influx of workers. In Ayliffe Street, the anonymous Mistress who kept the house provided for sixty adults who went out daily in search of work and returned for the night. Her house was clean and the beds made up.[1]

In the nearby parish of Christchurch, where 'Itchy Park' would become the unofficial nightly home of hundreds in Jack's time, a similar workhouse was set up in Bell Lane in the summer of 1728. Housing eighty-four paupers, including thirty children, most of the inmates were employed (as befitted a silk-weaving community) in winding Bengal silk, as opposed to the wool-winding and oakum-picking[2] carried out in other workhouses elsewhere. The old women knitted stockings while the children were taught to read and say their Catechism. The house diet included meat three times a week.

By the 1770s both workhouses had grown enormously, a reflection of the fact that London was now the largest city in the world. With an inmate population of nearly 600, the Whitechapel workhouse was one of the biggest in the country, dwarfing Christ Church with its 340. A map of 1830 shows the workhouses, one next to the charity school along Whitechapel High Street, the other (Spitalfields) north of St Thomas's Street and the Quaker's Burial Ground. There is a modern sheltered housing block on the High Street site and today it backs onto the old burial ground for the workhouse, which is now a small, open park.

1834 saw a turning point in the history of poverty management throughout the country. In that year, Lord Grey's Whig government, alarmed at the huge cost of outdoor relief[3] commissioned Edwin Chadwick to find a cheaper solution. His answer was an extension of the workhouse system coupled with the principle of 'less eligibility'. Conditions in the workhouses were to be so grim that a man would take *any* sort of work, no matter how badly paid, rather than go there. Christened 'Bastilles' by the poor after the Paris prison synonymous with corruption and suffering and which had been pulled down by the mob during the French Revolution, the stigma attached to the work-house would last as long as the system did – for another hundred years.

In Whitechapel, the Poor Law Union was set up in February 1837, under the supervision of twenty-five elected Guardians of the Poor and including nine East End parishes, three of which would contain the sites of the murders of 1888–9. In the 1831 census, these parishes' populations added up to 64,141 (Whitechapel alone being half that) and the expenditure in the financial years 1834–6 had been £23,036.

There was at first no new building and a doctor reported to the Poor Law Commissioners of Whitehall in 1838 on the appalling state of the Whitechapel institution. Of the 104 children there, all girls, eighty-nine had recently been hit by fever. This was partially explained by the fact that all of them slept in one dormitory 88 feet long, 16 feet wide and 7 feet high along with the four women in charge of them. Most beds housed four girls, some five. In the Infant Nursery, twenty-three two to three-year-olds were crowded into a single room which they rarely left, 'either for air or exercise'. In the main workhouse there were two fever wards (the forerunners of the Infirmary to which Annie Millwood staggered on 25 February 1888) with two patients per bed.

There was no ventilation in the room so that even visitors were at risk from infection. The privies (lavatories) were in a deplorable state, drainage was poor and the whole building did not possess a single bath.

By the time this report was written, serious economic hardship had hit Whitechapel and Spitalfields and the independent weavers who had been so prosperous in the previous century were now forced to take what work they could in factories and workshops, operating to the rhythm of steam-driven machines. Consequently, a larger new work house was erected on the site of the old one along Charles Street and Baker's Row in 1842. A map of 1860 shows the building clearly divided into two blocks occupying the site on the corner of Charles and Thomas Streets. This was upgraded in that year by the architect Thomas Barry and the new plan is faithfully recorded on a map of 1867. There was now a conventional 'H' shape to the plot, one block measuring 128 feet by 43 including the master's house, wards and kitchen. The other block, containing the receiving wards and laundry was smaller and a third a mere 50 feet by 31. The front of the building along Charles Street was a forbidding five storeys high and must have dwarfed the weavers' cottages and even some of the work shops nearby. Here stood the entrance hall and committee rooms and a central two-storey wing linked this to the rear arm of the 'H', a six-storey block with chapel, dining hall and accommodation.

In keeping with tradition, male and female wards were separate, women to the north, men to the south. The relieving offices were ranged along Thomas Street, with a separate laundry block to the north-east and a ward for imbeciles occupying the rear of the plot that backed onto a starch manufactory. The dispensary stood next to the male wards and probably formed the nucleus of the Infirmary.

When the medical journal *The Lancet* focused on workhouses in 1865 there was no actual visit to Whitechapel, but no doubt it suffered from the usual problems present elsewhere. There was a generic lack of ventilation; medical staff were too few and underpaid; there was very little furniture; there was one comb per ward and no games provided for the sick. *The Lancet* recommended that there should be a separate ward for sick children and that the labour ward be moved so that screams should not reach adjacent wards.

1867 saw yet more legislation for London's poor. Now workhouses had to build infirmaries on separate sites and this led to the building of a second workhouse (by 1872) at South Grove. The Clerk to the Governors in these years was William Vallance and his signature is all over the surviving documentation. Today, Baker's Row is called Vallance Road.[4] From now on the whole of the Charles Street/Baker's Row site operated as the Infirmary.

Our view of the Whitechapel workhouse is inevitably coloured by our own twenty-first-century sense of comfort and well being, which is aeons away from what Annie Millwood would have understood; and by the external viewpoint of sensitive souls like Jack London. Jack the Ripper was dead by the time of London's visit. The brilliant *People of the Abyss* was actually describing the Spike, the men's casual ward on the other side of Thomas Street. At first he was not allowed in, passing himself off as a down-and-out, because he had too much money in his pocket. Once accepted, however, he underwent an experience he would never forget. London joined the daily queue of the homeless before three o'clock to be told that only twenty-two would be admitted. By four there were over thirty and others turning up later drifted away realizing there would be no bed for the night for them. Men in the line spoke with bitter memories of the smallpox hospital with its loathsome food and its mortality rate of one in six. Each of them had been 'on the doss' for three nights and days and were now desperate for shelter. As desperate perhaps as Annie Millwood. People were known to inflict wounds on themselves to gain a 'hospital' bed for the night.

> 'Age and English hardship had broken them,' London wrote, 'and for them the game was played and up.'[5]

Thomas Street was twenty feet wide, with three feet wide pavements. Here the view from the houses every day was the pauper line of the 'Ins and Outs'; the children played around the paupers' feet –

> They had been born to the sight of the spike line and all their brief lives they had seen it.

At the gate, where porters like William Keep held sway, paupers had to give their name, age, place of birth, condition of destitution and last night's doss. London felt his pockets ransacked for knives, matches or tobacco, then realized that he had not been searched, but that a brick-hard loaf of bread had been shoved there. Every man denied having any of the above – matches started fires; tobacco was a source of a quarrel; knives could end it fatally. *But every man carried a knife.*

In the anteroom, London thought he was on his way to Hell. Shoes came off, blood-soaked, putrid rags were unbound from tired, aching feet. The food was appalling – three quarters of a pint of skilly (maize and hot water) into which hungry men voraciously dunked their bread. The general talk in the badly lit room was of the problem of getting 'tommy' (food) anywhere else and that the Polish and Russian Jews had come over, set up sweat shops and taken away a working man's livelihood.

At seven, everybody stripped off and in pairs went into the two tubs available. All twenty washed in the same water and London dried himself as best he could with a damp towel bloody with the sores from another pauper's back. He slept (eventually) in a canvas bed, six feet long, less than two feet wide and six inches off the floor. His head was higher than his feet and because all the beds in the narrow dormitory were attached to iron rails, movement in one bed caused them all to shake.

> The smell was frightful and sickening and my skin crept and crawled. While the shrill voices of children playing in the street continued til midnight, in the Spike it was all grunting, spitting, snoring and groaning like some giant sea-monster, the sound punctuated now and then by the screams of somebody's nightmare.

After a six o'clock breakfast of more bread and skilly, men were set to work, some picking oakum, others to scrubbing and cleaning. London was one of eight men sent across the road to the Workhouse Infirmary to scavenge. They emptied garbage cans from the sick wards and carried them down five flights of stairs to receptacles reeking of disinfectant. The inmates here, London reported, were of no use to anyone.

> They clutter the earth with their presence and are better out of the way.

At the bottom of what he called the Abyss, they were the first to be struck by disease, the quickest to die. And Jack London found himself sprinkling disinfectant in the new mortuary when the 'dead waggon' turned up with five bodies. These were clearly inmates from the Infirmary and it was generally believed that incurables were given a dose of 'black jack' or 'white potion' and were quietly 'polished off'.

'Breakfast' was a mass of scraps from the wards above –

> chunks of grease and fat pork... bones ... in short all the leavings from the fingers and mouths of the sick ones suffering from all manner of diseases.

London's co-scavengers plunged their hands into this and ate ravenously, anything left over thrust into handkerchiefs and hidden inside their shirts. Jack London ran away from the Spike because he could. He was after all staying some streets away in the comfortable house of Police Sergeant William Thick, and he knew he could bathe and change and try to forget. Most people in the Abyss were not so lucky.

Slightly less harrowing pictures could be found. A year after Annie Millwood was admitted, bleeding and shocked, to this place, Margaret Harkness (writing as John Law) wrote –

> The Whitechapel Union is a model workhouse; that is to say, it is the Poor law incarnate in stone and brick. The men are not allowed to smoke in it, not even when they are in their dotage; the young women never taste tea and the old ones may not indulge in a cup during the long afternoons, only at half past six o'clock morning and night, when they receive a small hunk of bread with butter scraped over the surface and a mug of that beverage which is so dear to their hearts as well as to their stomachs. The young people never go out, never see a visitor and the old ones only get one holiday in the month. Then the aged paupers may be seen skipping like lambkins outside the doors of the Bastille, while they jabber to their friends and relations. A little gruel morning and night, meat twice a week, that is the food of the grown-up people, seasoned with hard work and prison discipline. Doubtless this Bastille offers no premium to the idle and improvident habits; but what shall we say of the woman or man, maimed by misfortune, who must come there or die in the streets?[6]

One maimed by misfortune and an unknown assailant and who might have died in the street, was Annie Millwood. We have no record of who treated her or who called the police, but the Medical Superintendent at the time was Dr Herbert Larder. In the 1881 census, James Holt and Perkins Case were the resident medical officers and by 1885 they had been joined by a difficult colleague, Morgan Davies. They had a team of twenty-one nurses, all of them female. Edward Allen was probably on duty at the gate when Annie arrived and either he or his wife Elizabeth would have helped the injured woman into the waiting room.

At the bottom of the heap in terms of status was Robert Mann, who kept the Infirmary's mortuary. We have no hard evidence that Mann saw Annie Millwood when she was admitted or that he had anything to do with her, but the central thesis of this book is that it was this chance meeting that led to the Autumn of Terror and the start of a killing spree which still haunts the world a century and a quarter later.

What had happened to Annie Millwood? Had she been attacked by a random lunatic as she walked past him? Unlikely. We know that there were a surprisingly high number of dangerous men wandering the East End; some of them, as we have seen, were or are today, serious Ripper suspects. And it is possible that a pocket knife could have cut through a dress, petticoats and stays. Much more likely is that Annie's charms were on display when her attacker struck because she was a prostitute and he was her client. We do not know where the assault took place, but Whitechapel and Spitalfields, as we have seen, were hotbeds of open-air sex and even in the dusk of a cold February evening, any alleyway, yard, court or corner would do for a 'tuppenny upright'.

Annie was patched up and spent nearly a month in the Infirmary. We have no idea whether Robert Mann saw her again, talked to her, spent time with her. It is likely, given the strict segregation of the sexes, that he did not. But that did not matter – what mattered was that he may have witnessed her bleeding state, perhaps even seen her bloodstained clothes and something clicked in his brain. He would see the scars again in the near future...

It is noticeable that when Annie was discharged she did not go home to her doss in White's Row but to the South Grove Workhouse. Had her client/attacker robbed her as he stabbed, leaving her unable to afford even the 4d for her coffin-shaped bed in the doss? Ten days after arriving at South Grove, Annie was chatting to other inmates at the rear of the building when she suddenly collapsed. Death followed soon afterwards.

No reports mention the fact that Annie Millwood's body would have been taken to Whitechapel Infirmary, not to the main building but to the mortuary in Eagle Place along Old Montague Street, the mortuary kept by Robert Mann. And it was the pauper's job to strip corpses, to wash them, to lay them out for the post mortem and the coffin. Robert Mann would have had ample time to look at the partially healed wounds on the dead woman's body.

The coroner for south-east Middlesex, Wynne Baxter, who features prominently in the Ripper case, presided over her inquest on 5 April. Ironically, Annie's death had nothing to do with the attack on her. The cause of death was 'a sudden effusion into the pericardium from the rupture of the left pulmonary artery through ulceration'. Even if she had not met Jack the Ripper in the Whitechapel Workhouse, she would have died anyway.

What went on in Robert Mann's mind in February 1888? If the police had known that at the time, they may have been able to stop him before his killing spree started. But that would have been to ask the impossible and even today, with sixty years of the criminal psychology of serial killers to draw on, we still cannot identify the problem with certainty and our over-inflated, lopsided notion of human rights means that we can do nothing about it.

> 'All the while,' write Schechter and Everitt,[7] '[the serial killer's] hunger for blood is building inside him, his fantasies of torture and death are growing more urgent by the day. Suddenly, something pushes him over the edge from morbid daydream to murderous action, driving him to fulfil his lethal fantasies on living victims.'

This is the trigger and it is highly complex. Schechter and Everitt cite the 1981 example of David Bullock who went to a Christmas party at the flat of an acquaintance, Herbert Morales. In one single, incomprehensible sentence, Bullock summed up the bizarre nature of the 'trigger' – 'He started messing with the Christmas tree,' he told police, 'telling me how nice the Christmas tree was. So I shot him.'

The Whitechapel murderer was not, technically, the first serial killer in history, but he was among the first and he showed all the characteristics of what is actually a disease. Robert Mann's behaviour would have changed slowly between February and August 1888 as he entered what criminologists call the aura phase. As a long-term inmate of the workhouse, he had his well-developed routines – meals, exercise, work and bed followed a rigid timetable. Breakfast, eaten at six o'clock in the Infirmary in 1888, was a carefully measured five ounces of bread, half an ounce of butter and a pint of tea. Dinner (the midday meal) consisted of four ounces of cooked meat (five times a week), eight ounces of potatoes or other vegetable and three ounces of bread. Once a week, inmates were given fourteen ounces of suet pudding with their Irish stew and pea soup twice a week. The last meal of the day, supper, was a replay of breakfast, but with one ounce less of bread. Lights were put out at ten o'clock.

In the case of Mann it was slightly different. As the mortuary keeper, he could be summoned day or night to unlock the green-doored 'shed' at the end of Eagle Place off Old Montague Street to admit a corpse. This in itself gave him a sense of relative power and superiority over his fellow inmates. It would also explain, up to a point, his presence on the darkened streets of Whitechapel, should he ever be challenged by the police. As the records for 1889 in the London Metropolitan Archive show, the 'existing mortuary and Post-Mortem Room is not within the curtilage of the Infirmary but at a distance of some 300 yards therefrom'.

Deborah Gough was a night nurse who resigned two months after Annie Millwood's admission because she clashed with the matron who seemed bent on making life as difficult as possible –

> ... when a patient has died through the night I have been obliged to walk and get another patient to help me lay the body straight and put the large screens around the bed.[8]

In the August before the attack on Annie Millwood, forty-nine-year-old inmate Betsy Wilks cadged some matches from two boys who were looking over the wall of the yard at the back of the Infirmary. She set herself alight and ended up in the mortuary on Robert Mann's slab. So did Esther Shanley who died of rheumatic fever in the year of the

Ripper. It was not only dead workhouse inmates who were brought to the mortuary, but suicides from the Thames; the tragic poor who had died on doorsteps overnight from exposure, 'carrying the banner' as sleeping rough was called. And any victim of violent crime.

During the aura phase, although life went on as usual for Robert Mann, time would have seemed to slow down. His sense of smell would have become more acute and his skin extra sensitive. Sounds and colours became louder and brighter. This condition can last for a few moments or a few months. Dr Joel Norris of the University of Georgia, a world expert on serial killers, describes the aura phase as passing through a portal between two realities. One is the everyday, the commonplace – for Mann, the workhouse routines, the monotonous diet he had known for years. 'Laws are obeyed,' Norris writes, 'rules observed.' And apart from prison itself, there was nowhere by the 1880s more hidebound and ritualized in terms of rules than the workhouse. The other is the dark, unfathomable world of the killer. Here there are no rules, only the insatiable thirst for blood, the lust to kill.

> The serial murderer is translated into a different kind of creature. Whatever is human in him recedes for a while and he enters into a shadowy existence, a death in life which law and threats of death or punishment, morality, taboos or the importance of life itself, hold no meaning... he will not re-emerge into the world of the living until after the hallucination has broken or the ritual has been acted out.[9]

Chapter 6

Gone for a Soldier
~ Martha Tabram

The ritual was acted out on Tuesday 7 August, the day after a Bank Holiday. Polite society was horrified by the publication in *The Times* the previous day of a deal being struck between the Liberal politician 'Radical Joe' Chamberlain and the Irish leader, Charles Stuart Parnell. It is most unlikely that this news reached the inmates of the Whitechapel Workhouse Infirmary or would have meant much to them if it did. As for Robert Mann, although he was totally unaware of it, his strange psyche had now entered the trawling phase and he was in search of his first victim.

> '[Trawling],' writes Joel Norris, 'does not consist of random or accidental patterns. It is an unconscious compulsion, a deliberate cruising for the likeliest prey ... [It] is a series of compulsive, frenzied and paranoiac behaviour patterns in which the serial killer becomes very alert and focused... It is as if... there begins to operate a new level of behaviour programming which directs his every move.'[1]

Even so, this was not the fully formed Whitechapel murderer, not yet. We know today that serial killers develop and grow, probing the possibilities, weighing the options for their attack.

For Mann, the first problem would be actually getting out of the workhouse with its locked gates and gate-keepers. This was in fact surprisingly easy. As an inmate told Jack London in 1902, the Whitechapel Infirmary was 'the easiest spike going' and when London ran for it through the open gates, no one tried to stop him or gave chase. In October 1888, the Board of Guardians wrote to the residents of Queen Anne and Thomas Streets that ran to the east of the building that they would repair locks and gates 'to keep the road free from nuisance'. In the same year, twenty-year-old Edward Maloney escaped through one of these back doors. This was Robert Mann's physical portal into his other world, the door that led to a terrible destiny.

Would the inmates on each side of him have noticed that his bed was empty? Probably, but they were used to the man disappearing at odd hours on mortuary business and would have thought little of it. Mann would have put on his jacket and billycock hat, the workhouse uniform that looked for all the world like a civilian suit and checked that his clasp knife was in his pocket. Which route he took from the Infirmary is unknown, but it was probably south along Baker's Row, then west along Old Montague Street, past 'his' mortuary in Eagle Place. There was no moon and the streets, as we have seen, were dim and badly lit. It was probably two or three in the morning and drunks were meandering aimlessly from pub to pub. So too were the unfortunates, the prostitutes like Annie Millwood who would become the tragic targets of Jack the Ripper. One of these was Martha Tabram.

Constable 226H Thomas Barrett was walking his beat at the regulation two and a half miles an hour along Wentworth Street at about the time that Mann left the Infirmary. A Dorsetman from Sherborne, Barrett had been with H Division for five years. Along with all his colleagues, who were to face fierce criticism in the weeks ahead, he carried a 14-inch hardwood truncheon, a 'bull's eye' lantern and a whistle to summon assistance. Like all policemen, he knew his beat intimately – who belonged where and when and he was alert to strangers.

One such stranger was loitering near the entrance to the north end of George Yard. The man was aged between twenty-two and twenty-six, was about 5 feet 9 or 10 inches tall and wore the undress scarlet uniform of a Guardsman, with a good conduct stripe on one sleeve. When Barrett asked him what he was doing, he explained that he was waiting for 'a chum who had gone with a girl'. Such transactions were commonplace. Prostitution was illegal, but there were an estimated 80,000 street girls in London and the police simply could not cope with a volume of trade like that. Better to turn a blind eye. Barrett walked on.

The Ripper's first victim was Martha Tabram, who died on a first floor landing in George Yard Buildings, along what is today's Gunthorpe Street.

We cannot know how many potential victims Robert Mann walked past by the time he turned left into George Yard or precisely what he intended to do to the one he chose. In the event, that choice was made for him, in a way eerily like that of Annie Millwood. Stumbling out of the near-darkness towards him, clutching her chest, was thirty-nine-year-old Martha Tabram. Her dark hair was swept up in a bun, but rather dishevelled now and for all her plumpness, she looked a lot older than she was. She wore a black bonnet and a long black jacket, the colour of mourning, the colour of death. What riveted Mann however was the blood trickling over her fingers from a gaping wound in her sternum. Perhaps she called out to him, shocked, losing blood, dying. If so, she was calling to the wrong man.

The pauper inmate now flashed from one phase through another to a third. The murder of Martha Tabram was opportunistic and did not follow the classic pattern of modern serial killers. Mann became in profiling terms a 'raptor', attacking virtually as soon as he saw his victim. Perhaps the wooing phase, in which murderers 'disarm their victims by winning their confidence' lasted in this case mere seconds. Perhaps Martha collapsed into Mann's arms on the first floor landing, already dead. This is important, because somehow the killer's attention must have been alerted. Martha was physically *above* him when he was at street level and he must have climbed the steps to reach her. Once she was on the ground at his feet, like a cadaver on the slab, the wooing phase became the capture became the killing.

> 'The moment of murder itself,' writes Joel Norris, 'is the emotional high for most confessed serial killers. At this instant, when the victims were dying at their hands, many… report an insight so intense that it is like an emotional quasar, blinding in its revelation of truth. In those seconds of acting out the absolute pinnacle of their own anguish, some report spontaneous orgasms, a sexual release so complete that it is clearly their moment of triumph, a powerful statement of their own existence when they can face the collective demons of their past without the least trace of fear.'[2]

We do not know the exact order of events, but at some point, Mann hauled up the dying woman's green skirt and brown petticoat, forcing her legs apart before he opened his clasp knife and went to work. He stabbed her left lung five times, her right twice. One thrust hit the heart, five the liver, two the spleen and six the stomach. The breasts, the belly, the groin – the physical attributes that make a woman a woman. Clearly, police and doctors reasoned at the time, this was a sexual attack. Most of us would still accept this today, but in the case of Robert Mann, it was different. Frenzied though the thirty-nine wounds were, they were in a pattern. *The killer knew where to strike.*

The whole thing was probably over in minutes. Mann wiped his blade, closed and pocketed the knife and made his way down the staircase to the street. Now he was in the totem phase:

The murderer's fantasy has been so all-consuming that he is

drained after the crime and begins to slide quickly into depression.[3]

In an attempt to hold on to the high, many serial killers take a trophy or totem by which to relive the moment and there is evidence that Mann did this in the later killings. But this was not yet the Whitechapel fiend. He was an apprentice in murder, feeling his way. Certainly, he showed already the signs of the disorganized killer. He had taken a weapon with him and intended to do someone harm – showing a degree of organization – but the injured Martha Tabram had suddenly presented herself and Mann, on impulse, mutilated her. But now he made no attempt to conceal the deed, not even to give the corpse some dignity by pulling down her skirt. Perhaps, deep inside his twisted unconscious, he was rather proud of his work and wanted to display it.

Any killer's natural instinct is survival. Mann had to get back to the Infirmary before he was missed, checking as he walked the scum-cobbled streets that there was no blood on him. He probably returned the same way he had come, his heart skipping a beat as he saw the flashing helmet plate of Constable Barrett checking locks along Wentworth Street. It was probably nearly three o'clock by now and the market porters and labourers would be up soon, their hobnailed boots clattering on the cobbles.

One of them was John Reeves, on his way to work at the largest docks in the world, at 4.45 am. In early August, it was getting light by then and Reeves could see, on the landing below his home at Number 37, the mutilated remains of Martha Tabram. He dashed into the street and found Constable Barrett still patrolling and the two went back to the body. The policeman sent for a doctor and the first man to pronounce on the handiwork of Jack the Ripper was Dr Timothy Killeen, of 68 Brick Lane. It was now 5.30 am and Killeen estimated that the murder had taken place three hours earlier. This would chime with other testimony at the inquest when Joseph Mahoney and his wife deposed that they had climbed the stairwell at 1.40 and 1.45 respectively (Mrs Mahoney going out to a grocer's shop in Thrawl Street to buy some supper) and had seen nothing. Alfred Crow, however, a twenty-four-year-old cab driver from Number 35, had seen what was undoubtedly Martha's body lying on the first landing, at 3.30. In the dark, he assumed she was drunk or 'carrying the banner' and walked on. Dr Killeen, unknowingly, prolonged the totem phase for Robert Mann because he ordered the woman's body to be taken to the mortuary in Eagle Place, the mortuary where the man who would become known as the Whitechapel murderer and Jack the Ripper worked.

Bodies found in the street were placed in 'ambulances', basically two-wheeled biers large enough for a coffin or 'shell' and covered over with tarpaulin. A pair of policemen were usually detailed to take the sad load to whichever mortuary had been designated. In this case, they would have had to knock on the door of the Infirmary in Baker's Row and the keeper would have gone to the Male wards to rouse Robert Mann, the mortuary keeper. We do not know precisely where the key was kept, but it was probably hanging in an office where it could be easily reached. We can only imagine what terror rushed through Mann's mind when two policemen came for him some hours after he had stabbed a woman to death in George Yard Buildings.

Now, bizarrely, his victim was brought back to him and he had the leisure to survey his handiwork up close and personal. It is highly likely that Robert Mann, perhaps with an older inmate, James Hatfield, stripped and washed Martha Tabram. They would certainly do so in later murders and this was probably the accepted pattern, making life easier for the doctor when he came to perform his post mortem. There was of course nothing sinister in this. Mann was not attempting to destroy vital forensic evidence by handling the corpse. Fingerprint evidence lay four years in the future and it was not until 1905 that such evidence resulted in an actual conviction in court.[4] It would be nearly a century before DNA technology would be available. On the other hand, for a man with the mortuary keeper's psychosis, here was a golden opportunity for which many serial killers long.

The process of inquests emerged from the work of medieval 'crowners' (coroners) who permitted juries to view bodies of suspected murder victims. This was partly because of the suspicious belief that the wounds of a corpse would 'bleed anew' in the presence of a killer and that 'murder will out'. In a macabre way, of course, dead men *do* tell tales and this is the precise purpose of a post mortem today; to ascertain the exact cause of death. As early as 1861, Dr William Guy of King's College, London, wrote:

The great rule to be observed in conducting post-mortem examinations [is] to examine every cavity and every important organ of the body... even when the cause of death is obvious.

It is likely that Dr Killeen used the autopsy techniques advanced in recent years by Professor Rudolf Virchow and written in English by Sims Woodhead in 1883. The protocol began with observations at the scene of crime. This was followed by an external examination in the mortuary with the body clothed (when, in daylight, more could be observed). If, as I assume, Mann and Hatfield had already stripped and washed Martha Tabram, the procedure was already disrupted. The naked body was then examined with internal dissection of the wounds. Finally, in this order, the brain, thorax and abdomen were to be opened.

Killeen went to work that same day, Tuesday 7 August, behind the green doors of the Whitechapel mortuary. Though little better than a shed, it was brick-built, its murky windows allowing enough daylight for him to see by. Colour changes to Martha's skin would have been more difficult to see in artificial light. Killeen would have noted the position of the hands, whether the fingers were curled or not and whether there were any cuts which could be defensive wounds. He would have checked the clothing which Mann and Hatfield had probably removed, looking for dirt or blood. If the mortuary pair had already washed the body, bruising would be obvious. Martha Tabram's body would have been stiff from rigor mortis by the time it arrived at the mortuary and this process would continue for the rest of the day.

At this stage of course, no one in authority and not the men clustered around the corpse in Eagle Place, had any idea who Martha was, so any scars or moles would have been observed by Killeen to aid identification. The absence of a hymen proved that the dead woman was not a virgin and the obvious attacks to the breast, belly and genitals indicated the work of a sexual sadist; the sexual sadist who was standing at Killeen's elbow as he carried out his routine.

Killeen carefully measured the stab wounds and counted them. He was convinced that thirty-eight of the wounds were inflicted by a right-handed assailant using a pen or clasp knife, short-bladed and single edged. The thirty-ninth wound (actually, of course, the first) was different. It was deeper and wider, possibly made by a double-edged dagger or bayonet. This was the wound to the chest. The doctor cut Martha Tabram open, displaying the abdomen and thorax while her killer watched, rapt with attention in the uniquely prolonged totem phase. The vagina and uterus were checked for signs of recent sexual activity.

Mann's job would have been to provide buckets of water, both hot and cold, and to provide Killeen with a bottle of 1-20 carbolic acid, turpentine, linseed oil and any number of rags, sponges and towels. If rags were in short supply, newspapers would do – even those in the future that carried the latest atrocities in Whitechapel and letters from Jack the Ripper!

There is no evidence that Timothy Killeen was a police surgeon, and it is not clear why *he* was sent for by the police. There was a tendency for non-police surgeons involved in autopsies, today called pathologists, not to take their job too seriously. Killeen seems to have been thorough – hence his awareness of two weapons being used – but he seems only to have concerned himself with the wound areas. In other words, Martha Tabram's skull was not opened.

During the day of the post mortem, a photograph was taken of the dead woman, as Robert Mann would have seen her on the slab. We can imagine him clucking around the police photographer, arranging a blanket decorously to cover her modesty as if he were the most caring person in the world. In the photograph, the eyes are closed and the mouth is slightly open, as though she is snoring in her sleep. Someone – almost certainly her killer – has brushed her hair away from her face. The throat – the trademark of Mann's later work – appears untouched, but a report by Chief Inspector Donald Swanson in September refers obscurely to wounds 'on body, *neck* and private parts...' [my italics].

Meanwhile the police operation swung into action. Divisional Inspector Edmund Reid launched the inquiry that Tuesday. The *Weekly Dispatch* described him as 'one of the most remarkable men of the century'; he was an actor, singer, conjuror and balloonist and made the first parachute jump in British history at 1,000 feet above Luton. Such was his fame that he was used as a prototype for Detective Dier in the crime novels of Charles Gibbon. He and Constable Barrett visited the nearest barracks, at the Tower, but the constable failed to recognize the soldier he had seen loitering in Wentworth Street. Reid interviewed the residents of George Yard Buildings, an area described by the *East London Advertiser* as:

> ...a number of courts and alleys in which some of the poorest of the poor, along with thieves and roughs and prostitutes, find protection and shelter in the miserable hovels bearing the name of houses.

He talked to the Mahoneys, to Alfred Crow and to Francis Hewitt, the superintendent of the Buildings, whose wife had heard a cry of 'murder' earlier in the evening, both a reminder of the kind of area Whitechapel was and of the problem facing the police.

The next day, Reid and Barrett were back at the Tower and an identity parade took place. Although no one could know it at the time, this marked the first piece of sloppy police work in the hunt for the man who would become Jack the Ripper. Barrett picked out first one man, then another and immediately backtracked on the first, on the grounds that the man he saw wore medal ribbons – the soldier in the line did not. This man, who might have plunged his bayonet into Martha Tabram, was allowed to go without his name being taken. The second was John Leary who told police that he and a comrade, Private Law, had gone on a pub crawl that began in Brixton. From there, the pair had parted company and Leary had walked through Battersea, Chelsea, past Charing Cross and into the Strand, where he met up with Law again. The two had a final drink in Billingsgate some time around five before returning to barracks. When these men's stories tallied, the police were satisfied, blithely ignoring the fact that neither of them had an alibi for the time of Martha Tabram's murder.

The inquest which opened at 2 o'clock on Thursday 9 August in the Working Lads' Institute in Whitechapel Road was typical of those that would follow in the Whitechapel murders. The coroner, the larger than life Wynne Baxter, was holidaying in Scandinavia and his place was taken by his deputy, George Collier. The George Yard residents were called first, then Constable Barrett and Dr Killeen, following the pattern of involvement in the crime. There was still no definite name for the deceased, although Martha Turner had been suggested as a result of her description circulated to 116 infirmaries throughout London. Accordingly, Collier adjourned proceedings for two weeks.

The timing was unfortunate, because on the day of the inquest, husky-voiced prostitute Mary Ann Connolly, known as Pearly Poll, gave a definite name for the dead woman and had been with her on the night she died. She was Martha Tabram, otherwise known as Emma Turner; and Sergeant Eli Caunter, of H Division, whom the underworld knew as 'Tommy Roundhead' elicited more information from her friend. She and Martha had been drinking with soldiers in various Whitechapel pubs between ten and eleven forty-five on 6 August. Nobody was in any doubt about the way in which this would end. Pearly Poll took her soldier up Angel Alley, which ran parallel to George Yard into which Martha disappeared with hers.

Another identity parade was to be held at the Tower on 10 August, but Pearly Poll had disappeared. Relations between East End prostitutes and the police were naturally strained and would worsen in the weeks ahead, as the Met and eventually the City Force failed to provide any effective protection for working girls. Eli Caunter tracked Pearly Poll down at her cousin's home in Fuller's Court, Drury Lane and the identity parade duly took place on the 13th.

The less than helpful Mary Connolly now suddenly remembered that the men she drank with – the man she had sex with – had white cap bands. This meant that they were Coldstream Guardsmen, who were stationed at the Wellington Barracks and the whole Tower episode had been a waste of time. Misidentifications and muddle like this complicate any police enquiry, but somehow, Barrett's missing of *white* cap bands, even in the darkness of Whitechapel, is reprehensible.

The next day, 14 August, Pearly Poll picked out two men from the Coldstreamers. She identified one as the corporal who went up Angel Alley with her, except that he was actually Private George. The police again failed by meekly accepting his story, corroborated by his wife, that he was at home until 6 am on the night in question with her at 120 Hammersmith Road. To an untrained eye, of course, George's two good conduct stripes looked very like a corporal's chevrons. The other soldier, Private Skipper, could prove that he had been in barracks from 10.05 pm on the night that Martha Tabram died. Once again, we have inferior investigative work. Comrades back their comrades – the whole essence of army life depends on it.[5] Wives, too, lie for their husbands. The assumption that most Ripperologists have made, that Mary

Connolly wrongly identified the two men must therefore be questioned and it is highly likely that Private Skipper's bayonet was the weapon that thudded into Martha Tabram's breastbone on that dingy landing in George Yard. The rest was down to Robert Mann.

When the inquest re-opened under Collier on 23 August, a line could be drawn under Martha Tabram's murder. Information from that day and the diligent research of Ripper historians since has enabled us to piece together a portrait of Jack the Ripper's first victim. She was born Martha White, daughter of Charles and Elizabeth, at 17 Marshall Street, Southwark, on 10 May 1849. At that time, Robert Mann was fourteen and already living in the Whitechapel workhouse. Martha's father died suddenly – a reminder of the almost instant destitution that could befall families – in November 1865. On Christmas day, four years later, Martha married Henry Tabram in the Trinity Church, Newington and the couple had two children, Frederick born in 1871 and Charles the following year.

The Tabrams were a volatile couple, a situation by no means uncommon in the East End and rows were usually about her drinking. When Henry finally had enough and left her in 1875, Martha took up with another man. Tabram subsequently reduced his maintenance to her from a hefty 12 shillings a week to half a crown. At some point, Martha moved in with a William Turner in rented accommodation at 4 Star Place and used his surname, though it is doubtful if they ever married. He too had left because of her drinking and at the time of her death lived in the Victoria Working Men's Home in Commercial Street. Three weeks before she died, Martha had moved to 19 George Street. Turner had bumped into her three days before she met Robert Mann and gave her 1/6d for her to buy stock as a street hawker. She was known to have pestered other people for money, including her sister-in-law, Ann Morris. On one occasion she had been sentenced to seven days' hard labour for this offence.

The story of Martha Tabram is an all too tragic one and all too common in the Abyss. In fact her life – apart from putting her in harm's way on the street – has no bearing on her death. That is the fanciful stuff of conspiracy theorists. What I believe happened was this. Martha Tabram went up George Yard with Private Skipper of the Coldstream Guards shortly before midnight. There was a quarrel, probably about payment for her services and Skipper, furious, lashed out with a bayonet stab. He hurried back to barracks and would have got there before one o'clock, perhaps persuading his mates with some cock and bull story to lie for him. Shocked and badly hurt, Martha collapsed and passed out, coming to at some unknown time in the small hours. Perhaps she saw, through the mists of her pain, the shadowy figure of Elizabeth Mahoney, going up the stairs at George Yard Buildings with the supper she had just bought in Thrawl Street. It was now nearly two o'clock and Martha hauled herself up the stairs to where she knew there would be help. She was just a victim of street crime, an everyday event in Whitechapel. The coroner's jury's verdict? 'Murder, by person or persons unknown.' And that person, in the eyes of the deputy coroner 'must have been a perfect savage to inflict such a number of wounds on a defenceless woman that way'.

'A perfect savage' had to suffice for the general public of 1888. We have to get closer.

Chapter 7

'Never Such a Brutal Affair' – Polly Nichols

It takes less than three minutes to walk from Baker's Row to Buck's Row and there is only one way to do it. Robert Mann walked that way in the early hours of Friday 31 August. In terms of the genesis of a serial killer he was to grow a long way that night – for the first time he took on a healthy, alert adult and, subconsciously, he had to pass through the phases in a more conventional manner. He had found Martha Tabram to the south-east. This time, he walked south-west.

By the time he left the Infirmary, he had the key to the mortuary in his pocket. Why? Because now he needed a knife with a stronger blade than the pocket knife he had used on Martha Tabram and they were on display in the mortuary. Perhaps he remembered that last time, his clasp knife had not been up to the job. Perhaps, however, he needed the different knife for a different purpose. Either the catling or the cartilage knife, with their 5-inch blades, would be ideal.

Did he accost any other women at the east end of Old Montague Street? How much time did he *actually* take until he reached Buck's Row? If he entered it from the western end, he would have seen ahead of him, by the light of the quarter-full moon, the great looming building of the National School with the girls' entrance to the right and the boys' to the left. There were horses and stables to his right and weighing machines to his left. Beyond the warehouses that edged Buck's Row ahead of him were the manure works and the railway lines that ran behind his workhouse home.

Walking towards him, out of the darkness by Essex Wharf, was a middle-aged whore. Her name was Mary Ann Nichols and she would become the first 'canonical' victim of Jack the Ripper.

Mann was now in the wooing phase, that most tricky of operations which was almost wholly lacking in the case of Martha Tabram. It had been twenty-four days since he had killed her and the black mood was on him again. John Wayne Gacy offered his young male victims marijuana and killed them when they were high. Ted Bundy feigned a broken arm and asked young, long-haired girls to give him a hand. Both these modern serial killers used charm to lull their victims. How much charm did a workhouse mortuary keeper have? Was it the same for him as behavioural investigative advisor Professor Laurence Alison believes it was for serial killer Robert Napper:

> His paranoia about how they looked down upon him, finding him disgusting and repugnant, will have fed his anger, his self-loathing and his lust for their blood.[1]

The point at issue is that the Ripper's victims were considerably more vulnerable than any of those killed by Gacy or Bundy. These were desperate women, driven to prostitution by drink and bad luck. To avoid 'carrying the banner', they had a straight choice – the casual ward with all the hells that Jack London describes or earning their 4d for a bed in a doss; and that meant appeasing the clients who wandered drunkenly over the cobbles in the early morning air, 365 days a year.

For the last eight years of her life we can piece together the sad world of 'Polly' Nichols. Records confirm that she was in Lambeth workhouse in 1880–81. She was back there in 1882–3, spending two days in the Infirmary. She lived with her father that spring, but by May was back in the workhouse again. In the Autumn of 1887 she was living with Thomas Drew in York Street, Walworth, south of the river, but by October was in the St Giles Workhouse in Endell Street. From there she went straight to the Strand Workhouse in Edmonton and was known to be carrying the banner along with hundreds of others in Trafalgar Square.

In the previous year, on 19 November, 'Bloody Sunday' had erupted when crowds over 70,000 strong had marched to the Square to complain about the endemic poverty in the East End. They faced 3,500 constables, as well as mounted police and 300 Life Guards. In reserve were 300 Grenadier Guardsmen (including, no doubt, the men

Polly Nichols was murdered on the pavement at the entrance of Brown's
Stable Yard behind the National School along Buck's Row.

who would be quizzed later by Inspector Reid) and their bayonets were fixed. Not since the dark, revolutionary days of Chartism had London seen unrest and numbers like this. Realizing they were trapped in a cul-de-sac of authority, protestors (who were armed) began to fight their way out. There were 150 hospital cases and nearly 300 arrests. In December, Polly Nichols was one of those routinely cleared out by a battered and defiant Metropolitan Police. Christmas of 1887 saw Polly in Lambeth Workhouse again and from January to April of 1888 she was in Mitcham Workhouse, then Holborn Infirmary. She found good employment in the summer, but by the beginning of August was in the temporary workhouse in Gray's Inn Lane. On the 2nd, she was sleeping in a doss at 18 Thrawl Street and for the last week of her life at the White House, 56 Flower and Dean Street.

Unlike her killer, Polly Nichols was not a local. She was born on 26 August 1845, in Dean Street, off Fetter Lane when Robert Mann as a ten-year-old perhaps still lived in Hope Street, Whitechapel with his family. Polly's father, Edward Walker, was a locksmith. She married printer's machinist William Nichols at St Bride's Church, Fleet Street in January 1864. The couple lived with her father in Trafalgar Street, Walworth and moved in 1874 to some Peabody Buildings model dwellings for the poor, in Stanford Street, near Blackfriars Road. They had five children, three boys and two girls, but the marriage was over by 1880. The cause is uncertain. Certainly, William had an affair with a nurse and subsequently married her, but Polly left home at least five times before that, leaving her husband to cope as best he could with five children. As in the case of Martha Tabram, Polly's maintenance of five shillings was cut once her husband found out she was living with another man. That, briefly, was the blacksmith Thomas Drew, but Polly was drinking and he kicked her out in June 1886.

Her one chance – as it turned out her last – fell to Polly in May 1887 when she found employment as a servant with the Cowdray family in Rose Hill Road, Wandsworth. She wrote to her father, telling him what a 'grand place' the house was and that her employers were teetotal and religious. On 12 July she stole clothing worth £3 from the 'very nice people' and ended up in the East End.

Historian Philip Sugden sums her up accurately – 'inadequate, impoverished, a prostitute, probably an alcoholic' – Polly Nichols was not about to pass up the prospect of cash in hand that early morning along Buck's Row.

Hours before she met Robert Mann, Polly was drunk and was wandering along Whitechapel Road. It was 11.30 pm. An hour later, she left the Frying Pan pub on the corner of Brick Lane, even more the worse for drink. And at twenty past one she was knocking on the door of 18 Thrawl Street asking for her bed back. Perhaps she preferred the ambience to that of the White House, perhaps she had quarrelled with someone there. In the event she had no money and was turned away. Merrily tipsy, she called out, 'I'll soon get my doss money; see what a jolly bonnet I've got now.' If she'd bought the bonnet with her earnings that night, she poured the rest of it down her throat back at the Frying Pan. Her friend and fellow dosser Ellen Holland saw her at half past two on the corner of Brick Lane and Whitechapel High Street. She told her she had earned her doss three times already, but had spent it. She would not go back with Ellen to Thrawl Street, but instead staggered off towards Buck's Row and her meeting with destiny.

Drunk as she was, Polly Nichols probably had difficulty focusing on Robert Mann. He was wearing a shabby suit and a billycock hat and was watching her intently. Did she accost him with the time-honoured, 'Are you good natured, dearie?' Did she put her hand on his arm? His chest? In the body language of the street, the first move always came from the street girl. There would not be much 'wooing' involved; Polly Nichols was streetwise. There was a gap in the brickwork just behind her, where the wall curved inwards towards a stable door. Mann would have much preferred to be on the other side of that door, but it was padlocked.

It was between 3.20 and 3.30 and Mann may have seen Constable 973 John Neil patrolling the area fifteen minutes earlier. In that Buck's Row and Baker's Row were Neil's beat, it is even possible that the two men knew each other. It would have been vital then that Mann shrink out of sight in the shadows and his dark clothes helped him there. Mann struck with appalling speed and ferocity, gripping Polly's throat just under the jaw line with such power that she fell backwards to the pavement, losing consciousness as she did so. When she hit the ground, all the hesitant probing of the Martha Tabram incident vanished and with his right hand, Mann slashed her throat in two gashes, from ear to ear and back as far as the spine. Then he went to work on her body.

It was less than ten minutes later when Charles Cross, a carman on his way to work turned into Buck's Row from Brady Street. He would not have seen the mortuary keeper hurrying away in the opposite direction, but he did see what he thought was a tarpaulin in the gateway to Brown's Stable Yard. Just as he realized it was a woman, he was joined by Robert Paul, another carman going to work. Cross touched the woman's hands and told Paul that he thought she was dead. Neither man could detect signs of life and they decided to carry on to work and tell the first policeman they saw. One of them, out of decency, pulled Polly's skirts down to give her some dignity.

It was unlikely that Robert Mann saw the little huddle that followed, but had he done so, he would have noticed three men at the junction of Hanbury Street and Old Montague Street, which was on his way home. Two of them were Paul and Cross, the third was Constable 56H James Mizen. In one of those eerie slips of the tongue that are occasionally found in murder cases, Cross said, 'You are wanted in Baker's Row.' He meant of course, Buck's Row and quickly corrected himself. Robert Mann lived in Buck's Row and was at that moment getting himself into his dormitory bed, careful not to disturb his fellow inmates. Had Mizen actually gone to Baker's Row, he might have caught Jack the Ripper.

By the time Mizen got to Polly Nichols' body, Constable Neil was already there. He in turn had flashed his bull's eye to attract the attention of 96J John Thain patrolling at the far end of the street. Neil sent Thain to find Dr Rees Llewellyn at his premises at 152 Whitechapel Road. Mizen went to fetch an ambulance and summon further help from Bethnal Green police station. When Sergeant Kirby arrived with other officers, a house to house began. Walter Purkiss in the Essex Wharf building had seen nothing; neither had Emma Green of New Cottage, outside which the dead woman lay.

Llewellyn got there by four and noted the relatively little blood around the body – no more than a wine glass and a half, by a rough reckoning – and the woman's legs were still warm. He estimated the time of death at about 3.30. Under his instruction, Neil and Mizen loaded Polly onto the ambulance and together with Sergeant Kirby trundled it around the corner to Eagle Place, to the mortuary where

Robert Mann knew she would be brought. It cannot have been much more than an hour and a half later and the mortuary keeper was being asked to survey his handiwork in daylight. When he entered the mortuary yard in front of those green doors, he found Inspector John Spratling of J Division peering down at the corpse on the bier and making notes in the half light. Spratling boasted in the years ahead that he smoked blacker tobacco and drank blacker tea than anyone else in the Force; this obviously worked – he lived to be eighty-six. Mann must have watched with his own very personal brand of morbid curiosity as he saw Spratling lift the corpse's skirts to reveal her mutilated stomach with the intestines exposed. Spratling was appalled – 'I have seen many terrible cases,' he told the Press later, 'but never such a brutal affair as this.' He sent for Dr Llewellyn again.

Llewellyn's evidence has caused problems in the Ripper case. Although qualified in Obstetrics from London University in 1873, he was not a Police Surgeon and his notes on Polly Nichols have not survived. Spratling's report, presumably based on his own observations and those of Llewellyn in the mortuary explain that the throat had been cut from left to right with two distinct cuts – still, at this stage, the work of a relative amateur – that had severed the windpipe and spinal cord. The left cheek and right lower jaw showed bruising where Mann had gripped her before making the incisions. The abdomen was ripped open from the ribs to the groin and there were two distinct cuts to the vagina. The knife used was strong-bladed and the killer left-handed. By 19 October, a further report from Chief Inspector Swanson states that Llewellyn was now having second thoughts about this, but the right-hand/left-hand debate has caused endless controversy and is an example of the careless forensic work which often appears in the reports of non-Police Surgeons.

The sequence of events at the mortuary is not clear. Because Spratling was already there when Mann arrived, the mortuary keeper had no opportunity at that stage to wash the body. It is very likely he was told not to and when Dr Llewellyn arrived, the whole issue was out of his hands. Llewellyn carried out the post mortem that morning and it is at least possible that he did this soon after being summoned by Spratling. Mann would have assisted, stripping the body of the red-brown Ulster, the brown linsey frock, the white chest flannel, two petticoats, the stays, the black stockings and the men's side-sprung boots. The 'jolly bonnet' would have been placed with the rest, probably in a corner of the mortuary and somebody noticed the laundry mark on one of the petticoats – 'Lambeth Workhouse, PR', which would later help in identification.

At some point, however, Mann and his assistant, fellow pauper James Hatfield *did* wash the body, so there must have been a sufficient gap for all this to happen. This is an important piece of evidence because it is one of the only two times that Mann's name actually appears in the historical record, as we shall see.

The speed of events is dazzling. Coroner's inquests have always been held as soon as possible after an unnatural death. Wynne Baxter, now back from holiday, presided over this one, again at the Working Lad's Institute. Baxter was a vain and contentious figure, a flashy dresser who had been accused of electoral improprieties to obtain this post in the first place. He was critical of the police handling of the case and added to the invective against them that would grow in the weeks ahead. At the mortuary, Robert Mann and James Hatfield were busy, showing the corpse to various visitors. The sequence is unclear, but Mary Monk, an inmate of Lambeth Workhouse arrived at 7.30 pm on 31 August and identified Mann's victim as Mary Ann Nichols. It is likely that Ellen Holland made a similar sad pilgrimage. The next day, Inspector Abberline brought William Nichols to the mortuary. Mann scraped back the coffin lid and the dignified estranged husband was very moved. All he saw of course was what we can see today from the faded mortuary photograph, Mann's shroud tastefully covering the wounds he had inflicted. Polly's eyes are slightly open, as is her mouth. Her hair appears to have been brushed. 'I forgive you as you are,' Nichols mumbled, 'for what you have been to me.'[2]

During the inquest, Baxter and his jurymen arrived to view the body, in accordance with practice and Robert Mann would have come face to face with the men charged with pronouncing his guilt. Perhaps this was too much for him, because it was James Hatfield who took charge at this point, in that it was he who showed the jury Polly Nichols' stays. This of course implies that some and probably all of the dead woman's clothes were kept in the mortuary, which would horrify forensic officers today, but was probably procedure back in 1888.

Despite the horrific mutilations carried out on Polly, it had been three weeks since Martha Tabram's murder and few, if any links were yet made. There was no sense of outrage and terror – that would start to build a week later. The fullest report of the post mortem comes from *The Times*. Five of Polly's teeth were missing (although this had no connection with Mann's attack). One inch below the left jaw was an incision 4 inches long. Below that was a circular incision which terminated about 3 inches below the right jaw. This was about 8 inches long, severing all the vessels of the neck, down to the vertebrae. The murder weapon would have been long-bladed, 'moderately sharp and used with great violence'. The fact that Llewellyn reported no blood on the breast indicated that he was making his external examination after the body had been washed. The fact that there was no blood on the clothes at this point indicates that Polly was lying down when the throat wounds were made and that the blood ran outwards and downwards onto the pavement where we know it was washed away by the son of Emma Green who lived in the house outside of which the attack took place.

There was a jagged wound to the left of the abdomen, very deep and there were several incisions across the body. Others ran downwards and all wounds were made by the same knife. There is nothing in this version that implies Llewellyn followed procedure by opening up body cavities. Spratling's description of stomach wounds were probably visible externally. When Baxter asked the doctor if the killer had any medical skill to carry out these mutilations, his answer was, of course, absolutely correct; he 'must have had some rough anatomical knowledge, for he seemed to have attacked all the vital parts'. So had he in the case of Martha Tabram, but no one considered this, seeing only the frenzy of the thirty-nine stabs.

Having heard Llewellyn's testimony, Baxter adjourned proceedings until the Monday. Abberline was in attendance, as was Inspector Joseph Helson and Sergeant Patrick Enright, both of J Division. The *Telegraph* reported Enright as being from Scotland Yard, but this is probably a confusion with Abberline. Inspector Spratling was called as the first witness on that Monday (3 September) and explained his note-taking at the mortuary, the body appearing to have been unwashed for some time. He next saw it when it was stripped – the implication being that he must have left the mortuary at some time and Enright volunteered the information that that had been carried out 'by two workhouse officials' [Mann and Hatfield]. Baxter asked if they had any authority to do this and Enright was emphatic – 'No, sir; I gave them no instructions to strip it. In fact, I told them to leave it as it was.' Once again, we have an example of police sloppiness. Between them, Spratling and Enright left a murder victim to untrained amateurs. The fact that I believe one of them to be the Whitechapel murderer is an irrelevance. Baxter saw no problem with any of this – 'I don't object to their stripping the body,' – but he wanted to see the clothes. Enright mentioned the Lambeth Workhouse label and explained the 'PR' initials – Prince's Road. He was not in a position to say how the stays were adjusted. Spratling was. The stays were loose-fitting, he told the inquest and he could clearly see the wounds without unfastening them.

The rest of the police testimony that day concluded with the house-to-house enquiries and search of the area. Bearing in mind that this killing occurred closest of all to Mann's mortuary and the Infirmary, no one thought to make enquiries there. It was out of the killer's immediate orbit as far as the police of 1888 were concerned. Slaughtermen Harry Tomkins, James Mumford and Charles Britten, working in the slaughterhouse in Winthrop Street when the murder took place, heard nothing. Tomkins was quick to dissociate himself from the Unfortunate. 'Are there any women about there?' the Coroner asked. 'Oh, I know nothing about them; I don't like 'em.' Baxter, getting more irritable as the day wore on, snapped, 'I did not ask you whether you like them; I ask you whether there were any about that night.' There were, of course – Polly Nichols was one of them – but the slaughterers heard and saw nothing until Constable Thain told them there was a body nearby.

Inspector Helson first heard about the murder at quarter to seven that Friday morning. He viewed the still-clothed body in the mortuary, at which point the stays were still fastened. There was a little blood on the collars of the dress and Ulster, but no cuts to the cloth and no obvious signs of a struggle.

With Mary Ann Nichols positively identified by Ellen Holland and Mary Monk, Baxter adjourned the inquest until 17 September.

On that Tuesday, Dr Llewellyn was recalled. He had re-examined this body – exactly why and exactly when is unclear – and 'there was no part of the viscera missing'.[3] Polly Nichols was buried in Ilford cemetery on Thursday 6 September, her body very probably in the care of Robert Mann until that date. And Robert Mann emerges into the full glare of history as the eighth witness that morning. He told the coroner and his jury that the police came to the workhouse shortly before five o'clock. He unlocked the mortuary, took the body inside, locked the door and *kept the key* [my italics]. He then went for breakfast, that wholesome fare with its pint of tea and then went back with Hatfield and undressed the woman.

Baxter asked him if the police were there at the time. Mann said no, mentioning Inspector Helson by name.

Coroner:	Had you been told not to touch [the body]?
Mann:	No.
Coroner:	Did you see Inspector Helson?
Mann:	I can't say.
Coroner:	I suppose you do not recollect whether the clothes were torn?
Mann:	They were not torn or cut.
Coroner:	You cannot describe where the blood was?
Mann:	No, sir, I cannot.
Coroner:	How did you get the clothes off?
Mann:	Hatfield had to cut them down the front.
A juryman:	Was the body undressed in the mortuary or in the yard?
Mann:	In the mortuary.

I have quoted this dialogue in full because they are almost the only words we *know* to have been spoken by the Whitechapel murderer. Baxter delivered his bombshell immediately after Mann's answer to the juryman – 'It appears the mortuary keeper is subject to fits and neither his memory nor statements are reliable.' We will examine Robert Mann's fits later, but in that one line, Coroner Baxter dismissed him as a possible Ripper and consigned him to the dustbin of history. Other journalists reporting this inquest use casual phrases like 'poor old keeper' and so Ripper historians today have dismissed

Mann as a toothless imbecile, some grotesque Dickensian gargoyle, the caricature of a mortuary attendant, like Dr Frankenstein's crippled assistant Igor. Why should Wynne Baxter have made this statement? It can only be because he had cross-questioned Mann in his court before and must have made enquiries about him at the Infirmary. It was the only time that the authorities – albeit not the police – were actually investigating the Whitechapel murderer.

We do not know how Robert Mann reacted in the witness box, but a moment's reflection would have made him realize that he had been let off the hook. He would not receive another grilling or a cross-examination because the coroner, the high and mighty Mr Baxter, had effectively excused him from the story. Robert Mann was fifty-three when he appeared before the coroner, not the dribbling imbecile of popular fiction. It is possible that the reporters (who got a great deal wrong) confused Mann with his assistant James Hatfield. He was sixty-two and his performance in the witness box was no better than Mann's according to most experts' opinions.

When asked who was at the mortuary when they undressed Polly Nichols, Hatfield's answer was 'Only me and my mate.' Towards the end of his evidence, Baxter said, 'He admits his memory is bad' (although evidence of this appears nowhere in the newspaper's report) and Hatfield agreed. The answers he gave, however, were not as rambling and incoherent as has been assumed. He remembered the exact sequence of removing the clothes, and told the jury he had torn the petticoat and chemise with his hand. 'There were no stays.' Baxter asked him who had given authority to do this. 'No one gave us any. We did it to have the body ready for the doctor.' Baxter's rather fatuous question – 'Who told you a doctor was coming?' was answered with a polite, 'I heard someone speak about it.' Doctors *always* came to mortuaries in the cases of suspicious deaths and as Mann's assistant, Hatfield, would have known that. But an even sillier question came from the coroner next. 'Having finished, did you make the post-mortem examination?' There must have been a silence of disbelief in the Working Lads' Institute, but Hatfield saved Baxter's embarrassment by answering, 'No, the police came.' This is probably another example of Baxter's irascibility and was probably delivered in a sarcastic, contemptuous tone. Later in the proceedings he would rail against the inadequacy of the mortuary and its attendants. On Helson's instructions, Hatfield had cut the Lambeth Workhouse label out of the petticoat band. The next bizarre interchange came when a juryman, confused by Hatfield's assertion that there were no stays, reminded him that when the jury had viewed the corpse on 1 September, Hatfield had actually tried the stays on to show how short they were.

'We cannot do more,' sighed Baxter.

But we must. Mann's testimony can now be reassessed in the light of what we believe. He knew Helson perfectly well in that he used his name unbidden. He remembered that Polly Nichols' clothes were not cut because he had not cut them. He could not remember the blood because he had deliberately kept the memory of the blood fresh in his mind from its first appearance, warm and liquid, in Buck's Row, not as it appeared, crusted and brown in the mortuary. The rest of it – 'I can't say, I can't say' was a screen to hide what he really knew. And he couldn't say in case it incriminated him.

What is more interesting is that he consciously shifts attention to his 'mate', mentioning Hatfield by name, whereas Hatfield does not mention Mann at all, except that he went to the mortuary with him. And what were the jury to make of Hatfield's disturbing admission that he *tried on* the dead woman's stays? This one incident throws a bizarre spotlight onto the world of mortuary assistants.

If Robert Mann's testimony on 17 September was flaky, it is hardly surprising. Because in the early hours of Saturday 8 September, he had killed 'Dark Annie' Chapman.

Chapter 8

'I Must Pull Myself Together' – Annie Chapman

In his summing up at the inquest on Polly Nichols, Wynne Baxter referred to three other murders that formed a pattern. He was tangentially correct, but in making this assertion he was laying the foundations of the myth of the Ripper before the Press coined the name. By that time of course, Annie Chapman was dead and Baxter included what was actually a red herring, the attack on Emma Smith, on Tuesday 3 April. Smith, as we have seen, was a forty-five-year-old prostitute who was assaulted by three men near the Chocolate and Mustard Mill at the corner of Wentworth Street and Brick Lane in the early hours of the morning. When she got back to her lodgings in George Street, the deputy keeper took her at once to the London Hospital. Her face was bruised and her right ear almost torn off. A blunt instrument, perhaps a stick, had been forced into her vagina and her perineum had been torn. She fell into a coma and died from peritonitis on Wednesday 4 April.

The case is dissimilar from the attacks on the others. Serial killers do not operate in threes and the wounds were clearly the result of a beating. It is possible that this was some sort of pimp-related attack, the vaginal injuries making a symbolic point. This is certainly how the police saw it, but Baxter believed differently. All four victims – Smith, Tabram, Nichols and now Chapman – were 'of middle age, all were married and lived apart from their husbands in consequence of intemperate habits, and were at the time of their death leading an irregular life, in each case the inhuman and dastardly criminals are at large in society'.[1]

It is interesting that Baxter should refer to criminals (plural) perhaps because of Emma Smith's account of a three-man attack, but it also shows a complete lack of understanding of how a serial killer's mind works.

The murder of Polly Nichols unleashed the ghoul in ordinary people. They came in ones and twos to gawp at Robert Mann's green doors, totally unaware that this was the Ripper's lair. They stood on street corners and wandered up and down Buck's Row, looking for the exact spot where the body was found. There was nothing new in all this. ''Orrible murder' had been a staple diet of the London Press for three quarters of a century, but there was something about this spate of murders that made them special, out of the ordinary.

In the early hours of Saturday 8 September, the *lustmord* as German psychologists were beginning to call it, came upon Robert Mann again. The depression phase after the Nichols murder had left him with a sense of emptiness, almost disappointment.

> 'For days or weeks after the most recent murder,' writes Joel Norris, 'the killer will inhabit a shadowy world of gloom in which he feels his own sorrow. All the while he is going about the business of life as if he were normal... But soon the fantasies begin to assemble in his mind; his uncontrollable urges begin to overtake him again... Again, an unwary stranger will cross his vision, enter his corridor of death and the killing ritual will once more be carried out to its inevitable conclusion.'[2]

The unwary stranger was born Eliza Anne Smith in Paddington in 1841, when her killer was a six-year-old boy living in Whitechapel. She married coachman John Chapman in May 1869 at All Saints' Church in Knightsbridge and moved around the West End until 1881 when John got a job as coachman in Windsor, Berkshire. The union produced three children – Emily, Annie and John, but Emily died of meningitis when she was nine and John was born crippled. Perhaps it was this sad combination that led Annie senior to drink and by 1884 she had left John and ended up in Spitalfields.

Until Christmas, 1886, Annie received an allowance of ten shillings a week from John, but his death ended all that.[3] Perhaps the loss of allowance also ended a relationship she had with John Siffey – the pair had lived at 30 Dorset Street. By May 1888, Annie was usually to be found at Crossingham's dosshouse, at 35, so she had not moved far and made a living by selling flowers, crochet work and occasional prostitution. Annie was not well and her fierce temper got her literally into scrapes. In the days before she died, she had a nail-gouging, hair-pulling fight with another prostitute, Eliza Cooper, which began at Crossingham's and continued in the Britannia pub on the corner of Dorset and Commercial Streets.

On 4 September, Annie bumped into a friend, Amelia Palmer. She was still bruised from the fight and told Amelia that she intended to go to the casual ward to get help. Amelia gave the woman twopence and told her not to buy drink with it. We do not know if Annie Chapman actually went to the casual ward, but if she did, this would have been the Whitechapel Workhouse Infirmary and she may have met Robert Mann there. Evidence for her having got *some* medical help from *somewhere* would come later, but on Friday 7 September she met Amelia again, in Dorset Street. 'It's no good me giving way,' Annie said. 'I must pull myself together and go out and get some money or I shall have no lodgings.'

This was at five in the afternoon and at half past eleven Annie turned up at Crossingham's where the deputy, Timothy Donovan, saw her in the kitchen. Half an hour later, fellow lodger William Stevens saw Annie put two tablets into an envelope and place them in her pocket. The envelope bore the feather and garter crest of the Sussex Regiment and would become a classic Ripper red herring in the hours and years that followed. About half past twelve, another lodger, Frederick Stevens (no relation of William) drank a pint of beer with Annie, but exactly where is unknown. It was probably the Britannia. By 1.35 am she was back at Crossingham's eating a baked potato. Donovan asked her for the 8d for her bed (Annie always slept in a 'double' when she could afford it). 'I haven't got it,' she told him. 'I am weak and ill and have been in the infirmary. Don't let the bed. I'll be back soon.'

John 'Brummy' Evans, Crossingham's nightwatchman, saw her wander off towards Little Paternoster Row and Brushfield Street – 'I won't be long, Brummy,' Annie called to him. 'Make sure Tim keeps the bed for me.'

The next time anyone saw Annie Chapman she was standing outside No 29 Hanbury Street talking to Robert Mann. We have no idea when he left the Infirmary but again he took the mortuary key and helped himself to a knife. Dr George Bagster Phillips, who carried out the post mortem on Annie, doubted whether the murder weapon was of the type to be found in a post-mortem room. That said, he also denied that it was a bayonet, or a slaughterer's knife 'unless ground down' and we are left wondering what sort of knife he thought it was. Was Mann later than usual or had his trawl taken him longer? And why did he choose Annie Chapman?

In the case of some serial killers, physical appearance can be everything. Virtually all of Ted Bundy's victims had long, straight dark

Annie Chapman died in the back yard of 29, Hanbury Street. Today the site is dominated by a brewery, but houses across the road are little changed since 1888.

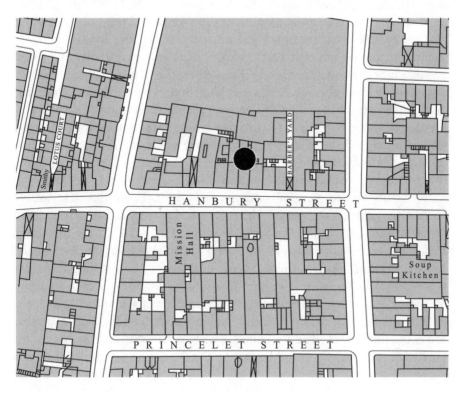

hair with a centre parting. On the other hand, the targets of Peter Sutcliffe, the Yorkshire Ripper, looked very different and ranged widely in terms of age and occupation. Peter Kurtin's victims were of all ages and of both sexes. In the sense that Mann's victims so far – Martha Tabram and Polly Nichols – were both forty-something and must have looked like bag-ladies, Annie Chapman was perfect. It is of course possible that she had gone to Whitechapel Infirmary – and been given her pills – and that Mann recognized her (it was, after all, only days earlier).

It was Elizabeth Long, also known as Darrell, who witnessed the conversation. The wife of a cart-minder living in Church Row, she was on her way to Spitalfields Market at half past five. She remembered the time because she heard the brewery clock in Brick Lane strike. Having visited the mortuary later to look at the deceased, she was certain that the woman she saw was Annie Chapman. She did not see the man's face (and that fact alone, of course, saved Robert Mann's life when they met in the mortuary) but was able to describe his general appearance. 'He was wearing a brown low-crowned felt hat. I think he had on a dark coat, though I am not certain. By the look of him he seemed to me a man over forty years of age. He appeared to me to be a little taller than the deceased.'[4] Pressed by the coroner, she could not comment on whether he was a working man, but he looked 'foreign' and 'what I should call shabby-genteel'. Both these almost throwaway phrases have led Ripperologists in two wrong directions. First, 'foreign' was usually a euphemism for Jew in the East End. Given that about 90% of the community was now Eastern-European Jewish in origin, this is not surprising; but it could of course be wrong. It was after all half past five in the morning and not fully light. The other description – 'shabby-genteel' – opened the way to the middle-class murderer down on his luck, someone 'slumming' in the East End for the sheer hell of it. And that in turn is only a relatively short step to the caped, top-hatted 'toff'. In fact the headgear of the man seen talking to Annie Chapman has become part of Ripper folklore. Most experts today, following the account for example of the *Suffolk Chronicle*, refer to a deerstalker cap of the type made memorable by Sherlock Holmes. Such headgear was usually called a cap, not a hat and as it has no crown at all, hardly fits Mrs Long's description as per the *Daily*

Telegraph. The low-crowned variety accords exactly with the billycock hat worn by workhouse inmates.

Elizabeth Long also heard a brief conversation. The man asked 'Will you?' and the woman answered 'Yes.' As she continued on her way to the market, Annie led Mann literally into Joel Norris's 'corridor of death'. It was the dingy passageway that led from the front of No 29 Hanbury Street to the enclosed yard at the back. This was a place often used by prostitutes as one of the house's inhabitants testified at Annie's inquest. Three stone steps led down from the back door of this passage and there was a locked door leading from the yard down to a cellar. There was a wooden fence nearly 6 feet high around the premises and a lavatory and woodshed in the far corner.

At about 5.20 am Albert Cadoche, a carpenter who lived next door at No 27 was in his own yard when he heard a thud as though something fell against the adjoining fence. Since seventeen people lived at No 29 and some operated a packing-case business, he thought no more of it. In fact, what he almost certainly heard was Annie Chapman, unconscious and partially throttled, hitting the fence as Robert Mann squeezed her throat. While Cadoche was walking back through his house on his way to work, the Whitechapel murderer was living up to his name.

The timings of Long and Cadoche do not add up, but if Mrs Long heard the brewery clock chime the quarter hour, not the half, then it all works. Alternatively one of the two clocks referred to (Cadoche cites Spitalfields church) was wrong. It was only a quarter of an hour later that John Davis got up. He was a carman who lived with his wife and three sons in one of the attic rooms of No 29. He had a cup of tea and then went to the yard, presumably to use the lavatory. There he saw Annie Chapman's body at the bottom of the three steps, with her head towards the house and her legs towards the woodshed. Her skirts had been hauled up to her groin and Davis did not wait to see more. He ran back along the passage into Hanbury Street, by which time Robert Mann was probably just returning by way of the mortuary having washed the knife and Davis bumped into two packing-case workers, James Green and James Kent. Henry Holland, a boxmaker from Aden Road, was also within hailing distance. A rattled John Davis led the three back to the yard, but only Holland had the nerve to descend the steps. Today, of course, he would be compromising a murder scene, but such niceties were beyond the forensic scope of 1888. At least he did not touch the body and the four men ran back to Hanbury Street again in search of a policeman. At this point, however, they seem to have scattered. Kent got as far as a pub and downed a brandy to settle his nerves. Green went to his workshop at Bailey's packing-case premises at 23A and did nothing, presumably in shock. Holland reached Spitalfields Market and found a constable there, but the man, following procedure, could not leave his fixed spot and refused to budge. Holland was so appalled that he reported the constable later that day at Commercial Road police station. Fatuously rigid though this policeman's activity seems by modern standards, he could not have intercepted the killer. It was by now six o'clock and Robert Mann was on his way with all the other Infirmary inmates to breakfast.

While the various inhabitants of No 29, none of whom had heard or seen anything suspicious in the night, were realizing that all hell was breaking loose on their premises, John Davis got to Commercial Road police station at 6.10, blurting out, 'Another woman has been murdered.' Inspector Joseph Chandler, already aware from the sound of running feet that there was an emergency, followed Davis to the murder scene.

The ghouls were already choking the passageway and the street outside No 29 when Dr Phillips arrived. With his surgery at 2 Spital Square, Phillips was the Police Surgeon for H Division and dominates the medical aspects of the Ripper killings from now on. By definition better qualified in ghastly crime than Llewellyn who had carried out the Nichols post mortem, Phillips made a careful note of what he saw at the crime scene. There was a piece of muslin and two combs, one in a paper case, near the body. These he described as 'apparently... arranged there' which gave rise to all sorts of Masonic speculation as we saw in an earlier chapter. In fact, Inspector Chandler, who of course witnessed the same scene a few minutes earlier, makes no mention of any 'arrangement'. It seems likely that the muslin, the combs and the pills in their Sussex Regiment envelope, had spilled out of Annie's pocket. Any such situation will tend to produce a pattern of sorts, and no one says any item was placed between the dead woman's feet.

As to the body itself, the left arm lay across the left breast and the legs were drawn up, and outwards, the feet on the ground. The swollen face was turned to the right and the swollen tongue showed signs of partial strangulation. The small intestines were lying on the right of the body above the shoulder and part of the stomach lay over the left. The body was cold (it was a chilly day) and rigor mortis was beginning to set in. The throat had been deeply gashed with a jagged cut and there were various patches and spatters of blood on the ground and fence which convinced Phillips that the woman had been butchered where she lay.

Inspector Chandler supervised the removal of the body by ambulance to the mortuary and examined the yard, taking charge of the items from Annie's pocket. At the inquest, he was quizzed about the envelope and whether the partially visible address was written in a man's hand. Chandler could only reply, 'I should imagine so.' Other items found in the yard had no relevance at all to the murder, especially a leather apron, soaking in water, which, it turned out, belonged to John Richardson, whose mother lived at No 29 and had placed the apron 'to soak' on the previous Thursday. 'Leather apron' is another of those infuriating red herrings that plague Ripperology, as we shall see.

Constable 31H Edward Badham accompanied Annie's body to the mortuary and somebody sent for Robert Mann. It was about seven o'clock when the mortuary keeper turned up and he and Badham waited until Chandler arrived, along with Detective Sergeant William Thick, with whom Jack London would lodge briefly thirteen years later. While Badham took down a description, probably from Chandler's dictation, two women came from 35 Dorset Street to identify the body. According to Badham's testimony at the inquest, only Thick touched the clothing. No one touched the body.

Look up Robert Mann in any Ripper book and he will be described as an inmate pauper who kept the Whitechapel Workhouse Infirmary Mortuary and appeared as a witness at the inquest on Mary Nichols. What it will not tell you is that he also appeared in court in the case of Annie Chapman. The dialogue from the *Daily Telegraph*'s edition of Friday 14 September is clear, that on the third day, Thursday 13 September, Mann told coroner Baxter of his involvement in the case.

This explains why Baxter was able to tell the jury in the *Nichols* inquest on 17 September that Mann was subject to fits and was unreliable as a witness. Something in his behaviour at the Chapman inquest must have made Baxter ask questions of the Infirmary staff. The reason that researchers have missed Mann is that *The Telegraph* reported his name as Marne, thereby causing confusion.

Inspector Chandler was recalled to explain that he arrived at the mortuary soon after seven. At that point the body had not been disturbed and he briefly left Constable 376H Barnes in charge with Mann. Mann testified that he stayed at the mortuary until Dr Phillips came. Since Phillips was not called to carry out his post-mortem work until after two o'clock, Mann was with Annie Chapman's body, alone for much of the time, for nearly seven hours. He said that the mortuary door was locked except when two nurses from the Infirmary – Frances Wright and Mary Simonds – came to undress the body. What he did not say was which side of the locked door he was. As in the case of Polly Nichols, the nurses claimed the police told them to do this and to wash the corpse; the police denied it. It eventually transpired that instructions came from the clerk to the Guardians and the matter was cleared up.

What was not cleared up was exactly what Mann was doing. One newspaper account says he left the mortuary while the stripping was being done – we shall discuss the possible significance of this later. Baxter had not yet let rip about the inadequacies of pauper mortuary attendants – in fact he would do so now and again four days later when he met Mann for a second time on the closing day of the Nichols inquest. Why, then, should the two nurses be sent for, in that Mann – and occasionally Hatfield – did this job routinely? Even more confusingly, according to the *Telegraph*'s account of the 14th, Mann passed his key to the police. Presumably, this was only a temporary measure and it would have been returned to him.

It was now that Baxter began his rant. He had already snapped at John Davis, and criticized the police for sloppy work. Now he turned his invective on the dead-house provision:

'The fact is that Whitechapel does not possess a mortuary... We have no right to take a body there. It is simply a shed belonging to the workhouse officials. Juries have over and over again reported the matter to the District Board of Works. The East-end, which requires mortuaries more than anywhere else, is most deficient. Bodies drawn out of the river have to be put in boxes and very often they are brought to this workhouse arrangement all the way from Wapping. A workhouse inmate,' he sneered, 'is not the proper man to take care of a body in such an important matter as this.'

The foreman of the jury then went off at a tangent on the matter of rewards and when Baxter returned to 'the witness' (Robert Mann) he asked him if he was present during the post mortem. The answer was yes and he said that he had handled the bloody handkerchief and put it in some water, on the orders of Dr Phillips. Mann assumed that the nurses had removed the handkerchief from the body.

'How do you know?' Baxter asked him.
'I don't know,' Mann admitted.
'Then you are guessing?'
'I am guessing.'
'That is all wrong, you know!' Baxter snapped, and to the jury,
'He is really not the proper man to have been left in charge.'

And the coroner for Middlesex was more accurate in that censure than he knew.

Dr Phillips' post mortem was far more complete than Llewellyn's on Polly Nichols. When he got to the mortuary at two o'clock he was surprised to find the body already stripped and on the table. To the coroner he complained again of having to work in the appalling conditions he found at Eagle Place and Baxter agreed, adding that 'at certain seasons of the year it is dangerous to the operator'. Annie Chapman had been partially washed. This may have been carried out by nurses from the Infirmary or it may have been done by Robert Mann. As we have seen, he witnessed the post mortem itself, helping Phillips out with the menial work while all the time enjoying the spectacle that lay before him.

Phillips noted the bruises caused earlier by the fight with Eliza Cooper, and opening the brain and other organs led him to believe that Annie was seriously ill – 'far advanced in disease of the lungs and membranes of the brain'. In other words, she would not have survived on the streets much longer, even if she had not met the man who now washed her bloody handkerchief in a mortuary bucket. So thorough was Phillips that he noted abrasions on the dead woman's fingers where rings had been removed. Were these taken by the Whitechapel murderer as a trophy as he killed her? Or were these taken by the Whitechapel murderer as he washed her corpse?

Annie's throat had been cut with such force as if the killer was attempting to separate the bones of the neck. The other mutilations were carried out after death, but Phillips deferred to the coroner as to whether the revolting details should be made public. The coroner needed to know in order to ascertain the cause of death and to try to understand motivation. Phillips' circumspection is a reminder that this was still Victorian England and the middle classes in particular who read the *Telegraph* did not want to be put off their breakfasts. In the event, the full technical details appeared in the *Lancet* where only medical men would read them.

On the crucial question of whether the killer displayed any anatomical knowledge, Phillips answered, 'My own impression is that... anatomical knowledge was only less displayed or indicated in consequence of haste.' The blade of the murder weapon was 5 or 6 inches long and Phillips said that for him to carry out a similar disembowelling i.e. for post-mortem purposes, would take him an hour. The killer had done it in less than fifteen minutes.

Baxter grew quite dramatic in his summing-up – 'here a few feet from the house and a less distance from the paling they must have stood. The wretch must have then seized the deceased, perhaps with Judas-like approaches. He seized her by the chin. He pressed her throat and while thus preventing the slightest cry, he at the same time produced insensibility and suffocation'... 'There are two things missing. Her rings had been wrenched from her fingers and have not been found and the uterus has been removed... There are no meaningless cuts... No mere slaughterer of animals could have carried out these operations. It must have been someone accustomed to the post-mortem room.'

Had Coroner Baxter left it there, the whole thrust of the police investigation at the time and of Ripper research ever since might have closed in on Robert Mann years ago. Instead, Ripperologists went down the 'mad doctor' line and Baxter himself, as unable as anyone to understand the totemic phase of the serial killer, made the assumption that the uterus was the motive for the attack and was actually for financial gain – the selling of wombs. He told the court that he had been contacted by the sub-curator of the Pathological Museum with news that months earlier he had been approached by an American who was prepared to pay £20 for a uterus and that he intended to give one away free with each copy of a book on which he was working. Bizarre as this story is, it does link in with the notorious Dr Tumblety.

Francis Tumblety was a Canadian quack whose name first appears as a possible suspect in a letter written by Inspector John Littlechild in 1913. Ripper experts Stewart Evans and Paul Gainey have built a plausible case against Tumblety, but we cannot actually place him in Whitechapel at all. He was arrested on charges of gross indecency with men and jumped bail, probably being in custody at the time of the Kelly murder. He was known to be a flamboyant dresser and with his height given at anything between 5 feet 10 inches and 6 feet 4, would have been *very* noticeable on the streets of the East End.

> '[The murderer's] anatomical skill,' Baxter concluded, 'carries him out of the category of a common criminal, for his knowledge could only have been obtained by assisting at post-mortems or by frequenting the post-mortem room.'

A careful reading of this eliminates the surgeon himself. Who it does not eliminate is the mortuary-keeper.

Chapter 9

'Anything But Your Prayers'
– Liz Stride

The brutal murders of two women in the same confined area in just over a week saw the Press go into overdrive. The stuff of fiction in the form of Penny Dreadfuls had somehow become reality and no one felt safe. A moment's thought would have convinced the affluent West End that the murderer's targets were so far removed from them that they might as well have been a different species, but killings like these do not sit well with rationalism and there was panic on the streets.

The day after Robert Mann killed Annie Chapman, William Piggott walked from Whitechapel to Gravesend in Kent and had a drink at the Pope's Head. His loud conversation was decidedly misogynist and the landlady called the police. Since he admitted to having had a fight in a Whitechapel dosshouse and had a hand wound and blood on his shirt and shoes, he was put into an identity parade by Inspector Abberline. Three witnesses, Mrs Fiddymont, Mary Chappell and Joseph Taylor had all seen a shifty, bloodstained man drinking in the Prince Albert in Brushfield Street the previous morning. Since none of them could be sure of their identification, Piggott had to be released. His whereabouts after that are uncertain, but it is possible he could have been sent to the Whitechapel Workhouse Infirmary, where an alleged Ripper could have broken bread with the real one.

On Monday 10 September, the best known of several pressure groups was formed, not trusting the police to get the job done. This was the Whitechapel Vigilance Committee whose sixteen original members met at the Crown pub in the Mile End Road, a stone's throw from the birthplace of the man they were determined to hunt down.

The builder George Lusk was president, B Harris was secretary and Joseph Aarons treasurer. Their brief was to be available in the Crown every morning to receive information from the public and they wrote letters to the police and the Press. On 27 September Lusk went so far as to send a petition to the queen urging her to intervene personally on the matter of rewards. Her Majesty's reply, via the Home Office, was that it would not be in anyone's interest. When rewards had been offered in the past, this had led to the perversion of justice in order to get rich quick. The whole issue of rewards festered throughout the Autumn of Terror and beyond.

That was the day they arrested John Pizer, known as 'Leather Apron'. A Pole, but British-born, the man lived on and off at his parents' home at 22 Mulberry Street. He was known to have a history of violence and had done time for assault. The name 'Leather Apron' first hit the headlines on 4 September, before the Chapman murder and Pizer's exact whereabouts on the night of Polly Nichols' death are uncertain. The newspaper stories described him as a threat to prostitutes and Scotland Yard had him in their sights. Detective Sergeant Thick arrested him at home – 'You're just the man I want' – and took him into custody at Leman Street police station along with his leather-working knives and hats. Once again, Mrs Fiddymont watched him in a line-up and once again failed to recognize anybody. The half-Spaniard, half-Bulgarian vagrant Emmanuel Violenia claimed that he had seen Pizer threatening a woman in Hanbury Street on the morning of 8 September. When invited to see the body of Annie Chapman in the mortuary, however, Violenia refused. Police concluded that he was either a busybody or someone hoping for a reward and Pizer was released.

Perhaps in view of the fact that the public were clamouring for his head and he had only one known friend in the world, Mickeldy Joe with whom he drank at the Princess Alice, Pizer was given a chance to clear his name at the same Chapman inquest which Mann attended, but on the Wednesday. In answer to Baxter's questions, he admitted to being a shoemaker with the nickname Leather Apron (although he had previously denied this to the police). The normally irascible Baxter appears extremely polite to Pizer, giving him a chance to say his piece. He either felt genuinely sorry for the man, caught up as he was in a frenzy of false accusation, or he knew how dangerous he was and was anxious to avoid trouble in his courtroom.

Pizer does not quite disappear off the radar. He received compensation from the *Star* for putting him in the frame and summonsed Emily Patswold on 11 October for calling him 'Leather Apron' and hitting him. The man seems to have been out of work in the months of the Ripper, perhaps because of ongoing hernia problems and he died of gastroenteritis at the London Hospital in the summer of 1897.

Having lost one suspect, the police picked up another, Jacob Isenschmidt.[1] The Press quickly dubbed him the Mad Pork Butcher. His business had failed and he had spent several months in Colney Hatch asylum the previous year. He was given to nocturnal wanderings and his profession clearly linked him in the public's mind with the mutilations involved in the murders. He was reported by two doctors in Holloway and subsequently arrested on Wednesday 12 September by officers there. 'The Holloway lunatic' was a Swiss national, at once ticking a lot of boxes as a knife-carrying foreigner, but he was clearly deranged (and harmless). He was sent to Islington Workhouse, then Grove Hall asylum and finally returned to Colney Hatch where he was still a resident when the later murders occurred.

Before those later murders, the police arrested Edward McKenna, a man resembling someone seen behaving oddly in Flower and Dean Street on the day after the Chapman murder. A Miss Lyon believed she had been accosted by 'Leather Apron' and did not care for the glint in his eye. Questioned by Abberline, McKenna's story that he had been asleep in a doss in Brick Lane at the time was corroborated and he was released.

Altogether more dangerous was Charles Ludwig, the hairdresser from Hamburg who had arrived in London only months earlier. This time, a scissors-carrying foreigner, he was an irresistible suspect for locals, but he was certainly genuinely antisocial. As we have seen, he knew the Minories well, having worked for Mr C A Partridge in the street and lodged nearby. Early in the morning of Tuesday 18 September he took one-armed prostitute Elizabeth Burns to Three King's Court near the Minories. There were railway arches here and it was clearly a regular haunt of prostitutes. He pulled a knife, but her shrieks of 'Murder!' brought City Constable John Johnson running to the scene. The policeman moved Ludwig on and he escorted Liz Burns to the end of his beat; only at that point did she tell him about the knife and by that time, the bird had flown.

It can only have been moments later, however, that he turned up at an all-night coffee stall in Whitechapel High Street and pulled his knife on bystander Alexander Freinberg. Ludwig was arrested by Constable 221H John Gallagher, charged with being drunk and disorderly and using threatening behaviour. He was remanded for over a fortnight because of his access to razors and his clearly unstable temperament. His dilemma was resolved by Robert Mann when he killed his next victim.

I have introduced these random suspects to show the problem the police faced. Whitechapel and Spitalfields were full of odd characters whose behaviour was, to say the least, unusual. What threw them suddenly into the spotlight was the work of the real Whitechapel murderer, quietly going about his business at the Whitechapel Infirmary. *No* report could be ignored. *Any* strange behaviour had to be followed up. The upshot of course, is that it made the police appear ridiculous, as if they jumped at every shadow and were so clueless that their operations were directed by media scaremongering. It was brilliantly lampooned by *Punch* four days later –

A Detective's Diary à la mode

Monday   Papers full of the latest tragedy. One of them suggested that the assassin was a man who wore a blue coat. Arrested three blue coat wearers on suspicion.

Tuesday   The blue coats proved innocent. Released. Evening journal threw out a hint that the deed might have been perpetrated by a soldier. Found a small drummer-boy drunk and incapable. Conveyed him to the station-house.

Wednesday   Drummer-boy released. Letters of anonymous correspondent to daily journal declaring that the outrage could only have been committed by a sailor. Decoyed petty officer of Penny Steamboat on shore and suddenly arrested him.

Thursday	Petty officer allowed to go. Hints thrown out in correspondence column that the crime might be traceable to a lunatic. Noticed an old gentleman purchasing a copy of *Maiwa's Revenge*. Seized him.
Friday	Lunatic dispatched to an asylum. Anonymous letter received, denouncing local clergyman as the criminal. Took the reverend gentleman into custody.
Saturday	Eminent ecclesiastic set at liberty with an apology. Ascertain in a periodical that it is thought just possible the Police may have committed the crime themselves. At the call of duty, finished the week by arresting myself!

And as if this situation was not bad enough, on 26 September John Fitzgerald added another kind of 'lunatic' to the mix by giving himself up to the police and confessing to the murder of Annie Chapman. He was a bricklayer's labourer and incoherently drunk. None of his confession made sense and he was proved to be elsewhere at the time. He was released on the 29th.

And by the 29th, Robert Mann was probably already in the aura phase and the need to kill rose in him at the very time that the 'Dear Boss' letter arrived at the Central News Agency and the murders were on everyone's lips. This was reflected in the increasing numbers of police patrols and vigilante groups in the area and definitely had an effect on Mann's behaviour in the killing zone.

This time, the killing zone was further south than usual. Absolutely in keeping with the geographical profile we noted earlier, he was venturing further afield, confident in his abilities, sure of his ground; and he was travelling due south away from the Nichols and Chapman murder sites. It is possible though that it was the very presence of the police, effectively (and ironically) carrying out Robert Peel's original remit of them as a preventative force that sent Mann in that direction. Because although the line drawn by the Commercial Road was within his profile, it did not fit the boundaries of the Old Montague Street mortuary. Any corpse found here would be sent to St George's-in-the-East. Mann was also out earlier in the night than usual and we do not

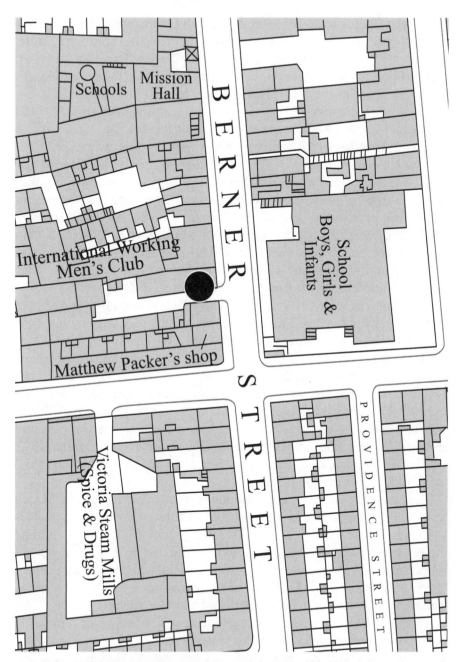

The first killing on the night of the double event – Liz Stride was murdered at the entrance of Dutfield's Yard along Berner Street.

know why. Perhaps the urge was irresistible, perhaps he saw a window of opportunity vis-a-vis the mortuary key or the surgeon's knife. Whatever the reason, I believe he was in Berner Street by half past midnight on 30 September. Somebody else who was there was Mann's fourth victim, Elizabeth Stride. But she was not alone.

The last moments of Liz Stride are shrouded in mystery and confusion, but we know a great deal about her life. She was born in Torsland, Sweden in November 1843 when the man who would kill her was an eight-year-old boy in Whitechapel. Elizabeth Gustafsdottir was a domestic servant by the age of seventeen, but the Swedish police knew her as a prostitute (Sweden, even then, had a system of registering prostitutes) and she gave birth to a stillborn child in April 1865. She came to London the following February and married John Stride three and a half years later. The pair ran a coffee house in Poplar, but the marriage broke down. Stride's business must have collapsed and he died in the Poplar Workhouse in October 1884.

The problem with Liz Stride, as with many women of the Abyss, is their propensity for lies. This no doubt explains why friends and even relatives who gave evidence at inquests give confusing and often contradictory testimony. 'Long Liz' as she was known, perhaps because of her height (at 5 foot 7 inches the tallest of Mann's victims) or because of her married name, Stride, had a missing roof to her mouth.[2] This may have been congenital but Liz's version was that it was the result of an accident when she was on board the pleasure steamer *Princess Alice* that sank in the Thames on 3 September 1877 with an astonishing loss of 527 lives. She claimed that her husband and two children were among them.

The 'real' Liz Stride was an inmate of Poplar Workhouse in March 1877 and by 1882 was living in a doss in Flower and Dean Street. It was where she was for six days in December–January 1881–2 that most interests us. She was admitted with bronchitis to the Whitechapel Workhouse Infirmary where she may have met Robert Mann. From 1885 onwards, Long Liz had been living with a short-tempered waterside labourer and frequent drunk named Michael Kidney. The pair lived at 35 Devonshire Street and their relationship was rocky. She complained to the police about his violence towards her in April 1887 and two years later he spent three days in gaol for being drunk and disorderly.

Sir Charles Warren, Commissioner of the Metropolitan Police, resigned on the day Mary Kelly's body was found.

The Ripper murders gave the London Press a great opportunity for increasing sales. *Punch*, October 1888.

Sir Robert Anderson was Head of the CID and left tantalizing clues as to the Ripper's identity.

Sir Melville Macnaghten became Head of the CID in 1891 and suggested three possible Ripper suspects – all of them wrong.

Inspector Frederick Abberline knew Whitechapel as well as the killer, having served there for many years before secondment to Scotland Yard.

Today's Gunthorpe Street was George Yard, known by the locals as 'Shit Alley', where Martha Tabram took a soldier client in August 1888.

The Ten Bells on the corner of Fournier Street was a favourite haunt of Mary Jane Kelly.

The churchyard of Nicholas Hawksmoor's Christ Church was called 'Itchy Park' by the locals in 1888 and was a sleeping place for down-and-outs, hence the name.

A vicious crime floating in the Whitechapel air, from the satirical magazine *Punch*, September 1888. Note that the door and steps in the background are taken from the murder scene of Annie Chapman.

All that remains of the huge Whitechapel Workhouse Infirmary is this wall dividing modern flats along Vallance Road.

Annie Millwood, the trigger, lodged at No 8 White's Row. The building shown here is not original, but interestingly the numbers have been retained.

Durward Street as it is today. The National School is now a block of flats and Polly Nichols' body lay on the pavement next to the motorbike.

Buck's Row as it looked in 1888. The National School loomed over the murder site of Polly Nichols, whose body was found on the pavement in the centre of the picture. Behind the gates was Brown's Stable Yard.

AMPUTATING INSTRUMENTS.

Fig. 17.

Amputating Knife (Liston's), single-edged, 6-in., Fig. 17 £0   7   0
    Ditto   ditto   7-in.   ...   0   8   0

Fig. 18.

Amputating Knife (Liston's), single-edged, 8-in., Fig. 18   0   8   6
    Ditto   ditto   9-in.   ...   0   9   0

Fig. 19.

There is debate over the type of knife used by the Ripper. From the length and depth of the wound it is likely to have been similar to one of these from Arnold's Medical Catalogue, 1888. Courtesy of Thackray Museum.

Dr Rees Llewellyn was called to the murder scene of Polly Nichols in Buck's Row.

Chief Inspector Donald Swanson was put in overall charge of the Ripper case.

Coroner Wynne Baxter, who presided over most of the Ripper inquests and dismissed Robert Mann as 'unfit to be in charge of such important matters'.

An artist's impression of the Whitechapel Workhouse Infirmary mortuary at the end of Eagle Place, September 1888. Note the small child banging on the doors.

The murder site of Annie Chapman as it was in 1888. The door to the right of the drainpipe is the front door of No 29 and leads through to the yard at the back where she was killed.

Annie Chapman's murder site today. The blank wall of Truman's Brewery has replaced the shabby houses along Hanbury Street.

Dr George Bagster Phillips, surgeon to H Division, carried out the autopsies on most of the Ripper victims.

The author standing in an alleyway off Regal Close, the former site of Robert Mann's mortuary.

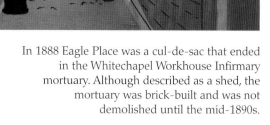

In 1888 Eagle Place was a cul-de-sac that ended in the Whitechapel Workhouse Infirmary mortuary. Although described as a shed, the mortuary was brick-built and was not demolished until the mid-1890s.

A more realistic impression of Robert Mann's mortuary, from 1891.

ON GUARD OUTSIDE THE MORTUARY.

Henriques Street today. The entrance to Dutfield's Yard has been widened to allow access to the school. Liz Stride's body was found just inside the original gates.

Berner Street as it was in 1888. The entrance to Dutfield's Yard was fronted by two wooden gates with a small door on the right-hand side. The building on the right was the International Working Men's Club at No 40 and Matthew Packer's fruit shop is marked by the window on the extreme left.

The mortuary of St George's-in-the-East as it is today. For a while a nature study centre for East End children, it is now derelict.

The mortuary of St George's-in-the-East as it was in 1888 when the body of Ripper victim Liz Stride was brought here.

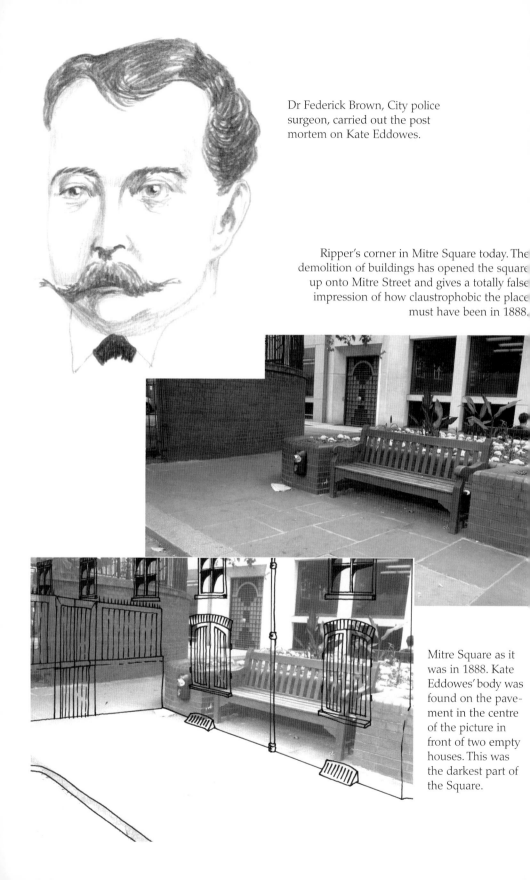

Dr Federick Brown, City police surgeon, carried out the post mortem on Kate Eddowes.

Ripper's corner in Mitre Square today. The demolition of buildings has opened the square up onto Mitre Street and gives a totally false impression of how claustrophobic the place must have been in 1888.

Mitre Square as it was in 1888. Kate Eddowes' body was found on the pavement in the centre of the picture in front of two empty houses. This was the darkest part of the Square.

The site of the Goulston Street graffito today. The doorway was in a direct line with the Ripper's lair.

The entrance to Wentworth Model Dwellings, Goulston Street in 1888. Inside the stairwell someone had written the chalk message which had nothing to do with the Ripper killings. The standpipe where Kate Eddowes apron was dumped was close by.

Dorset Street today has disappeared under the multi-storey car park in parallel White's Row. The road with the parked vehicles runs right through Miller's Court and has no name.

Dorset Street in 1888. The archway in the centre of the picture marked the entrance to Miller's Court where Mary Kelly lived at No 13. The landlord, John McCarthy, had a shop to one side of the entrance.

Dr Thomas Bond who officiated at Mary Kelly's post mortem was the first to present a profile of Jack the Ripper.

Castle Street today was Castle Alley in 1888. The building in the foreground was the Public Baths and the alley was the width of the pavement. Alice McKenzie, last of the Ripper victims, died here in July 1889.

These houses stood behind the Pavilion Theatre and looked out onto Robert Mann's mortuary in Eagle Place.

Gentrified weavers' houses in today's Wilkes Street. Robert Mann would have been born in a similar house where his father was a silk weaver.

The Old Montague Street graffito, 2009. Who had written this and why?

It is inconceivable that Mann would have remembered the woman from a brief period six years before he killed her and still more inconceivable that he would have deliberately sought her out. But once again, as with Annie Chapman, who had also been to the Infirmary, there had to be *some* reason for the choice of victim. Liz was not quite Mann's usual physical type, although her age was right. She was tall and slim with a mass of curly hair. This time there were difficulties in the wooing phase, as we shall see.

One man who was not called to the subsequent inquest on Stride, but should have been, turned into Berner Street from Commercial Road at 12.45 on that Sunday morning. He was the Hungarian Jew Israel Schwartz. As he reached the open gates that led to Dutfield's Yard, he saw a man and a woman standing there, talking. They were clearly arguing, but as Schwartz's English was not good, he could not make any of it out. The actions were clear enough, however. The man spun the woman round and threw her to the pavement. She screamed three times not very loudly and Schwartz crossed the road to avoid involvement in what today might be called a 'domestic'. On that side of Berner Street stood another man, appreciably taller than the first, lighting a pipe. The assailant shouted 'Lipski' and Schwartz started running, convinced he was being followed by 'pipe-man'.

This sequence of events has caused Ripperologists considerable grief because it is open to so many interpretations. What we can certainly establish is that the woman *was* Liz Stride because Schwartz identified her corpse in the mortuary later. One possible explanation is that her assailant was the Ripper and the pipe-smoker an accomplice. The name Lipski almost certainly refers to Israel Lipski or Lobulsk, a Polish-Jewish immigrant who was hanged in the previous year for poisoning fellow-lodger Miriam Angel with nitric acid in Batty Street. Feelings ran high against the poisoner at a time of a huge influx of Eastern European Jews and it is likely that the name was used as a generic anti-Semitic term, rather like 'Yid'.

The most likely interpretation of the scene, all of it probably witnessed by Robert Mann, skulking in the shadows, is that Liz Stride was attacked by a client, perhaps over money, perhaps because she refused to lie down for sex on the now wet ground.[3] It is even possible that what Schwartz saw was literally a 'domestic' and that the assailant, described by Schwartz as about thirty, with a moustache, fair hair, dark jacket, trousers and a peaked cap was Michael Kidney, Liz's lover with whom she had quarrelled days earlier. At the inquest, Kidney denied any such separation, but if he had really knocked her down in Berner Street, this testimony would not be too surprising. The second man, 'pipe-man', may well have been the client's friend, whether it was Kidney or not and the assailant's shout to him was simply to let him know there was a nosy Jew crossing over to him with the implication to get rid of him, which of course worked.

In essence, the exact meaning of the street altercation is irrelevant. There is little doubt that Berner Street was Liz Stride's patch, although various locals at her inquest denied that the area was used for immoral purposes. She was definitely the woman seen by William Marshall, a bootmaker of 64 Berner Street, in conversation with a stout, peaked-capped individual dressed rather like a clerk, in the street at about 11.45 pm. The pair were kissing and Marshall heard the man say, 'You would say anything but your prayers.' They walked off in the direction of Dutfield's Yard. An hour later, James Brown, of 35 Fairclough Street, passed a woman and a man standing by the school wall opposite Dutfield's Yard. 'No, not tonight,' he heard her say. 'Perhaps some other night.' Yet a third sighting was reported by Constable 425H William Smith whose beat included Berner Street. At around 12.30 am, Smith saw Liz Stride, who he correctly remembered wore a flower pinned to her jacket, talking to a man opposite Dutfield's Yard. He was 5 foot 7 inches tall, with dark clothes, was clean-shaven and about twenty-eight years old. He wore a dark deerstalker hat. Most interestingly of all, he was carrying a newspaper-wrapped parcel about 18 inches long and 6 or 8 inches wide. The next time Smith reached Berner Street, half an hour later, a woman was dead and yet another East End hue and cry was under way.

If all these sightings and timings are correct, and bearing in mind the gloom of a wet night and the notoriously faulty observational powers of the average witness, the sequence runs something like this. Liz kissed and cuddled with a client who made a crack about her prayers at 11.45. Forty-five minutes later, Constable Smith saw her with the parcel-carrying man. Fifteen minutes after that, Israel

Schwartz saw the quarrel and heard the shout 'Lipski' at *exactly the same time* that James Brown heard Liz apparently turning down a client with 'No, not tonight, some other night.'

The man with the parcel can be bracketed with the shiny black bag we have met already in Ripper folklore. No actual murderer stalks the streets with a weapon so prominently displayed (assuming the parcel to contain a knife). Either Brown was wrong about the time of his sighting or Schwartz was. I am inclined to opt for Schwartz. His English was poor and it must have been easy for mistakes to have been made in translation.

What I believe happened in Berner Street was this. Liz had sex with the 'prayers' clerk and possibly others (she does seem to have been very busy) before meeting the parcel carrier. If he was a client, the business was over quickly and Liz was then accosted by a second man, with his tall, pipe-smoking friend, who rowed with her and threw her to the ground. The bruises subsequently found on the dead woman's shoulders were almost certainly caused by this. Robert Mann saw all this and once again, saw his chance. This was his wooing equivalent; Martha Tabram had staggered towards him, hurt and he had taken advantage of that. Now, he did the same thing to Liz Stride. She was not badly hurt, but obviously shaken and he went over to her, helping her up. Perhaps he asked her for sex, the only way to get her off the street where there were too many witnesses. 'No,' said Liz. Up close, Robert Mann may have shown all the signs of the workhouse, even the mortuary with its distinctive smell. 'Not tonight, some other night.' James Brown saw him – Jack the Ripper. And all he could remember was he was about 5 foot 7 inches tall (Liz's height), stout and wore a long coat.

As Brown moved on to eat his supper at home, Mann would not take 'no' for an answer. He grabbed her and pushed her through the open gates of Dutfield's Yard where she had probably already been several times that night. He seized her throat in what was now the fully formed MO of a serial killer and forced her to the ground on her back by yanking hard on the silk scarf she wore around her neck. The spot was far from ideal. Behind him as he cut Liz Stride's throat, there was music and laughter coming from the lighted windows of the International Working Men's Club at No 40, the side of which overlooked the Yard. He may have pondered that he should have gone further into the darkness of the Yard, where there were water-closets and more seclusion. But in fact it was actually darker where he was and his knife was already slicing along the Swedish woman's neck and it was too late. Blood spurted away from him as he cut through the left carotid artery. He hacked again, this time less deep. Now he would go for what he really came for. And in his mind he was in the mortuary again, his lair, the place that gave him his purpose.

Like a lightning bolt, he realized the danger. His ears caught the rattle of the trap, slowing as it took the corner. This was no passing vehicle. It was turning into the Yard, coming right towards him. His heart thumping in his chest, Mann darted behind the left-hand gate, the knife still glistening in his hand.

He could see nothing now but the rough bricks of the wall to his left and the back of the gate to his right. He heard the whinny as a horse shied, its hoofs clattering and scraping on the cobbles. He heard a voice, harsh, snarling in a language Mann could not understand. He heard hobnailed boots crunch on the ground and the whisper of a Lucifer that lit up the ghastly scene. A silence followed when two men's hearts – and no woman's – thudded in respective breasts. The owner of one had just stumbled over a body. The owner of the other was Jack the Ripper.

Mann heard cries of murder and mayhem. He had been interrupted, certainly, but not caught. The cries died away with the footsteps. Whoever had come across his handiwork had crossed the Yard and rattled up some stairs, almost certainly to get help. Mann popped his head cautiously around the gate. All was clear in those few seconds. He jumped over the body of Liz Stride and ran for his life.

The body of Elizabeth Stride had been found by Louis Diemschutz, a hawker of jewellery who was just returning from a hard day's selling in the market at Weston Hill, Crystal Palace. When his horse had shied at the entrance to the Yard, Diemschutz had prodded the dark bundle on the ground with his whip, then dismounted and struck a match. Oddly, he assumed the woman lying there was his wife and rather than looking more clearly at the face went into the International Club in search of her. He went back to the body, armed with a candle and accompanied by a friend and fellow Club member, Isaac Kozebrodsky. Mrs

Diemschutz had gone with them and began screaming hysterically at the sight of so much blood.

Diemschutz and Kozebrodsky went off in a fruitless search for a policeman and a large crowd now gathered in and around Dutfield's Yard. Morris Eagle, who had turned left out of the gates when the other two turned right, bumped into Constable 252H Henry Lamb and reserve Constable 426H Edward Collins in Christian Street and they returned to the scene. Lamb sent Collins in search of a doctor and Eagle to Leman Street Police Station. Lamb felt some warmth still in the dead woman's cheek, but there was no sign of a pulse.

In the event it was not Dr Frederick Blackwell who arrived with Collins, but his assistant, Edward Johnston, who reached the Yard soon after ten past one. Johnston noted the slashed throat and that the body, with the exception of the hands, was warm. He unfastened the woman's blouse, checking for body warmth and saw her bonnet lying near her head. It was only minutes later that Dr Blackwell arrived – he timed his arrival at 1.16 by his watch – and made very careful observations, bearing in mind that Blackwell does not seem to have been a Police Surgeon.

The dead woman was lying on her left, facing the Club wall. Her feet were nearest to the gates and her right hand rested on her chest, covered in blood. Her left hand lay on the ground beside her with a small packet of cachous – perfumed sweets often used as breath fresheners – wrapped in tissue paper and partially held by the fingers. Her face looked calm, indicating that the attack was incredibly fast. Her mouth was slightly open. Blackwell put the time of death at between 12.46 and 12.56. When Police Surgeon George Phillips arrived half an hour later, he estimated that the woman would have taken up to a minute and a half to die and pushed the time frame earlier to the assault being delivered between 12.44 and 12.54.

By the time Phillips came to this conclusion, Robert Mann was already killing another woman, in Mitre Square.

Chapter 10

'Goodnight, Old Cock' – Kate Eddowes

Robert Mann had the luck of the devil. But he probably did not think so as he made his way west. We cannot know what riot of emotions tumbled through his head. He had psyched himself up to kill Liz Stride and the knife in his pocket was still sticky with her blood. Whatever was still rational in him at that moment would have told him to turn left out of Dutfield's Yard and scuttle along Berner Street, to cross Commercial Road and lose himself in the labyrinth of streets that led to the mortuary and beyond to the sanctuary in Baker's Row.

But the killer in him held him back. It may have been a momentary decision to turn right out of the Yard, but it was the correct one. This was the way Diemschutz and Kozebrodsky would run moments later, searching in vain for a policeman. And by turning right into Fairclough Street, Mann would not have run into Eagle or the two policemen he found, nor Edward Spooner, standing with his 'young woman' outside the Beehive pub and drawn to Dutfield's Yard moments later out of sheer curiosity.

The killer in Robert Mann would not let him go home because he had unfinished business. He had cut the throat of the whore in Dutfield's Yard, but he had not carried out the rest of his work and that impulse pushed him on. He moved ever further west and we do not know why. Geoprofiler Spencer Chainey believes that he *did* turn north up Berner Street onto the Commercial Road, weighing the risks as he went. Certainly, there would have been more people here, including police patrols, but Robert Mann could blend 'for England' and he had walked away from murder scenes before, a bloody knife in his pocket. Why would he have done this? Because, Chainey believes, this was his comfort zone and he knew that area like the back of his hand. The labyrinth of alleyways to the south-west of Berner Street may have been relatively unknown to him.

Instinctively he had to get away from the murder site. It was around one o'clock now and he must have known that the whole area would soon be jumping with policemen, doctors and locals. Who knows how many patrols he almost ran into? How many beat coppers walked past him. He was experienced by now, an old hand at the killing game. In his dark billycock hat and old overcoat, he would not have attracted undue attention as long as he kept his pace brisk. Loiter and a copper might notice. Run and the boys in blue would have had him.

Spencer Chainey's argument is persuasive, but I still believe Mann walked south-west, down Backchurch Lane and across the railway sidings at Hooper Street. Once there it would be natural to carry on along Great Prescott Street and on to Goodman's Yard and the Minories. Anywhere along this route, he may have paused at the sight of a woman standing on a pavement, weighed his options, made his choice. That one was wrong; there was too much light there; that one was with two men. Serial killers are high risk merchants, but there are limits even for them. He turned right up the Minories and left along George Street. Another choice: Jewry Street or the Crutched Friars? He chose right and crossed Aldgate.

Now he was not only out of his killing fields, his comfort zone, he was in the jurisdiction of the City Police. He probably did not know that and certainly did not care. All that mattered to him was to find another victim, to finish the job he started in Dutfield's Yard. Somewhere in the tangle of streets around Aldgate, he saw a woman, middle-aged, touting for custom. Perhaps they talked business on the pavement briefly before she took him down a dark alleyway. It was part of her regular patch, ideal for the purpose. Perhaps he looked up at the iron plate on the wall and saw the name Mitre Square. It was ideal for his purpose too.

On the last day of her life, Catherine Eddowes, known as Kate, joined her lover, a market porter called John Kelly, at the workhouse in Shoe Lane. Unlike many couples whom the conditions of the time drove apart through deprivation and drink, Kelly and Kate seem to have been relatively loyal and happy. They had been hop-picking in Kent the previous week and although the work was back-breaking, it usually provided cash and was regarded by most Eastenders as the equivalent of a holiday. Two days earlier, Kate had gone to the casual ward at Mile End while Kelly dossed in Cooney's lodging house in Thrawl Street. In one of those infuriating red herrings that dog Ripper studies, Kate told the deputy at Cooney's – 'I have come back to earn the reward offered for the apprehension of the Whitechapel murderer. I think I know him.' The deputy urged Kate to be careful she did not become a victim – 'No fear of that,' she said.[1]

On that Saturday morning, Kate took a pair of Kelly's boots to a pawn shop in Church Street and got half a crown for them. She got a ticket in the name she had given – Jane Kelly – sending Ripperologists into a flurry of conspiracy mania; Mary Jane Kelly would become Robert Mann's next victim. Between ten and eleven, Kelly and Kate had breakfast with tea and sugar they had bought, but by two o'clock their money had gone. Kate left Kelly in Houndsditch and went to Bermondsey to scrounge some cash from her married daughter, Annie Phillips, but couldn't find her.

By half past eight, however, Kate was lying drunk on the pavement outside No 29 Aldgate High Street with a small crowd around her. This was of course a common occurrence; most of those who stumbled upon Mann's victims assumed at first that they were drunks. City Constable 31 Louis Robinson and Constable George Simmons bundled Kate off to Bishopsgate Police Station. When the desk sergeant, James Byfield, asked her her name, she replied sullenly, 'Nothing.' It could almost sum up women of the Abyss in the way the rest of society regarded them.

By quarter past twelve, when Robert Mann was on his way to Berner Street, Kate was awake and happier. She was singing quietly to herself in her cell. A quarter of an hour later she tried to persuade Constable George Hutt that she was capable and at one o'clock, by which time Mann was on his way west, Hutt finally cracked. 'Too late for you to get any more drink,' he told her, knowing full well that closing time in the East End was no more than a serving suggestion. 'I shall get a damned fine hiding when I get home,' she said, a reminder of the daily reality of domestic relations for the working class. She gave her name as she left as Mary Ann Kelly and her address as 6

Fashion Street. 'All right,' she called to Sergeant Byfield at the door of the station. 'Goodnight, old cock.'

These were the last recorded words of Catherine Eddowes. She was seen at 1.35 am by three men: Joseph Lawende, a cigarette salesman; Harry Harris, a furniture dealer; and Joseph Levy, a kosher butcher, who were all on their way home from a night at the Imperial Club down the road. Kate was talking to a man and had a hand on his chest.

The information forthcoming from these men, especially Lawende, who was regarded by the police as an excellent witness, would be brought into sharp focus just over ten minutes later when City

The second killing on the night of the double event – Kate Eddowes was butchered in Mitre Square, the most westerly of the Ripper's murders.

Constable 881 Edward Watkins got back to the Mitre Square section of his beat. He had been there fourteen minutes earlier, at 1.30, and had seen nothing unusual at all. The Square was very quiet, with only two houses (one occupied by a City policeman, 922 Richard Pearse) and dominated by various warehouses belonging to Kearley and Tongue. Horner and Co also had warehouses there and a Mr Taylor ran a shop at one of the three entrances to the Square itself.

Having tramped his usual beat of Duke Street, St James's Square, King Street, Greenchurch Place, Leadenhall Street, Mitre Street and back to the Square, Watkins flashed the bull's eye lantern on his belt into the corners and saw Kate Eddowes lying on her back with her clothes thrown up. Her throat was cut and her stomach ripped open. Without touching the body, Watkins dashed across the Square to Kearley and Tongue's, the door of which was ajar and called to the watchman, George Morris, who was sweeping the steps inside. 'For God's sake, mate, come to my assistance,' a shaken Watkins blurted. 'Here is another woman cut to pieces.'

The City Police, unlike their Metropolitan counterparts, carried no whistles, but Morris did. Having checked the body with Watkins, the nightwatchman ran along Mitre Street into Aldgate, blowing his own whistle. He met Constables 814 James Holland and 964 James Harvey on their respective beats adjacent to Watkins and Holland ran for a doctor. The nearest was George Sequeira at 34 Jewry Street and Holland knocked him up at 1.55.

That was the time when Inspector Edward Collard, on duty at Bishopsgate, got the call. He telegraphed to headquarters and sent a runner to the City's Police Surgeon, Dr Frederick Brown, who wrote the fullest medical notes of any of Robert Mann's victims, as we shall see. Collard reached Mitre Square at three minutes past two. Sequeira was already there and handed to Collard the debris of the murder – black boot buttons, a thimble and a mustard tin containing pawn tickets.

Sequeira noted that the corpse lay in the darkest corner of the Square, but that there was enough light for the killer to carry out his mutilations. From the state of the body he believed the woman had died no more than a quarter of an hour before he arrived.

Dr Brown's sketch of what he saw has survived and backs up his crime scene description. The woman who had been Kate Eddowes lay on her back, her head turned to her left. The arms had flopped to her side, with palms upwards and fingers bent. Her bonnet was underneath her head and the upper part of her dress had been torn open. The body, which was still warm, had been subjected to appalling mutilations. The throat was cut across and the intestines drawn out to a large extent and placed over the right shoulder. Part of this, about two feet long, had been placed between the body and the left arm, Brown thought deliberately. The face was gashed and bloody and the right ear almost cut off. Brown ordered the body to be taken to the mortuary.

We have already seen that Robert Mann killed Kate Eddowes out of his killing zone. That meant that this time there would be no prolongation of the totem phase. He could not gaze in admiration at his handiwork, because the job of mortuary keeper at the Golden Lane mortuary fell to his counterpart, a Mr Davis.

While the police carried out house-to-house enquiries in and around Mitre Square, which, as usual, yielded nothing, there was more bustle of activity further east. Plain-clothes man Sergeant Robert Outram was in conversation with his colleagues Constables Daniel Halse and Edward Marriot at the corner of Houndsditch and Aldgate High Street when they heard Morris's whistle. They reached the Square and then scattered in search of the killer. It was Halse who, unknowingly, was on Robert Mann's trail.

The mortuary keeper's frenzy in Mitre Square meant that he had been less careful than usual. He had blood and excrement on his hands and a uterus and a kidney in his pocket, along with a knife. He must have known he would not have long before the next police patrol arrived, so he had sliced off a piece of the dead woman's apron and had taken it with him, wiping his hands as he went. He got to the standpipe along Goulston Street, near the Wentworth Model Dwellings, Number 108–119, and rinsed his hands and perhaps the knife there, throwing the bloody rag down before moving on.

The risk he took now was huge. He was carrying parts of a woman's body and a murder weapon and he was trudging through the nightmare of what Ripperologists call the 'double event'. Robert Mann was at last on his way home, the Ripper going back to his lair. He would have been relatively calm by now, his lust sated, at least for a while. He must have become aware of increased activity, police patrols everywhere, people clustering at street corners and outside pubs, rumours flying in the blood-spattered night. We cannot be sure of times, but it was probably somewhere around 2.30 that Mann reached the standpipe. Where he had been in the forty-five minutes since he killed Kate is unknown. Perhaps he was hiding in the shadows, ducking police patrols, blending with the nightly flotsam of the East End. Perhaps the timings given by Constable 254A Alfred Long were incorrect.

Long testified at Kate's inquest that when he passed the Goulston Street standpipe at 2.20, there was no sign of the apron. On his return at 2.55 it was there and chalked on the black tiles of an entrance leading to a staircase in Wentworth buildings the infamous words 'The Juwes are the men that will not be blamed for nothing.'

More ink has been wasted on this irrelevance than on any other single 'clue' in the Ripper case. Constable Halse, who saw it too, believed the writing was fresh, but his version was worded slightly differently, according to the notes he made at the time – 'The Juwes are not the men who will be blamed for nothing.' Either way, the double negative has caused huge confusion over the years. Convinced that this had a bearing on the Whitechapel murders, the Metropolitan authorities, ultimately Sir Charles Warren himself, ordered the writing removed, especially as, on Sunday morning, the Jewish stallholders were already setting up for their street trading in what was still called Petticoat Lane, the whole area of Wentworth and Middlesex Streets. There is little doubt that Warren's decision was a sensible one in the sense that race relations were a problem and the recent murders had added to the tension, but it should have been photographed first. In the event, I believe the 'Goulson Street Grafitto' to have no more import than John Richardson's leather apron in the back yard of 29 Hanbury Street. Urban crime scenes – even rural ones – have items in the vicinity which are totally unconnected with the crime. Contrary to popular fiction and the conspiracy theories so beloved by Ripperologists, the most successful serial killers do not advertise, do not stand out. They are merely faces in the crowd and that is why they are so difficult to catch.

While Dr Brown prepared for the post mortem he would conduct on the dead woman, police enquiries focused on her identity. The pawn tickets should have been clinchers, but both of them were for false names. One was marked Emily Birrell, 52 White's Row and the other Jane Kelly, 6 Dorset Street. Certainly Joseph Jones, the pawnbroker of 31 Church Street, remembered the woman who had pledged the boots two days earlier, but it was the tattooed initials on the dead woman's left forearm that brought proof. 'T C' stood for Thomas Conway. It was under the name of Conway that Kate had been admitted to the Whitechapel Workhouse Infirmary in June 1887 with a burnt foot. At that time she had given her address as Flower and Dean Street. Once again, the Infirmary; once again, a possible contact with Robert Mann.

John Kelly, coming from Cooney's doss in Flower and Dean, viewed the body in the mortuary and identified the deceased from the TC initials. He had heard that Kate Conway, as she sometimes called herself, had been taken in drunk to Bishopsgate and so had not been unduly alarmed when she had failed to make their four o'clock rendezvous in Houndsditch. The rest of it was pieced together by weeping relatives at the inquest, by dosshouse deputies and by dedicated teams of Ripperologists over the years, to the extent that the theme of the 2007 Ripper Conference was Kate Eddowes.

She was born on 14 April 1842, when Robert Mann was a little boy still in the bosom of his Whitechapel family, to George and Catherine Eddowes of Wolverhampton. When she was two the family moved to Bermondsey and on the death of her mother when Catherine junior was thirteen, the family was scattered, Catherine returning to an aunt in Wolverhampton. Unhappy, the girl ran away to Birmingham to live with an uncle, Thomas Eddowes. At some point in her late teens or early twenties, Kate met an Irishman, Thomas Conway, an ex-private in the 18th Foot (Royal Irish) and they lived together in Wolverhampton from about 1864.

The common-law union produced three children and the pair made a precarious living selling chapbooks that Conway may have written himself. It is not known when the 'Conways' came to London, but they were there by 1881 when the relationship ended. It was then that Kate met John Kelly in one of the Flower and Dean dosses and although they had the occasional tiff, were by and large together until the day she died. Kate's three sisters, one of whom, Eliza Gold, gave a tearful character reference at her inquest, all lived in London and her daughter, Annie Phillips, admitted that when she (Annie) moved last, she did not tell her mother because of Kate's habit of scrounging money off her.

The problem with accuracy in the backgrounds of women of the Abyss is not helped by friends' and relatives' testimony. We shall see a classic example of this later in the inquest on Liz Stride, but there are examples of it in the Eddowes' inquest too. John Kelly swore Kate did not go out 'for any immoral purpose' and that, though occasionally drunk, never drank to excess. Dr Brown's post mortem would prove him wrong on the second count and her murder by Robert Mann on the first. Frederick Williamson, the deputy at Cooney's, believed that Kate earned her money by hawking and charring. She was a jolly woman, always singing. But she wasn't when Dr Brown saw her on the slab in the Golden Lane mortuary.

We cannot help noticing that the inquest on Kate Eddowes was in every way superior to those presided over by Coroner Baxter in the Metropolitan district. To begin with the Coroner's Court was next to the mortuary, a rather imposing building and rather than allowing Robert Mann virtually a free hand, as at Eagle Place, mortuary-keeper Davis was supervised as he stripped the body and laid it out, both by police and a medical team. 'Team' is the operative word here because Brown was observed at work in the mortuary by Dr Sequeira and by George Phillips who of course had handled the post mortems on Mann's earlier victims. Sedgwick Saunders analyzed the dead woman's stomach contents. This doubling up of medical expertise was deemed desirable by the practice of the day because it made mistakes less likely. What it also did, however, was to increase the areas of dissension and disagreement with which defence counsel at any subsequent trial could have had a field day.

With Brown working at half past two that Sunday afternoon, Kate's body was showing marked signs of rigor mortis. Her face was badly mutilated, with a gash over the bridge of the nose that extended to the cheek and cut through to the jaw bone. The tip of the nose had been removed and a cut had split the upper lip. There was a triangular flap cut into each cheek and the eyelids had been nicked vertically. An ear fell off as Davis removed her clothing.

Kate's throat had been cut with a sharp, pointed knife, with a gash 6 or 7 inches wide. The larynx was severed below the vocal cord so that she would have been unable to cry out in Mitre Square. The jugular vein was opened and there was a hole in the left carotid artery. Death would have been caused by haemorrhage and would have been virtually instantaneous.

The post-mortem mutilations to the body were extensive. The front walls of the abdomen were laid open from breastbone to groin, with an upward, ripping motion. The liver had been stabbed and slit. The killer had cut in a jagged line, changing direction at the navel and slicing to the right of the vagina and rectum. The groin had been stabbed to a depth of one inch and there was a 3-inch cut on the perineum. The left thigh was also cut, as was the right, the muscles here sliced right through. Because all these hideous wounds had been made after death, the amount of blood on the killer would not have been great. He knelt or crouched on the right side of the fallen woman to carry out the mutilations.

Kate's stomach contents were examined by Sedgwick Saunders, the City analyst. He was particularly looking for traces of poison which might explain why Kate was so easily overpowered, but found none. Part of her colon had been cut away and the left kidney had been removed, leaving the renal artery in place. 'I should say,' Brown wrote, 'that someone who knew the position of the kidney must have done it.' While the vagina and cervix were uninjured, the womb itself had been taken away.

In an attempt, perhaps the first by a medical man, to decide on a possible motive for this butchery, Brown believed that the perpetrator had 'considerable knowledge of the positions of the organs in the abdominal cavity and the way of removing them ... It required a great deal of medical knowledge'. Unlike Wynne Baxter, who thought that Annie Chapman's uterus may have been removed for financial gain, Brown knew that the 'parts removed would be of no use for any professional purpose', and again admits the Victorian lack of understanding of serial killer motivation – 'I cannot assign any reason for the parts being taken away.' But then Brown led the world in the wrong direction by his statement, 'Such a knowledge might be possessed by someone in the habit of cutting up animals.'

What is impressive about Brown is that he noted that 'there were no indications of connexion'. In other words, although perhaps his own reasoning would not have taken him this far, the Whitechapel murders are not directly sex-related. Robert Mann's psychology was far more complicated than this.

Dr Sequeira, who observed the post mortem, disagreed with Brown – 'I think that the murderer had no design on any particular organ of the body. He was not possessed of any great anatomical skill.' Allowing for the fact that Sequeira's *exact* meaning may have been that he thought that the killer had a *certain* anatomical skill, the semantics in doctors' responses to coroners' questions are important. To them, 'anatomical knowledge' was not the same as 'medical skill'. The medical fraternity, then as now, was a close-knit community, where backs were scratched and operating-room errors covered up. The slur of the 'mad doctor' was utterly rejected by medical practitioners; no one who had taken the Hippocratic oath could slaughter women in the streets. And in trying to protect their own, doctors like Sequeira were also protecting Robert Mann.

Three photographs of Kate Eddowes were taken in the Golden Lane mortuary. In the one of poorest quality, she is lying naked in her coffin, the gash clearly visible in her throat. In the others, she has been propped against a wall and the photograph shows all the injuries having been stitched up roughly by Brown. The neatest stitches, extending from the navel to the throat, are Brown's closure after his post-mortem procedures. Kate's face is an appalling mess. And no one has combed her hair.

The 'comedy of errors' that was Liz Stride's inquest opened on Monday 1 October and continued until the 5th. Her body had been taken to the mortuary at St George's-in-the-East (a building which still stands, now in ruins) and the indefatigable Wynne Baxter held forth at the Vestry Hall in Cable Street. There were twenty-four jurymen and they all trooped through the mortuary to gawp at Liz's corpse. The only existing photograph shows her wild, uncombed hair and clear damage to her mouth. Bearing in mind that her other nicknames were Hippy-Lip Annie and Mother Gum, the post-mortem findings on her intact palette make no sense. The various witnesses, passers-by, police and doctors, gave the testimony we have already heard, but two people caused the proceedings to turn into farce.

It had not yet been fully established who the dead woman was. After all, she had only been in the mortuary for forty-eight hours and a tearful Mary Malcolm appeared to tell the court that the deceased was her sister, Elizabeth Watts. Mary was a tailor's wife, living in Holborn and told the tragic tale of her sister, who had married the son of a wine merchant from Bath, but had been unfaithful to him. She turned to drink and frequented low lodging houses. On the night of the 'double-event', Mary was in bed and about twenty past one felt pressure on her breast and three distinct kisses – a phantasm of the dying. Mary had visited the mortuary and identified Elizabeth from an old snake bite on her leg. So dissolute was Mary's sister that she once left one of her children as a baby naked on her doorstep. She was constantly asking for hand-outs.

On Tuesday the 5th an outraged Elizabeth Watts, now Stokes, having remarried, was in court to refute furiously everything that Mary Malcolm had said about her. They had not seen each other for years and she was clearly very put out that her sister should slander her. Since all the other testimony, of dosshouse deputies and officials of the Swedish church who kept careful records, proved that Elizabeth Stride lay dead in St George's mortuary, we can only wonder at Mary Malcolm's testimony. Was she merely an attention-seeker, drawn out by the bizarre events of the Autumn of Terror, longing for some kind of limelight, however brief? Whatever the motives, the Mary Malcolms of this world merely add to the litany of nonsense that dogs the Whitechapel murders.

Michael Kidney was another example. Whether or not he was the assailant who had pushed Liz Stride to the ground outside Dutfield's Yard, his behaviour in court was certainly odd. On Monday (he deposed on Wednesday) he had gone to Leman Street Police Station with information that he had on the killer. He wanted to catch the man himself, however, and needed a 'young, strange [i.e. unknown to Whitechapel] detective' to get the job done. Inspector Reid reminded the court that Kidney was drunk at Leman Street and the coroner reminded Kidney that he could not go about hiring policemen for his own amusement. Even at this stage, Kidney refused to pass any information on.

In the more relevant and rational world of medical evidence, George Phillips also testified on the Wednesday. He had performed the post mortem two days earlier and noted the mortuary temperature – 55°. He clearly carried out a full necropsy, referring to the skull, brain, heart and stomach, even though none of these had been damaged. The stomach contained partly digested food, including cheese and potatoes.

Phillips was recalled the next day and had been asked to re-examine the body. This was largely in response to another Mary Malcolm-like busybody whose evidence has tainted Ripper enquiries for a century and a quarter. Matthew Packer was not called to the inquest but was an old grocer living at 44 Berner Street, two houses away from the Dutfield's Yard entrance and he gave evidence to J H Batchelor and Mr Grand, private detectives of the Strand, who had been employed by both the *Evening News* and the Whitechapel Vigilance Committee. All three men went to Scotland Yard and spoke personally to Charles Warren, whose handwritten notes of Packer's testimony still survive. The grocer explained that he had sold grapes to a woman answering Liz Stride's description and described the man she was with. Since the matter of rewards was now being hotly discussed (the City of London offered one in the case of Kate Eddowes) and since Grand, if not Batchelor, had a long list of aliases and shady dealings, we can ignore Packer's testimony altogether. All the details, such as the flower that Liz wore, he could have gleaned from the Press that week and Packer often contradicted himself. The last word, though, was Phillips's – 'Neither on the hands or about the body of the deceased did I find grapes, or connection with them. I am convinced that the deceased had not swallowed either the skin or seed of a grape within many hours of her death.'

The cases of Mary Malcolm, Michael Kidney, Matthew Packer and Messrs Grand and Batchelor, fascinating though they are as glimpses of the frailties of human nature, should be thrown into the Ripper shredder once and for all.

Chapter 11

'Oh, Murder!'
– Mary Jane Kelly

The 'double event' according to one reporter, seemed to bring the entire population of the East End – all Jack London's half a million souls – onto the streets. The police had sealed off Mitre Square and Dutfield's Yard, but the streets leading to them were solid with sightseers all Sunday and in lesser numbers for several days to come. Likewise, the inquests on the two women were mobbed and disappointed ghouls turned away at the doors jostled as close as they could to the buildings to catch snippets of news.

Where possible, women no longer 'carried the banner' but queued to enter the Spikes all over the East End. Those still out on the streets, in stairways and doorways and Itchy Park, armed themselves with knives or hatpins if they could. The terror gripped Whitechapel and Spitalfields as surely as the thick fogs that came with the middle of October. Historian Philip Sugden lists tragic people who hanged themselves – Mrs Sodeaux of Hanbury Street in a state of alarm over the murders; a man named Hennell who believed the police had him in the frame for them. Elsewhere, ghouls made money, as such people always had out of 'orrible murder – not least the journalists of various newspapers. Penny gaffs put on tableaux with 'Jack the Ripper' lit by naphtha flares. As early as September, Margaret Harkness, writing as John Law in the *Pall Mall Gazette*, complained

> ...there is at present almost opposite the London Hospital a ghastly display of the unfortunate women murdered. An old man exhibits these things and while he points them out you will be tightly wedged in between a number of boys and girls, while the smell of death rises into your nostrils.[1]

A pavement artist in Whitechapel Road drew crowds with his brilliant red-chalk drawings. The committee of the International Working Men's Club, good socialists all, charged admission to its premises so that the curious could gaze out of the windows at the murder scene in Dutfield's Yard.

A fearful and tearful East End buried Elizabeth Stride on 6 October and Catherine Eddowes two days later. But it was what happened at the end of the week that brought the nightmares screaming back. On Tuesday the 16th, George Lusk, chairman of the Whitechapel Vigilance Committee, received a three-and-a-half-inch square cardboard box in the post. It was wrapped in plain brown paper and the almost indecipherable postmark probably read 'London E'. With it was a letter, badly written and poorly spelt with the address which has become part of Ripper folklore – 'From Hell'.

> Mr Lusk
>
> Sor [it said in stage Irish]
>
> I send you half the Kidne I took from one women prasarved it for you tother piece I fried and ate it was very nise I may send you the bloody knif that took it out if you only wate a whil longer
>
> Signed
>
> Catch me when you can
>
> Mishter Lusk

This was very much in the vein of dozens of letters now flooding in to the police, the Press and prominent people whether or not they were directly involved in the Whitechapel case. What made this letter different was what else the box contained. It was a kidney.

Pages and pages have been written on this macabre package and it is as frustrating as the Goulston Street graffito. The letter and the kidney both have their 'armed camps' in attack and defence. Dr Thomas Openshaw, Curator of Pathology at the London Hospital to whom members of the Whitechapel Vigilance Committee took the kidney, believed it to be human and taken from the left side of a body. He noted that it was preserved in wine, not the spirits usual in a cadaver required for medical students' experiments. Major Smith of the City Police to whom the kidney was sent after Abberline had examined it at Leman Street, was in no doubt that it was indeed ripped by the killer from Kate Eddowes and sent to the high-profile George Lusk as a taunt. The other side of the argument, from Dr Frederick Brown who also examined it, rests on the fact that he was uncertain whether it was a right or left kidney. Brown also believed that the wine-based spirit which hardened the organ could only have achieved that level of hardening in a week (not the three since the Eddowes murder).

What ought to have been a decider was the evidence of Bright's disease, from which Kate Eddowes was believed to be suffering, because of Brown's description of the 'pale' kidney that remained in the body. Openshaw was at first quoted as saying the kidney was from a female of about forty-five years old and 'ginny' i.e. showing alcohol abuse. He subsequently retracted this and today, the medical jury is still out.

Did Robert Mann write the letter and send the kidney? The postmark is probably right, even some of the spellings/pronunciations in the letter – 'prasarved' – are nineteenth-century Cockney. The spelling, while odd – 'knif', 'nise', 'kidne' – could be from someone with a basic National School education a long time before or from someone who had been taught his letters in the workhouse. My natural instinct was to dismiss this letter as just another hoax, but having discussed it with Professor Laurence Alison of Liverpool University, I am now inclined to believe it is genuine. Graphologist Patricia Marne thinks so too, finding in its chaotic form and erratic rhythm the hallmarks of a psychopath. The long downstrokes to the 'g' and 'y' show signs of aggression, the 'periodic pressure reveals anger with emotional instability, leading to violent mood variation'... 'The muddled and jumbled lines with the letters running into each other demonstrate inability to control intense emotion.'[2] As to the level of decomposition in the Lusk kidney, this could be explained by Mann being able to preserve it in a wide variety of fluids in the Whitechapel mortuary. He actually says so in the text.

What about other pointers in the letter? 'From Hell' speaks for itself as to Robert Mann's inner torment. He is at last furious that other people are cashing in on *his* killings and he does not deign to use the most chilling sobriquet of any serial killer in history, instead going for the 'catch me when you can' variant. This is not a cry for help, but a rare glimpse of an otherwise anonymous man's arrogance. Did he actually eat the rest of the kidney? Did he really intend to send his murder weapon? I very much doubt it. He was merely making a point.

One week later, Openshaw received a letter and Ms Marne and others believe it was written by the same hand. I do not. It is addressed 'Old Boss' like scores of others and signed 'Jack the Ripper'. It spells 'nife' differently and uses obvious stage Cockney – 'them cusses of coppers' and 'along of er bloomin throte'. Above all, it appends the rhyme:

> Oh have you seen the devle
>   with his mikerscope and scalpel
>   a lookin at a kidney
>   with a slide cocked up.

Robert Mann may have regarded any doctor in his mortuary as the equivalent of the devil. He may even have watched them using microscopes and knew what a slide was, but the doggerel is too fanciful for a man used to the shadows. With the exception of his brief appearances in the inquests of Nichols and Chapman and this one burst of petulance over the Lusk letter, he is like the wallpaper that no one notices; that is why he was never caught.

The police and the inhabitants of the East End were experiencing a lull throughout October, although of course they could not relax. Patrols, especially at weekends, the killer's preferred time, were at their peak. Hysteria followed hysteria as an armless, headless and legless female body was found in the building site of New Scotland Yard on the third day of the Stride inquest. House to house enquires continued, rumours flew. In connection with the Eddowes murder, the police focused their attention on the three friends going home from the Imperial Club, because one of them had seen Jack the Ripper.

Because of the timings involved in the murders of Annie Chapman, Liz Stride and Kate Eddowes, the most likely eyewitness descriptions of the Whitechapel murderer came from Elizabeth Long, James Brown, Israel Schwartz and Joseph Lawende, although as we have seen, Schwartz was frightened off and is less reliable than the others. Lawende's description was of a man of medium build and shabby appearance, with a pepper-and-salt loose jacket, a grey cloth cap and reddish neckerchief. He was aged about thirty and had a fair complexion and a moustache. We must question Lawende's accuracy, however, since *The Times* reported him as saying that the suspect was 5 foot 9 inches, not the 5 foot 7 inches that is referred to in the Home Office files. If we take Mrs Long's and Lawende's descriptions together, they clearly cannot have been the same man. It was very dark at the entrance to Mitre Square and Lawende admitted he would not know the man again. On the other hand, Mrs Long and James Brown could be describing the same person. If, of course, we accept Laurence Alison's caveat that 'so fallible are our memories it is almost a wonder that eye-witness accounts are given the credence they are within the criminal justice system',[3] then *all* such evidence should be discounted.

What has given Lawende prominence in the folklore of the Ripper is that various people have assumed that the 'witness' referred to by Sir Robert Anderson in his memoirs is Lawende. We have already noted the unreliability of the memoirs written years after the event. Anderson claims that his witness was 'the only person who ever had a good view of the murderer'. If Chief Inspector Swanson was right (in the 'marginalia' he wrote in Anderson's book) the witness was male and Jewish. Ripper historians therefore have concluded that Anderson meant either Israel Schwartz or Joseph Lawende, with Lawende's friend Joseph Levy as a possible third. However, since nearly all the City Police files on the case were destroyed in World War Two and a sizeable percentage of the Met records are missing too, there is every possibility that there were other Jewish witnesses whose names we do not know.

Whatever the accuracy of Lawende's account, it led to no arrests and throughout October Robert Mann went about his daily routines. For him the 'double event' must have been an extraordinary roller-coaster of emotions. Deprived of his objective with Liz Stride, he unleashed his fury on the body of Kate Eddowes, and this, for a while, must have satisfied him. How long he kept her kidney and her womb we do not know, but in the chaotic mismanagement of the mortuary 'shed' in Eagle Place, it would be easy to hide it 'in plain sight'. He did not kill again in October because the madness had not returned and because the acid fog worsened the cough that had been irritating his throat and chest for some days. It was not until the clearer November that his mood changed and he seemed preoccupied, far away; at least, as far away as No 13, Miller's Court, Dorset Street.

This was the shabby, one-roomed (12 feet square) 'home' of Mary Kelly, fifth and last of the 'canonical' victims of Jack the Ripper – sixth and penultimate victim of Robert Mann. The murder of Mary Kelly is the most confusing of all the Whitechapel murders because Mary was twenty years younger than the other victims and was the only one killed indoors. Those who believe that the killings ended with her murder have taken their leaf from the memoranda of Melville Macnaghten:

> A much more rational theory is that the murderer's brain gave way altogether after his awful glut in Miller's Court and that he

Mary Kelly was the only one of the Ripper victims to be killed indoors, at 13 Miller's Court, off Dorset Street.

immediately committed suicide [opening the door to M J Druitt] or, as a possible alternative, was found to be so hopelessly mad by his relations [enter Cutbush and several more] that he was by them confined in some asylum.[4]

When Melville Macnaghten wrote this, Robert Mann was still living in the Whitechapel Workhouse Infirmary, although how much work he was now able to do, is debatable.

Where was he on the night of Thursday/Friday 8–9 November 1888? All that we can say for sure is that he was at Miller's Court at some time around three o'clock in the morning and Mary Ann Cox, who lived at No 5, probably heard him leaving at 5.45 am. That would have given him a mere fifteen minutes to be back at the Infirmary for breakfast, which is tight, allowing for his having to return the knife to the mortuary first. But, as we have seen throughout, the Whitechapel murderer thrived on fast times, with sudden disappearances being his speciality. As *The Astrologer* put it in 1888:

> How does this diabolical monster succeed in his infernal work time after time, in the midst of teeming millions of individuals? No one, out of all those multitudes, so far as we are aware, ever get a glimpse of him.[5]

Several people said they saw men talking to all the victims prior to the attacks, but no one saw anyone *leaving* George Yard, Hanbury Street, Dutfield's Yard or Mitre Square. And no one saw him leave Miller's Court either. It is partially this that has led to the legend of Jill the Ripper – the police and vigilantes were looking for a man, whereas they should have been looking for a woman. It is also occasioned by the fact that however much doctors at inquests explained that the killer would have little blood on him, the average member of the public – and the average copper on the beat – was still looking for a blood-soaked maniac with rolling eyes.

What Robert Mann left behind in that room in Miller's Court was the most enigmatic of his victims. She was at once Marie Jeanette; she was 'Black Mary', 'Fair Emma', 'Ginger'. She was Irish, she was French, she was Welsh. She had a six-year-old son. She was linked to the royals via the nonsense of the 'highest in the land' and was at one time a maidservant to the artist Walter Sickert. She was pregnant when

Jack found her. Some of this is the nonsense created by Ripperologists over the years; some of it is the nonsense of 1888 and the gossip of the streets.

So what do we *know*? She was born in Limerick, Ireland, about 1863, by which time her killer was possibly working as a labourer in London Docks; Robert Mann would then have been twenty-eight. Mary's father was John Kelly (no relation of Kate Eddowes' partner) and he had a large family. The 1860s were a bad time for the Irish (which decade was not?) with Fenian agitation coming to mainland Britain exactly as the Kellys did. They probably settled in Carmarthenshire where John worked as a foreman in an ironworks. When she was about sixteen, Mary married a collier named Davis who was killed in a mining explosion. The Irish girl drifted to Cardiff and became involved in prostitution, spending several months in Cardiff infirmary, but exactly why is unknown.

From there she came to London and worked at a high class bordello, possibly in Knightsbridge where the madame paired her up with a Frenchman who took her to Paris. Although she soon returned, she adopted the French-sounding Marie Jeanette as a result. All of this sounds the stuff of fairy story, but pretty girls like Mary from the country *did* end up in West End prostitution. At their highest levels, they were courtesans like Catherine Walters, known as Skittles, and had aristocrats and even royalty as their 'patrons'. We are once again faced with the tall tales and embellishments of a street woman, like those of Liz Stride. For them, elaborate stories of elegance and splendour were a kind of escapism.

Whatever the truth, Mary was in the East End by 1885 living briefly with a Mrs Buki in St George's Street,[6] north of the docks. She may or may have not lived with a man named Morganstone before moving into what may have been a brothel at Breezer's Hill, St George's-in-the-East run by a couple named McCarthy (no relation to her future landlord). There may have been another lover, Joseph Fleming, to whom Mary seemed quite attached.

She met Joseph Barnett, a Billingsgate market porter, on Good Friday 1887, while she was dossing at Cooley's in Thrawl Street. At the Kelly inquest, Barnett mentioned Mary's family, with estranged parents, and brothers scattered all over London and a 'respectable' sister who travelled from marketplace to marketplace. There is an air of superiority about Mary Kelly. Some reported her as very bright and a good artist. One said she spoke fluent Welsh. Walter Dew, who, as a young detective knew her by sight, found her pretty and not much of a drinker. Others said that drink turned her from a quiet woman into a terrifying harpy.

Kelly and Barnett moved from lodgings to lodgings, getting drunk and failing to pay rent until they came to 13 Miller's Court, a single-roomed apartment that was actually at the rear of 26 Dorset Street. This was one of the worst areas of the Abyss, described as a 'cesspool' by the social reformer Charles Booth the following year. Mary's rent was 4/6d a week and when she died she was several weeks in arrears.

On the last day of her life, Mary spent the afternoon and early evening with Lizzie Albrook who also lived in Miller's Court. Lizzie was only twenty and remembered Mary warning her gently not to turn out as she had. Between 7.30 and 8.00 pm Joe Barnett turned up. He had left Mary on 30 October because she persisted in bringing prostitutes to stay. If her line to Lizzie can be taken at face value, it may well be that, ironically, Mary was trying to give up prostitution and do what she could for her 'scarlet sisters'. Not unnaturally in a room as small as No 13, Barnett resented this intrusion and left. He may have disliked the way that Mary made her living and Ripperologist Bruce Paley has put him in the frame for the five Whitechapel murders, the other four being attempts to frighten Mary off the streets. He was in a friendly mood that night, however, and the next we hear of Mary Kelly she was with Barnett and Julia Venturney, another Miller's Court resident, drinking in the Horn of Plenty down the road. She may also have been in the Britannia at the other end of the street with another prostitute, Elizabeth Foster.

By a quarter to midnight, she was weaving her way drunkenly back to Miller's Court, in the company of a client. Widowed prostitute Mary Ann Cox from No 5, and who had a record for assault, described Kelly's client as wearing a billycock hat, carrying a pail of ale and wearing shabby clothes. He was in his thirties and had a carroty moustache and blotchy face. As Mary Cox called 'Goodnight', Mary Kelly told her she was going to sing. The client closed the door of No 13. Through the thin-partitioned walls, Cox could hear the music-hall favourite *Only a violet I plucked from my mother's grave* warbled by Kelly as Cox went out at midnight in search of a client. When she came back at one, Mary was still singing.

It is the next witness that has raised most eyebrows in the case of the Kelly murder. George Hutchinson, a military-looking man who lived in the Victoria Home in Commercial Street, met Mary in Thrawl Street at about two in the morning. Clearly they knew each other because Mary addressed him by name and asked to borrow sixpence. Probably she'd just drunk away the money from the blotchy-faced client, but no one seems to have seen her in a pub between one and two. Hutchinson could not help, as he was broke and watched her pick up a client along Thrawl Street. They laughed together and the snatches of conversation that Hutchinson remembered were Mary saying 'All right' and the client saying 'You will be all right for what I have told you' (presumably her 'fee'). Hutchinson was standing against the lamppost outside the Queen's Head and noticed that the man was carrying a small parcel with a strap.

Hutchinson watched them walk past him, then followed them to the corner of Miller's Court. More conversation – 'All right, my dear; come along, you will be comfortable,' she said. It was the typical mock-affection of a prostitute and client and the pair went into the Court, presumably to Mary's room. Hutchinson waited outside the court for forty-five minutes. Since the client did not come out, Hutchinson went away.

His description of the man with Mary Kelly defied belief, because it is impossibly detailed. He was 'foreign' i.e. Jewish, with an astrakhan-trimmed coat, dark jacket and trousers, light waistcoat with a Homburg-style hat ('turned down in the middle'), button boots, spats, a black tie with horseshoe pin and a thick gold chain. He was mid-thirties with dark hair and eyelashes [!] and a moustache curled up at the ends. And this, at night, in dim lamplight when most people can do no better than the vaguest outline. It is likely that George Hutchinson was a time-waster. He missed the inquest but no doubt enjoyed the limelight of his time talking to the police and the Press. He may have been a voyeur, hoping to watch Mary and her client in bed, or perhaps he was an ex-client with a grudge against a particular individual he wanted to frame. If so, it backfired – historian John

Eddleston believes that he, Hutchinson, may have been the Ripper!

At about 3.45 am (Hutchinson, according to his own estimation had left about 3) two residents in Miller's Court both heard a single weak cry, 'Oh, murder!' Sarah Lewis had had a row with her husband and gone to stay with Mrs Keyler at No 2. She arrived at 2.30 by the Christ Church clock. It is likely that this witness was the same Mrs Kennedy who talked to the Press because 'both' women (Lewis and Kennedy) described a would-be assailant with a shiny bag who threatened them in Bethnal Green Road days earlier. This sighting, with its archetypal knife-containing bag is typical of the now-terrified mindset of East End women. If Hutchinson's timings (although not description) are correct, then the man and woman Sarah Lewis saw across the road from Miller's Court at 2.30 have no bearing on Mary Kelly's murder; she was already in her room with the client by then. The man she saw, apparently waiting or looking for someone, was probably Hutchinson. The other witness, who appeared at the inquest, was Elizabeth Prater, the wife of a boot machinist, who lived above Mary's room (her husband having left her five years before). Probably a prostitute herself, she came home at one o'clock that Friday morning and stood on the corner for twenty minutes. She popped into McCarthy's chandler shop and then went to bed. There was no light in Mary's room. By half past one Elizabeth was in her bed, her door barricaded with two tables – either this was her habit or the Ripper scare was being taken very seriously by some women of the Abyss. She was woken by her scampering kitten at half past three or quarter to four and heard the 'Murder' cry. It was common enough to hear such words in the early hours and Elizabeth went back to sleep. She was up again by quarter to six and drinking in the Ten Bells, diagonally opposite Dorset Street.

Another huge red herring flopped into the Ripper net when Caroline Maxwell, wife of a dosshouse deputy, insisted she talked to Mary Kelly some four hours after medical evidence said she was dead. She was very definite about it, even remembering details of the conversation, with Mary feeling ill because of drink. Nothing else fits, so either Caroline had the wrong woman or the wrong day or both. Even this honest mistake has been seized upon by Ripperologists, who claim that a 'ringer' died in Miller's Court and that Mary was somehow spirited away.

The inquest into the death of Mary Kelly opened and closed on Monday 12 November. It was held at Shoreditch Town Hall with Dr Roderick Macdonald, Coroner for North-East Middlesex presiding. Before proceedings got under way, a juror protested over jurisdiction. 'I do not see why we should have the inquest thrown upon our shoulders, when the murder did not happen in our district, but in Whitechapel.' Macdonald was furious and tried to put the juror in his place. He would not shut up however – 'Mr Baxter is my coroner.' Politics reared its head here. Macdonald was an MP, a Scotsman with a radical bent who had lost out (perhaps through impropriety) to Wynne Baxter. Macdonald slammed the juryman, telling him, quite correctly, that the jurisdiction for coroners lay where the body was taken, not where it was found. Since Mary Kelly's corpse had been taken to Shoreditch mortuary, that fell into Macdonald's jurisdiction. If it had gone to Robert Mann's mortuary in Eagle Place, of course, then Wynne Baxter would have handled proceedings.

The inquest was extraordinarily brief, not helped by the fact that the coroner and at least some of his jury were at odds from the start. Some Ripperologists have seen Macdonald's early closure as being part of a massive police cover-up. Others have excused it because Macdonald had previously been Police Surgeon to K Division and perhaps disliked the juicy forensics that Baxter seems to have enjoyed. Either way, it was woefully unsatisfactory and meant that witnesses like George Hutchinson, who went to the police that same day, did not take the stand.

Thomas 'Indian Harry' Bowyer told Macdonald's court that he had gone, on behalf of his boss, landlord, shop-owner and probable pimp, John McCarthy, to collect Mary's overdue rent on the morning of Friday 9 November. There was no reply to his knock, but Bowyer parted the flimsy curtains beyond a broken windowpane and saw two pieces of flesh lying on the table. Then he saw the body. Shocked and appalled, he fetched McCarthy and the pair ran to Commercial Street police station. From there, Inspector Walter Beck followed them back to the crime scene, possibly with Badham and Godley and Constable Dew. Abberline was there by half past eleven.

The long-suffering Dr George Phillips was there already, but all proceedings were held up by police dithering at the highest level and an argument about whether bloodhounds should be brought in. It was Lord Mayor's Day in London and many East Enders were making their way west to St Paul's and the Mansion House to see the gilded carriages and the pikemen of the Honourable Artillery Company. It is likely that some sort of treat was laid on for the inmates of the Whitechapel Workhouse Infirmary. It was also the day that Charles Warren resigned as Commissioner of the Met, which added to the delay.

Eventually, by 1.30 pm, Superintendent Thomas Arnold of H Division arrived to tell the waiting Abberline there would be no dogs and ordered the door to be forced. Between Abberline's inquest evidence and Dr Phillips', we have a clear picture of the murder room. 'The mutilated remains of a woman,' Phillips deposed, 'were lying two-thirds over [the bed] towards the edge of the bedstead, nearest the door. Deceased had only an under-linen garment upon her and by subsequent examination I am sure that the body had been removed, after the injury which caused death, from that side of the bedstead... nearest to the partition.' Cause of death, Phillips said, was loss of blood from the right carotid artery. Abberline took an inventory of the room's contents and noted that a large fire had been lit in the grate, so hot that a kettle's spout had melted. The ashes revealed pieces of women's clothing, part of a hat and a skirt. He put forward the idea that the fire may have been to light the killer's work as the only other light source in the room was a solitary candle.

It was at this stage, with no medical details of mutilation given, that Macdonald urged the jury to come to a decision. They did, of course, bullied by the man, and it was the by now inevitable 'wilful murder by some person or persons unknown'.

And so it has remained.

Dr Thomas Bond's post-mortem report on Mary Kelly was not delivered at her inquest. Curiously, it was one of those original documents that vanished from the archive, fuelling all sorts of conspiratorial speculation. It was returned, anonymously, in 1987 and makes grisly reading, even in précised form:

The body was lying naked [although the in situ photograph of the corpse clearly shows a chemise around the shoulders] in the middle of the bed, the shoulders flat but the axis of the body inclined to the left. The head was turned on the left cheek. The left arm was close to the body and rested on the mattress, the elbow bent and the forearm supine with the fingers clenched. The legs were wide apart, the left thigh at right angles to the trunk and the right forming an obtuse angle with the pubes.

The whole of the surface of the abdomen and thighs was removed and the abdominal cavity emptied of its viscera. The breasts were cut off, the arms mutilated by several jagged wounds and the face hacked beyond recognition of the features. The tissues of the neck were severed all round down to the bone.

The viscera were found in various parts viz: the uterus and kidneys with one breast under the head, the other breast by the right foot, the liver between the feet, the intestines by the right side and the spleen by the left side of the body. The flaps from the abdomen and thighs were on a table [these would show clearly in the second photograph in Mary's room].

The face was gashed in all directions, the nose, cheeks, eyebrows and ears being partly removed. The lips were blanched and cut by several incisions running obliquely down to the chin. There were also numerous cuts extending irregularly across all the features.

The neck was cut through the skin and other tissues right down to the vertebrae, the 5th and 6th being deeply notched. The skin cuts in the front of the neck showed distinct ecchymosis [indicating bruising made by a slow, deliberate cut]. The air passage was cut at the lower part of the larynx through the cricoid cartilage.

Both breasts were removed by more or less circular incisions, the muscles down to the ribs being attached to the breasts. The intercostals [muscles] between the 4th, 5th and 6th ribs were cut through and the contents of the thorax visible through the openings.

The skin and tissues of the abdomen from the costal arch to the pubes were removed in three large flaps. The right thigh was denuded in front of the bone, the flap of skin, including the external organs of generation and part of the right buttock. The left thigh was stripped of skin, fascia and muscles as far as the knee.

The left calf showed a long gash through skin and tissues to the deep muscles and reaching from the knee to 5 inches above the ankle.

Both arms and forearms had extensive and jagged wounds. The right thumb showed a small superficial incision about 1 in. long, with extravasation of blood in the skin and there were several abrasions on the back of the hand moreover showing the same condition.

On opening the thorax it was found that the right lung was minimally adherent at the apex and there were a few adhesions over the side. Her pericardium was open below and the heart absent.

Although this is Bond's report, the post mortem at Shoreditch was actually carried out by the ubiquitous Dr Phillips, with Bond, Brown and possibly doctors Dukes, Hebbert and Clarke in attendance. The number of medical men there is testimony to the hysteria the Ripper was causing and the unparalleled butchery involved. The most controversial line in Bond's narrative is the last one – 'the heart absent'. A number of Ripperologists have taken this to mean that the heart had been cut out of the body, but, like other internal organs, was elsewhere in the room. Since Bond comments on the lungs and stomach contents, it is clear that he and Phillips carried out a complete necropsy, examining all organs under the Virchow method. He would therefore have described the condition of the heart had it been anywhere in the room. It is possible that the killer burnt it along with the clothes in the fireplace, but it is far more likely that it was slipped into his pocket by Robert Mann on its way to another glass jar in his mortuary.

Luck had followed Robert Mann again, although he could not have known it. The timings in the early hours of the morning mean that the only sound of his leaving was Kelly's door closing at 5.45 (although Elizabeth Prater could not be totally sure it *was* Kelly's door). Since

Hutchinson left his spot opposite Miller's Court at about three o'clock and Mary Cox saw no light in Kelly's room at the same time, then she was probably still entertaining the man whose incredibly detailed description Hutchinson gave to Inspector Abberline.

Medical experts at the time and since have estimated that the killer spent two hours hacking Mary's body to pieces. This means that she had gone out again, after three o'clock and met Robert Mann. We have always assumed that the man seen watching Miller's Court earlier was George Hutchinson, but what if it wasn't? Did Robert Mann linger in the shadows, accost Mary Kelly (already drunk and probably not very choosy) and go with her into her room?

As she turned to take off her coat, did she see the look on Mann's face and just have time to scream 'Murder!' before his fingers closed on her throat?

Chapter 12

The End of the Road – 'Clay Pipe' Alice McKenzie

Robert Mann struck again thirty-three weeks after killing Mary Kelly in 13 Miller's Court. It was the longest gap between his killings but after the extent of the mutilations carried out on Kelly, this is hardly surprising. There may have been another reason for the time lag, however, and this will be discussed later.

Such was the hysteria in the East End – indeed all over London – that any new outrage was likely to be attributed to Jack, and the extraordinary police presence by November underlined the seriousness of the situation. Apart from the uniformed patrols which were so important as a deterrent, the number of plain-clothes officers on patrol rose from twenty-seven in September (after the murder of Annie Chapman) to 143 after the discovery of Mary Kelly's body. By the January of 1889, they were cut to 102 and in the next month to forty-seven. By March they had stopped altogether.

The first attack that was wrongly attributed to Jack by some newspapers took place only eleven days after Mary Kelly's murder. Annie Farmer was a forty-year-old prostitute who usually dossed at Satchell's, No 19 George Street. It was here she took a client on the night of 20 November and paid for a double bed. As we have seen in a previous chapter, attitudes of lodging-house keepers varied enormously. Some knew their customers very well, others barely at all. Whoever was overseeing Satchell's that night turned a blind eye to the fumblings in the narrow wooden box-bed until there was an ear-piercing scream and Annie Farmer staggered into the kitchen with blood seeping from a throat wound. Her client was already on his toes, still fully clothed and he dashed off into Thrawl Street.

The description of the man given to police is yet another in the long list of men who were not Jack. He was about thirty-six years old, with a dark complexion and a black moustache, stood 5 feet 6 inches tall and wore a shabby suit and a round black hat.

The client was real enough, but the attack probably was not. 'Married' quarters in lodging-houses usually afforded some privacy, so we only have Annie Farmer's word for what happened. Her throat wound was very superficial and had been carried out with a dull-edged knife. Annie admitted to having coins in her mouth and the police realized that this was a case, actually very common, of a prostitute robbing her client. By slicing her throat and screaming 'murder' she hoped to keep the cash and get rid of its owner in one fell swoop. It almost worked.

It was a month later that a much more serious attack took place and this time, it led to murder. Rose Mylett, also called Catherine, 'Drunken Lizzie' Davis and 'Fair Alice' Downey was twenty-six when she died in the early hours of Thursday 20 November. At her inquest, her mother filled in the sketchy details we have heard before on women of the Abyss. Rose had been married briefly to an upholsterer named Davis and gave birth to a son, probably in 1881.[1] The boy was at school in Sutton, South London, when his mother died.

Rose had a number of different addresses. Sometimes she lived in Limehouse or Poplar; sometimes at 18 George Street, just across the road from Satchell's, making her a neighbour of Annie Farmer. Her most sinister neighbour, however, was Robert Mann, because sometimes she stayed with her mother in Pelham Street, off Baker's Row, in the shadow of the Workhouse Infirmary.

On the night she died, Rose was seen talking to two sailors in Poplar High Street, near Clarke's Yard. This was about 7.55 pm and the witness was Charles Ptolomay, who was walking along England Row on his way to work as a night attendant at another infirmary, that of the Poplar Union Workhouse. She seemed fully sober, but Ptolomay heard her shout 'No, no, no!' to the two men. At her inquest, Ptolomay described the shorter of the two men, who seemed to be in earnest conversation with Rose, as about 5 feet 7 inches. His friend was much taller, perhaps 5 feet 11 and looked like a 'Yankee'. Presumably the sailors were in uniform and locals like Ptolomay would have seen all the uniforms of the world sailing into the busiest docks on earth.

Rose may have been haggling over a price or perhaps she was not prepared to have a threesome on what was probably a cold night.

She was seen alive once more, outside the George pub in Commercial Road, by Alice Graves, who clearly knew her. Rose seemed to be drunk, but Alice could not provide a better description of the two men she was with other than the fact that they were sailors.

The next time a passer-by saw her, it was Constable Robert Goulding patrolling his usual beat through Clarke's Yard. By now it was 4.15 am and Goulding's bulls-eye shone on what appeared to be a bundle of rags in a corner. At first, the constable concluded that here was another Unfortunate, someone 'carrying the banner' who had frozen to death or died of malnutrition. Rose lay on her left side, her body still warm and there was no sign of injury or assault, her clothes were in place and, it would be revealed later, 1 shilling and 2 pence in her pocket.

Death was certified by Dr Harris, the assistant to Dr Matthew Bromfield, the Police Surgeon of K Division who lived at 171 East India Dock Road. Inevitably, it was his post-mortem report that was presented at the inquest:

> 'Blood was oozing from the nostrils,' Bromfield wrote, 'and there was a slight abrasion on the right side of the face... On the neck there was a mark which had evidently been caused by cord drawn tightly round the neck, from the spine to the left ear... There were also impressions of the thumbs and middle and index fingers of some person plainly visible on each side of the neck. There were no injuries to the arms or legs. The brain was gorged with an almost black fluid blood. The stomach was full of meat and potatoes which had only recently been eaten. Death was due to strangulation. Deceased could not have done it herself ...'

This extraordinary finding opened a can of worms. Sir Robert Anderson, anxious to prove that this was suicide, not yet another probably unsolvable murder that would damage his police force, took the unusual step of visiting the Poplar mortuary to examine the corpse himself. In rapid succession, while Bromfield and Harris were carrying out the post mortem, Dr Alexander McKellar, the Met's surgeon-in-chief and Dr Hebbert, assistant Police Surgeon of A Division both turned up to lend their considerable medical weight.

The arguments over whether Rose was murdered or committed suicide raged on throughout the January of 1889. Anderson clearly did not trust Bromfield's judgement. He had found no traces of alcohol in the dead woman's stomach, even though Alice Graves had sworn she'd seen Rose drunk. And medically, there was no sign of a birth, despite Rose's mother's testimony. The mark on the dead woman's neck was very faint and Anderson had observed for himself at the crime scene that there was no sign of a ligature or of a struggle. He put pressure on Dr Thomas Bond, the usually reliable ex-Police Surgeon of A Division and the man abruptly changed his mind – 'death was due to strangulation; it was produced accidentally and not by homicidal violence'. In other words, Rose had choked in a drunken stupor and strangled herself with the stiff collar of her dress.

The coroner, Wynne Baxter, was furious with all this police and medical interference, having clashed with the Met as we have seen in previous chapters. Accordingly, he made sure that the jury returned a verdict of 'murder by person or persons unknown'.

The whole thing was very unsatisfactory, but what was ludicrous was the fact that Rose Mylett was officially logged as an alleged Ripper victim. Laying aside the rather implausible accident or even suicide suggestion, *nothing* about Rose's death fits the pattern of the earlier killings. There was no use of a knife, no mutilation, not even disturbance of clothing. The most plausible theory remains that one or other of the sailors lost his temper with Rose and strangled her. This was not a sex crime in the accepted sense and it certainly was not Ripper-related. This was just part and parcel of the endemic violence of the East End. Only the New York *World* laid the next outrage at Jack's door, removed from the scene as the paper inevitably was by some 3,000 miles.

What had Robert Mann been doing in the weeks since he butchered Mary Kelly? As after all the other killings, he would have experienced acute depression. Perhaps after Kelly, with its unparalleled violence, the depression was worse than ever. As Dr Joel Norris puts it:

No real power is achieved and the killer is left feeling as empty, forlorn and damned as he had throughout the entirety of his life.[2]

In this mood, Mann may have contemplated giving himself up to the police. He might have considered writing a confessional letter such as those that were now flooding in to various newspapers and police stations. One written in block capitals and posted to Leman Street Police Station was sent with a London EC postmark on 10 November, the day after Kelly died. 'Look out for the next,' one of these letters warned. The next would be Clay Pipe Alice.

By the summer of 1889, the fantasies that drove Robert Mann to murder were crowding in his brain again. But by now, the bottom had fallen out of his world. We have already noted the condemnation of the unsatisfactory mortuary in Eagle Place by coroners of the day. The Infirmary authorities, no doubt stung by this, pushed for extra funding and the buildings were refurbished. This included the erection of a new mortuary within the Infirmary grounds. Since Alice McKenzie's body was taken to the old 'shed', in Eagle Place,[3] we must conclude that the new building was not ready. When the day came that the old mortuary, Mann's mortuary, the Ripper's lair, was taken out of use it would have a profound effect on the Whitechapel murderer.

Alice McKenzie came from Peterborough; like so many women of her class, drifting from job to job and man to man until she met the Irish porter John McCormack, who also used the surname Bryant, and worked casually for Jewish tailors along Hanbury Street. This was in 1883 and the couple lived as man and wife in various dosshouses in the Spitalfields area. Friends of the woman whose inquest they attended on 17 July claimed that she earned her living by charring. The police knew, however, that from time to time she turned to prostitution. She also drank to excess and was in the habit of smoking clay pipes.

At the time of her encounter with Robert Mann, Alice and McCormack were living at Tenpenny's Lodging House, 52 Gun Street. He came home from work at about 4 pm and gave Alice 1 shilling and 8 pence before going to bed. The 8d was to pay for their bed that night, but they had a row and Alice stormed out. It would be the last time McCormack saw her alive. He woke up between 10 and 11 pm to find that Alice had not paid for the bed. Elizabeth Ryder, the wife of the deputy, told McCormack he could stay put despite the lack of money. After all, he was a regular. He went back to bed and rose again at 5.45 am. By this time, Alice was dead.

Can we log her last movements? About 7 pm she had met George Dixon, a blind boy she obviously knew, a fellow lodger in Gun Street, and she took him to a pub near the Cambridge Music Hall. At some point while they were there, Dixon heard Alice asking a man to buy her a drink. The man had said 'Yes'. She still may have had McCormack's cash on her or she may have spent it, but this was a standard ice-breaker prior to picking up a client and perhaps she arranged to meet the man later. She took Dixon back to No 52 and went out again.

By 8.30 pm, Alice was back at Tenpenny's, the worse for drink. Elizabeth Ryder, to whom she did not speak, saw her leaving once more. Just over three hours later, the last sighting took place. Margaret Franklin, who had known Alice since she came to the East End, was sitting with Catherine Hughes and Sarah Mahoney on the front step of a barber's shop at the Brick Lane end of Flower and Dean Street. It was 11.40 pm on 16 July. Margaret asked Alice how she was doing. 'All right,' Alice answered. 'I can't stop now.' To Margaret, she appeared to be sober. An hour later she would be dead.

Robert Mann probably left the workhouse by the usual back door sometime around midnight. There was a marked difference from his last sortie back in November. The massive police presence he'd seen then had gone. Instead, he saw the usual bobbies, ambling purposefully at their steady 2½ miles an hour, checking locks and door catches, nodding to the odd passer-by. Nor did he see any of the obvious plain-clothes men, trying to blend, to look like any other denizen of the Abyss, but actually standing out like sore Metropolitan thumbs.

Once again, Robert Mann had a choice. And clearly, we do not know which one he took. If he went south along Charles Street, that would take him to the busy Whitechapel Road with its larger selection of whores. If he went west, along Old Montague Street, the range would be smaller but the alleyways darker, the gas lamps fewer – his ideal killing ground.

He had acted out in his mind again and again the thrill of his crimes – the initial resistance of skin to his knife-tip, the rush of blood, the hacking through sinew. He would have known all their names by now, his victims, either because he had read them himself or because it would have been the talk of the Infirmary. Now, as 16 July became the 17th, Mann was focused, alert. His exact route may be unknown to us, but it was not random. He knew this area like the back of his hand and knew that a corpse from here would be brought to his mortuary. Perhaps he saw Alice along Whitechapel High Street or Wentworth Street that runs parallel to it. She was exactly his type – short, mousy-haired, middle-aged. He probably couldn't see her freckles in the gaslight. He approached her, picked her up as he had the others. She was drunk, relatively helpless; his. They would have discussed his needs and agreed a price. He would have flashed a coin from his pocket to prove he was good for it. All this would have taken two, perhaps three minutes. She knew a place, she may have told him, up Castle Alley.

His heart probably sank when he saw it. Along the twisted length of the alleyway, cluttered with carts and rubbish there were four gas lamps. It was too bright, and perhaps too public, for what Mann had in mind. But now, in a sense, it was too late for them both...

Sergeant Edward Badham, Warrant No. 65001, knew Robert Mann and he was no stranger to his handiwork either. He may have been the Sergeant Betham reported in some newspapers as having accompanied Inspector Walter Beck to 13 Miller's Court to see the body of Mary Kelly. He was certainly one of the officers who had taken Annie Chapman's body to the Eagle Place Mortuary and would have met Mann there. But by the time Badham rendezvoused with Constable Walter Andrews outside the Three Crowns pub on the corner of Old Castle Street and Castle Alley, Mann was already making his way home.

Badham was a beat sergeant and was doing his rounds at 12.45, meeting Andrews at the pre-arranged time and pre-arranged place. 'All right?' 'All right, sergeant.' All was well, Badham walking away north-west up the alley towards Wentworth Street; Andrews in the opposite direction, south-east towards Whitechapel High Street. It could only have been a minute or two later that Andrews came upon the body of Alice McKenzie lying near a gas lamp *between two costers' carts*. It took him seconds to realize that this was another Ripper victim. The woman's throat had been cut, with dark blood still oozing

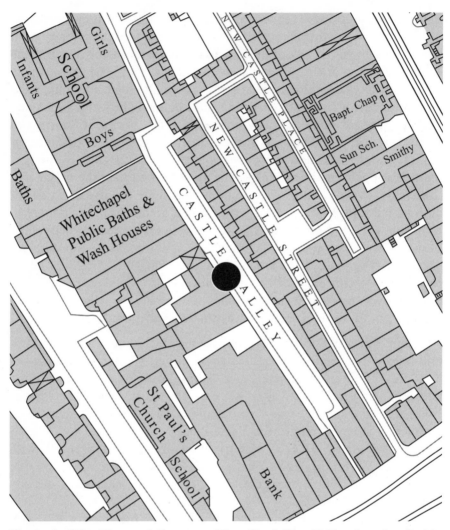

The last of the Ripper victims was 'Clay Pipe' Alice McKenzie, who died in Castle Alley between two costers' carts.

from the wound. Her heavy skirts had been hauled up above her abdomen and there was a great deal of blood there. Andrews touched the woman's skin. Still warm. Then he heard the footsteps.

It was probably the secret ambition of every copper in the Met and

City forces to catch Jack the Ripper. Perhaps because of this and the freshness of the corpse, Andrews broke every rule in the book by not staying with the body and summoning aid with his whistle. Andrews, a Suffolk man, had been with the Met for eight years, but now he was chasing Jack experience and procedure went out of the window. Now he *did* blow his whistle and almost at once came upon a man carrying a dinner plate walking towards Wentworth Street. He was Isaac Lewis Jacobs, who lived at 12 New Castle Street and was on his way to McCarthy's chandler's shop in Dorset Street to buy some supper.

Conspiracy theorists would have a field day with this coincidence. We know enough about the milieu of the East End not to be surprised by a man going out to an all-night grocer, nor even that he was carrying a plate expecting to buy some hot food. John McCarthy of course had been Mary Kelly's landlord. Surely, Jacobs could have found a nearer shop than Dorset Street for his purposes? Whatever suspicions Andrews had of the man, he marched him back to Alice McKenzie's corpse.

It was raining by this time and Sergeant Badham came at the run, having heard Andrews' whistle. He examined the corpse briefly, ascertained who Jacobs was and told Andrews to stay put this time. Badham went in search of the other two beat coppers, Joseph Allen and George Neve. Constable 423H Allen had already talked to Andrews and had paused under the lamppost where Alice now lay at about 12.15 am. He had seen nothing then. Now, Badham sent him running back to the station along Commercial Street for the duty inspector and, if he could, to rouse a doctor. Constable 101H Neve was detailed to search the area, rummaging in the rain behind carts, costermongers' barrows and hoardings. He found nothing. The only thing to find, the murder weapon, was in Robert Mann's pocket.

By ten past one, Dr George Bagster Phillips arrived, in the pouring rain and made his preliminary observations. The dead woman's head was turned to the right, revealing a gash on the left side of the throat. There were various cuts, including a deep one to the abdomen, but no attempt at actual disembowelling. He ordered officers to load the corpse onto the ambulance and take it to the Whitechapel Workhouse Mortuary. By that time, Inspector Edmund Reid had arrived and sent his men in all directions asking questions in dosshouses about anyone who had recently arrived with bloodstained hands.

We cannot know what was going through Robert Mann's twisted mind. On the one hand, according to the now well-known pattern, he was in the totem phase. Had he actually taken a totem or trophy from Alice McKenzie? When the police had lifted the body, they found a clay pipe lying on the still dry road. Was that her only pipe – or had Mann helped himself to another, now in his possession? Outwardly, of course, the mortuary attendant pauper was in control again, hanging his wet coat up before slipping back to his bed via the back door.

There is no record of whether Mann was actually called back to the mortuary by the officers with Alice's body, but as the mortuary attendant, this was highly likely. As before, he got up when roused by the superintendent or night staff and no doubt went straight into his assumed role of horror-struck member of the public. Only he can imagine his own sensations as his latest handiwork was rolled past him over the cobbles at Pavilion Yard to the slab. Whether he washed or laid out the body is unknown, but he would certainly have had *some* opportunity to remind himself that *this* time, the work had not been quite what it was. The mutilations were limited because he'd heard the tread of Andrews' size tens and had dashed away more silently than he'd come, south to Whitechapel High Street. From there, an unhurried 'normal' walk would have seen him home in ten minutes. But the wounds to the throat... a shadow of the Ripper in his prime only eight months ago.

Perhaps Mann was still there later that morning when the police took a photograph of Clay Pipe Alice. She looks asleep, her lower lip protruding slightly, her wiry hair turning grey. She has dimpled cheeks and blankets around her to cover her modesty. And her hair has been combed.

Dr Phillips must have carried out his post mortem in the leaky old shed that same day because he gave evidence the day after, the second day of the inquest. The overworked Wynne Baxter began proceedings again at the Working Lads' Institute on Whitechapel Road later that first day, 17 July, calling in succession, John McCormack and Elizabeth Ryder, both to prove who the dead woman was and to establish some pattern for the last day of her life. It speaks volumes for life in the Abyss that having lived with the woman for over seven years,

McCormack had no idea whether she'd been married or had children.

The third witness at the inquest was Constable Neve who confirmed that Alice worked as a prostitute around Brick Lane, Gun Street and Dorset Street. Lastly came Sarah Smith, the manageress of the Whitechapel Baths and Washhouses on Goulston Street. The back of these premises (where Mrs Smith lived) looked out onto Castle Alley, in fact the exact spot where Mann had killed Alice McKenzie. The luck which surrounded him like an aura was with him once more. Mrs Smith had gone to bed between 12.15 and 12.30 am and had sat up reading. Her windows were closed and she heard and saw nothing. Feet from where she lay, Jack the Ripper was now claiming his last victim. The first that Sarah Smith knew anything was wrong was when she heard the shrill sound of Andrews' whistle.

The inquest continued the next day, with Inspector Reid outlining operations of his team in the area. Dr Phillips gave a brief report, in keeping with the policy adopted at the Mary Kelly inquest. This served to dampen the ever-growing prurience of the Press and to prevent any possible copycat work. Phillips' report, completed by 22 July, was as full as ever. Mann's mortuary must have been very crowded on the 17th with Phillips, Chief Surgeon McKellar (who brought a friend!), Dr Gordon Brown, the City Police Surgeon and a Mr Bostwick who seems to have been a morbidly curious ghoul who was not allowed to stay long. There would have been a rich irony indeed if it was mortuary keeper Mann who showed him off the premises.

The cause of death in the case of Alice McKenzie was severance of the left carotid artery, caused by the two jagged wounds Phillips found there. Each one was no more than four inches long and the windpipe had not been severed. Bruising on the chest and abdomen suggested pressure marks caused by a right hand with the knife wounds being inflicted with the left. It was this, as well as the superficiality of the stomach cuts, that led Phillips to believe that Alice had not been killed by the same assailant who had murdered the others. He was careful to state that this was his opinion only on 'anatomical and professional' grounds.

The police thought differently. The age and occupation of the deceased, the speed and silence of the attack all screamed 'Ripper'. Police Commissioner James Monro wrote:

I need not say that every effort will be made by the police to discover the murderer, who, I am inclined to believe is identical with the notorious 'Jack the Ripper' of last year.

In essence, Jack was back and to that end Dr Thomas Bond, very familiar with the earlier murders, was brought in by Anderson. His report read:

I see in this murder evidence of similar design to the former Whitechapel murders, viz. Sudden onslaught on the prostrate woman, the throat skilfully and resolutely cut with subsequent mutilation indicating sexual thoughts and a desire to mutilate the abdomen and sexual organs.

In other words, all that had prevented Mann from his usual ferocious mutilations was the arrival of Constable Andrews. In fact, it was not that simple...

Robert Anderson did not accept Bond's findings, writing many years later in his memoirs that Clay Pipe Alice was 'an ordinary murder and not the work of a sexual maniac'. When we read nonsense like this, it is not remotely surprising that Mann was never caught. An 'ordinary' murder does not exist and *any* attack on the genitals is sex-related. Coming from a lawyer whose police career specialized in 'matters relating to political crime' (particularly Irish activities) the lack of understanding is perhaps not surprising, but Anderson was the officer in charge of the Whitechapel murders investigation and ultimately his word was law. Robert Mann was lucky again.

Apart from Margaret Franklin, who had called to Alice along Flower and Dean Street less than one hour before her death, the only other witness called on the second day of the inquest was Margaret Cheeks, another inmate at 52 Gun Street and another prostitute. The sole reason for her appearance seems to be that she had vanished on the night Alice died and there were briefly fears of another 'double event'. In fact Margaret had gone to visit her sister and there was no harm done.

On the second day of the inquest, William Wallace Brodie walked into Leman Street Police Station. He had been drinking and wanted to confess that he was the Whitechapel murderer, his conscience plagued particularly by the killing of Alice. The police of course had been here before, more than once, but because Monro in particular believed that the Ripper was on the streets again, patrols were stepped up once more and no stone was to be unturned. Brodie's statement must have left the recording officer open-mouthed. In one section he claimed to have walked from Land's End to London in half an hour. When this was queried by the officer, Brodie conceded this might have been forty-five minutes.

Just in case, Brodie was detained to appear in the police court on 20 July charged with the murder of Alice McKenzie. A week later however, police enquiries had proved that Brodie had taken ship to South Africa on 6 September 1888, the day Polly Nichols was buried. He did not return until 15 July 1889, so he could not possibly have killed Annie Chapman, Liz Stride, Kate Eddowes or Mary Kelly. When he appeared again on the 27th he was discharged but re-arrested immediately for wasting police time.

In the world of Ripperology, opinion is divided over the murder of Alice McKenzie. Stewart Evans and Donald Rumbelow believe it was a 'cover-up' killing, that Alice was murdered by someone she knew and that the relatively feeble mutilations were an attempt to pass the buck to the notorious Jack and allay suspicion. Philip Sugden believes that Alice may well have been a Ripper victim and John Eddlestone is sure of it. So am I.

But why, then, were the wounds not identical? Part of the answer, as we have seen, is that Robert Mann was interrupted before he could finish his work. He had made one 7-inch gash in Alice's stomach already and then he heard the thud of Constable Andrews' boots. And, of course, he too had been here before with the murder of Liz Stride, when travelling salesman Louis Diemschutz had arrived in Dutfield's Yard as Mann crouched, literally red-handed, behind the wooden gate. Then he had gone on to finish the work, his blood up, his lust uncontrollable, on Kate Eddowes in Mitre Square. There is no evidence of a second attack on 16/17 July, despite the temporary disappearance of Margaret Cheeks.

I believe that the difference in the throat wound – two cuts rather than a single deep slash that led to near-decapitation – is caused by the fact that Robert Mann was now ill. This may also explain an inability to follow up the crime à la Eddowes. By the summer of 1889 Robert

Mann was already suffering from phthisis, the lung disease which would kill him six years later.

The symptoms of tuberculosis, a major killer well into the twentieth century, can be felt five or six years before death. In the most likely form that Mann had – fibrous phthisis – there is coughing, a hoarse, rasping voice and a shortage of breath. Exertion – for instance ripping throats and abdomens – causes immediate exhaustion.

Because we know so little about Mann, of course, we cannot know whether he was coughing by now. In the workhouse and on the streets of Whitechapel *everybody* coughed. Interestingly, the remedies of the day involved avoidance of alcohol (Mann couldn't have afforded it), a simple diet (which was all the workhouse offered) and a cold environment (the workhouse was rarely anything else).

Ripperologists and historians have racked their brains to explain why the killings stopped when they did. Because most are obsessed with Macnaghten's observations on the 'canonical five', to them the last death is of course that of Mary Kelly. Serial killers, they contend, do not merely give up killing and take up a less obnoxious hobby like stamp collecting. To explain this, a number of solutions have been put forward: Jack died (Montague John Druitt, who committed suicide in the Thames); or he was incarcerated (Aaron Kosminski, sent to Colney Hatch Lunatic Asylum); or he emigrated ('Dr' Francis Tumblety, effectively, going home to America).

We need not look for anything so dramatic. And the whole issue turns on the pattern of serial killing and the length of time such a killer lies dormant. Because the Whitechapel murders happened in such a cluster – six in twelve weeks in the Autumn of 1888 – we naturally assume that this rollercoaster would have continued. This is wrong. What Melville Macnaghten called 'the awful glut' in Miller's Court sated Mann for thirty-three weeks. And after that, he remained dormant, probably because his disease would not let him do anything else. Albert de Salvo, the Boston Strangler, killed thirteen women in eighteen months; then he reverted to rape, letting his victims live. The compulsion to kill had gone. 'Il Monstro', the 'Monster of Florence' killed sixteen people between 1968 and 1985, but there was a gap of six years between the first and second murders and seven years between that and the third. And there were minor consolations along the way. On the morning of Friday 13 February 1891, the body of Frances Coles, known as 'Carrotty Nell' was brought in an ambulance to Mann's mortuary. He would have officiated, if he was well enough, as Dr Phillips carried out the post mortem. She was a prostitute and her throat had been cut but she was not a victim of the Ripper.

To say that Robert Mann had committed the perfect murders would be far from true. To say that he committed seven murders and got away with them all is at once astonishing and yet, to historians of the nineteenth century, no surprise at all.

Chapter 13

'Oh, Have You Seen the Devil?'

What kind of killer were the police looking for in 1888–9? Two days after the murder of Mary Kelly, they arrested the White-Eyed Man. That night, a Mrs Humphreys, going about her business in George Yard (which may or may not have been prostitution) was terrified by a bespectacled man who leapt out of the fog at her. She had the presence of mind to ask who he was and what he was doing; he laughed and ran away. When she screamed 'Murder!' however, a particularly alert crowd appeared from nowhere and grabbed him. He was rescued by the police who held him overnight, ascertaining that he was Dr William Holt, of St George's Hospital and that he was a lone vigilante wandering the streets in search of Jack.

The importance of this story is not Holt himself, but the fact that Mrs Humphreys, the Whitechapel mob and the police were all on the lookout for just such a man. It was the media who christened Holt 'the white-eyed man' because it was better copy than 'man with glasses'. To them, the Whitechapel murderer would be heavily bloodstained after each killing, would probably be carrying his murder weapon in a parcel or bag and would be a raving maniac with mad, staring eyes. Any number of stereotypes like this were reported by frightened women and worked up into ever more unlikely caricatures by the Press. And in this, the average man in the street, be he policeman, carman or journalist was consciously or unconsciously following the scientific orthodoxy of the day.

In 1890, Henry Havelock Ellis wrote *The Criminal* in which he lamented the fact that England had not kept up with the science of criminal psychology which was burgeoning elsewhere. He believed that criminals were of certain types – 'political', 'by passion' and 'insane'. About 100 people a year were imprisoned under the category of 'insane' and Ellis admitted to being in the dark about causation:

> The lunatic may be influenced by the same motives that influence a sane person, but he is at the same time impelled by other motives peculiar to himself and to which we have no means of access.[1]

Italians Enrico Ferri and Napoleone Colajanni included 'cosmic' causes such as temperature and diet. Biological causes covered anatomy, physiology, psychology. The social factor depended on the price of beer and the price of bread. Others were looking at physical characteristics – the sexual offender, wrote Ottolenghi, '...presents the most rectilinear nose, though he shows the undulating profile of nose more frequently than any other group of criminals'. Marro, also working in Italy, believed that sex-offenders were usually full-bearded; rapists had fair hair and blue eyes. The greatest authority of all, Cesare Lombroso, believed that the typical sex offender had bright eyes, a cracked rough voice, swollen lips and eyelids. He was occasionally hump-backed or deformed. 'The eye of the habitual homicide is glassy, cold and fixed; his nose is often aquiline... the jaws are strong; the ears long; the cheek bones large; the hair dark, curly, abundant; the beard often thin; the canine teeth much developed; the lips thin.'

Had Jack been caught, he would probably have had long arms, a weak chest or heart disease. He may or may not have been among the 20% of murderers who blushed. He would probably have been a smoker and may have been unusually sensitive to change in the weather. And he would have shown no remorse. The French authority Despine noted an Albanian killer who resented the fact that the traveller he had killed and robbed had less on him than the cost of his bullets. When Thomas Wainwright was asked how he could murder such an innocent girl as Helen Abercrombie, he said, 'Upon my soul, I don't know, unless it was because she had such thick legs.'

Whereas Havelock Ellis does not mention the Ripper at all, Richard von Krafft-Ebing does. His book *Psychopathia Sexualis* appeared in German in 1886 but later editions cite the Whitechapel murders as Case 17. It is not actually very helpful because Krafft-Ebing was probably working from newspaper accounts and gets the number of murders wrong:

> On December 1 1887 [there is no such attack but this is
> probably a variant on the non-existent 'Fairy Fay', a creation of
> the media], July 7 [no such attack], August 8 [Tabram],
> September 30 [Stride and Eddowes], one day in the month of
> October [no such attack] and on the 9th November [Kelly], on
> the 1st of June [possibly the torso of prostitute Elizabeth
> Jackson, not a Ripper killing] the 17th of July [McKenzie] and
> the 10th of September [the Pinchin Street torso] 1889, the
> bodies of women were found in various lonely [sic] quarters of
> London ripped open and mutilated in a peculiar fashion. The
> murderer, known as Jack the Ripper, has never been found. It
> is probable that he first cut the throats of his victims, then
> ripped open the abdomen and groped among the intestines. In
> some instances he cut off the genitals and carried them away;
> in others he only tore them to pieces and left them behind. He
> does not seem to have had sexual intercourse with his victims,
> but very likely the murderous act and subsequent mutilation of
> the corpse were equivalents for the sexual act.

This is an early and classic explanation of Robert Mann's motives, up
to a point. We know today that rape and what Krafft-Ebing calls
'lustmurder' (a killing with clearly intended mutilation of the genitals)
is not directly about sex, but about power and control over his victims.
Of the 238 cases that *Psychopathia* details, only thirteen involve
lustmurder and most of these were carried out on children by
inadequates. He lists the deeply deranged Joseph Vacher, who
assaulted both sexes. Inevitably dubbed the 'French Ripper' because of
his disembowelling signature, he was precisely the sort of dribbling
lunatic everybody was hunting in London in 1888. Spurned by a lover,
he had shot himself in the face in an attempted suicide as a young man
and was deaf and facially paralyzed as a result. He was caught in
August 1897 and guillotined, aged twenty-nine.

Other examples that Krafft-Ebing cites have echoes of Robert
Mann. Vacher's signature was very similar, with strangulation and
throat-cutting as the MO. Vincenz Verzemi, another serial killer,
carried pieces of clothing and intestines away from his victims 'because

it gave him great pleasure to smell and touch them'.[2] The Italian also described to his doctors how he felt during the killing, which fits the phases psychiatrists understand today – '...while committing his deeds he saw nothing around him (apparently as a result of intense sexual excitement, annihilation of perception/instinctive action)'. After such acts he was always very happy. 'I am not crazy, but in the moment of strangling my victims I saw nothing else.'

Even more instructive in the case of Robert Mann was a 'certain Gruyo'. He had led a blameless life until he was forty-one when he began strangling middle-aged prostitutes. He killed six, setting about 'his horrible deeds with such care' that he remained undetected for ten years. He strangled his victims and tore out intestines and kidneys.

The farmhand, simply called 'E' by Krafft-Ebing, was a child-killer who began having convulsions from the age of five. He had no memories of these convulsions or of committing his crimes and could not explain why he had done what he did. An unnamed former soldier in the Algerian army killed a middle-aged prostitute – 'The abdomen was ripped open, pieces of intestines were cut out, so was one of the ovaries – other parts were strewn around about the corpse.' The MO was strangulation.

It must be said that Krafft-Ebing's work, like Havelock Ellis's, is a strange mixture of accurate, even modern, psychiatric awareness and almost medieval mumbo-jumbo. Krafft-Ebing is still looking at shapes of heads in sexual offenders and implies that masturbation is the first step on the road to lustmurder (clearly something that senior Scotland Yard men believed too). Did any of his ideas permeate through to the police on the streets of Whitechapel? Probably not, but in September 1913, in response to a query from the journalist George Sims, ex-Detective Inspector John Littlechild of Special Branch said of Dr Tumblety 'Although a "Sycopathia Sexualis" subject he was not known as a "Sadist" (which the murderer undoubtedly was)' and this corresponds to many of Krafft-Ebing's cases which cover crimes of exhibitionism, bestiality and homosexuality, but not violence or murder.

As psychiatry developed as a science and as the serial killer became more common, there were further opportunities to study the behaviour of such people. Fritz Haarmann and Peter Kurtin, the monsters of Weimar Germany, were perhaps the most notorious, and in England, John Christie and Gordon Cummings in the war and post-war years were classic examples. But there was one early attempt at what today we call profiling and that was on the Whitechapel murderer himself in the report by Dr Thomas Bond. Although he only actually witnessed one post mortem (Kelly) he nevertheless had access to all the medical reports and under the aegis of Robert Anderson would have been able to talk personally to Phillips and the other doctors concerned. How right was he in the case of Robert Mann?

'The murderer must have been a man of physical strength.' Mann was the son of a silk weaver and may have been brought up even as a small child to use the loom, which required very strong wrists. A dock labourer at various stages in his life, he would have been hauling weights on and off ships and as a mortuary attendant would have been lifting literally dead weights on and off mortuary slabs and in and out of coffins as a matter of routine.

'...and of great coolness and daring.' Undoubtedly; look back over the events of the killings and note how close he was to being caught on every occasion, except perhaps Mary Kelly.

'There is no evidence that he had an accomplice.' Except in very unusual circumstances, serial killers work alone. That fact by itself should have stopped such fanciful 'highest in the land' type stories in their tracks.

'He must in my opinion be a man subject to periodical attacks of homicidal and erotic mania. The character of the mutilations indicate that the man may be in a condition sexually that may be called satyriasis.' This is the male equivalent of nymphomania and we now know that serial sexual murder motivation is more complex than that. Bond is right about the periodical, almost cyclical nature of the compulsion, however. He rejected religious mania as a motive, although the Press of the day did not. The Yorkshire Ripper, Peter Sutcliffe, a century after Jack, saw himself as 'the street cleaner', prompted by God to rid the world of prostitutes.

'The murderer in external appearance is quite likely to be a quiet, inoffensive-looking man, probably middle-aged and neatly and respectably dressed.' Robert Mann was fifty-three and wore the 'shabby-genteel' suit of a pauper inmate.

'I think he must be in the habit of wearing a cloak or overcoat or he could hardly have escaped notice in the streets if blood on his hands or clothes were visible.' In this, Bond has obviously not taken into account the fact that Mann understood enough about arteries and blood-flow to avoid saturation in blood. He almost certainly wore an overcoat, at least in the autumn because of the weather, but ironically Bond's suggestion of a cloak has opened the door to the red herring of the gentleman-killer.

'...he would probably be solitary and eccentric in his habits.' Robert Mann, by definition, worked alone. He did have James Hatfield as his assistant in the mortuary, but we know from the historical record that he just as often worked by himself. His 'eccentricity' may be measured by Coroner Baxter's view of him, as being unreliable with a bad memory and not fit to be in charge of such important matters as murder victims.

'... also he is most likely to be a man without regular occupation, but with some small income or pension.' As a workhouse inmate, until 1872, he would have been an 'in-and-out' man, seeking work in the docks and elsewhere. After that his only work would have been picking oakum, winding wool or, from an unknown date, tending the dead in the Eagle Place mortuary. In that capacity, his 'small income' may have been derived from distraught relatives and friends of the deceased (not to mention police photographers) who may have given him tips.

'He is possibly living among respectable persons who have some knowledge of his character and habits and who may have grounds for suspicion that he is not quite right in his mind at times.' Certainly, Robert Mann's fits would have been recognized and I will discuss those later, but equally, the withdrawal association with both the aura and the depression phases of the serial killer would fit this pattern. No one would doubt that the staff at the Whitechapel Infirmary would be 'respectable persons', but I doubt that many Victorians would have included pauper inmates in the same category.

Fast-forward to 1988, the centenary of the Ripper. In that year, Special Agent John E Douglas, of the Behavioral Science Unit of the FBI, based at Quantico, Virginia, was asked to provide a profile of Jack for a television programme. How well does this fit Robert Mann?

'An asocial loner.' Because we know so little about Mann, it is impossible to be accurate on this. Only two other men from the East End had been in the Whitechapel Infirmary as long as he had, but that does not make them all friends. James Hatfield referred to Mann as 'my mate', but that probably meant work-partner in the mortuary rather than any term of endearment.

'Employment in positions where he could work alone and experience vicariously his destructive fantasies, perhaps as a butcher or hospital or mortuary attendant.' Bingo! Mann must have spent hours alone with corpses, including victims of street violence and especially his own targets.

'Dress neat and orderly.' As we have discussed, this fits the garb of the workhouse.

'Sexual relationships mostly with prostitutes.' This is a grey area for Mann. His life in the workhouse was by definition celibate; Whitechapel, along with most others, had segregated wards. He was born in an area infested with prostitutes and there is every possibility when he was out working in the docks that he used their services.

'May have contracted venereal disease.' Once again, we simply do not know. All forms of sexually transmitted diseases were common-place among the low life of the East End and several of the silly theories on the Ripper's identity turn on it. Of the actual victims, only Liz Stride was mentioned as having treatment for it, but Mary Kelly's stay in a Cardiff infirmary may have been linked with the disease.

'Aged in his late twenties.' This is the most difficult aspect to come to terms with. We know that Mann was fifty-three in the autumn of 1888 but we do not know of earlier attacks. Serial killers do not suddenly commit murder as part of a mid-life crisis, but Douglas, like all behaviourists today, bases his findings on twentieth/twenty-first century killings. So American profilers will say that most serial killers are white and many are addicted to pornography. Neither of these has any relevance for 1888 when the coloured community in London was tiny and pornography was impossibly expensive for the ordinary man. It may of course be that Robert Mann *did* have a history of violence before the Autumn of Terror but the record has not yet thrown this up. Experts have estimated that in the Victorian period, large numbers of crimes, especially of a sexual nature, went unreported and only 8%

ended in a conviction in court. In 2006, Stephen Wright, the Suffolk strangler, killed five prostitutes in and around Ipswich at the age of forty-six.

'Employed since the murders were mostly at weekends.' For the 'canonical five' this is true, but neither Martha Tabram (Thursday) nor Alice McKenzie (Wednesday) fit this pattern. It has led Ripperologists to speculate on visiting sailors whose ships were in port, but it may simply be that a more lax gatekeeper on duty gave Mann access to the mortuary key and so his murder weapon.

'Free from family accountability and so unlikely to have been married.' Ironically, Mann did live with a family of sorts in the workhouse, but since I believe he had no genuine friends and could explain his nocturnal wanderings, this was irrelevant. Workhouse records, however, show that he was unmarried.

'Not surgically skilled.' Douglas has gone along with Dr Bond's opinion, but most doctors, especially the police surgeon Phillips, disagreed. In my view, Mann showed a considerable degree of anatomical knowledge (which may not be the same thing as surgical skill) and this is evident in all the killings. He cut throats so that his victims could not cry out. He cut away from his own body, so that he was not bloodstained. He removed two uteri, a kidney and a heart, all except the heart done at speed and in very poor light. How can *anyone* doubt that the Ripper did possess some surgical ability?

'Probably in some form of trouble with the police before the first murder.' Again, this is unknown. Ironically, he was in trouble with the police *after* the murder of Polly Nichols because of washing her body when told not to.

'Lived or worked in the Whitechapel area and his first homicide would have been close to his home or place of work.' This goes to the very heart of this book; Robert Mann's workhouse home and even more his mortuary lair were only three minutes' walk away from Buck's Row where Polly Nichols died, five from the murder site at 29 Hanbury Street and so on.

'Undoubtedly the police would have interviewed him.' Of course, they did; not as a suspect, but as a mortuary attendant and it was not so much an interview as a general conversation.

In 2000, John Douglas stood by his earlier analysis and in *The Cases*

That Haunt Us elaborated further. He analyzed the canonical five murders one by one, drawing valuable clues from each one. The attack on Polly Nichols was of the 'blitz attack' type, suggesting a killer who was unsure of himself and 'has no confidence in his ability to control her or get her where he wants her through any kind of verbal means – an inadequate personality'. Mann was no suave Ted Bundy, and he failed to get Polly *exactly* where he wanted her, in the tight-space confines of Brown's Stable Yard. Douglas sees the abdominal mutilations, the signature, as symptoms of a frenzy of anger and a release of sexual tension. The deep cuts to the throat, perhaps suggesting an attempt at decapitation, imply true dementia.

The attack on Annie Chapman was carried out, says Douglas, by a 'fairly unsophisticated offender... a combination of a violent and sexually immature and inadequate personality'. Let us not read 'sexually immature' to mean a very young man. It may be that because of his long years in the workhouse, Mann's sexual experience was virtually nil.

Interestingly, Douglas refers to Chapman's wounds as showing 'a perverse anatomical curiosity'. The removal of her uterus is explained by Douglas as being done by 'someone who hates women and probably fears them [remember that when the nurses arrived to wash Annie's body, Mann left the mortuary]. By removing the victim's internal sexual organs, he is, in effect, attempting to neuter her, to take away that which he finds sexually threatening.'[3] Laurence Alison is describing the killer Robert Napper, but the comparison with Mann is compelling – '...and finally, choosing to interact with other human beings by tearing them apart, exploring their body cavities and reducing them to nothing more than meat'.[4]

Douglas agrees with most people that the 'double event' was the work of the same man (others believe that because Liz Stride was not mutilated, she was killed by someone else, perhaps even pointing to a 'domestic' involving her partner, Michael Kidney). Then, unaccountably, Douglas claims that Stride was killed with a short-bladed knife and that leads him into all sorts of 'linkage' difficulties. Was Jack carrying two knives? Were there two lustmurderers on the streets of London that night? There is, in fact, nothing in the Stride inquest or medical reports to suggest a shorter blade and if the cuts seem shorter, we must remember that the killer was interrupted by Louis Diemschutz.

In his overview profile of 2000, Douglas has changed his mind about the killer's medical skill. He now says 'indicated some anatomical knowledge or curiosity' which of course fits Robert Mann very well. The Whitechapel murderer was a disorganized killer, leaving his victims displayed with no attempt to hide them. I would claim that he is actually a mix of disorganized and organized, in that he took the murder weapon with him and returned it after use, ready, as it were, for next time. Interestingly, Douglas clings to the white male killer because there are no recorded cases of females killing in this way and because all the victims are white. This is typical intraracial killing and explains why Anderson et al were wrong when they thought that a Jew was responsible; none of the seven victims was Jewish. Douglas opts for the likely age of the killer as being between twenty-eight and thirty-six, but admits that 'age is a difficult characteristic to categorize... we would not eliminate a viable suspect exclusively because of age'.[5]

Douglas expected the Whitechapel murderer to come from an unstable family with an absent father or domineering mother. By the time Robert Napper hit his teens his 'attitude towards his parents would have brimmed with unbridled hatred and he would have developed a loathing of siblings, peers and the world in general'.[6] The census of 1841 shows the Mann family living in Hope Street, Whitechapel, on the edge of the focus of Jack's activities, as outlined by geo-profiler Spencer Chainey. The area would have been exactly within Robert Mann's 'mental map', a comfort zone he had known from early childhood. His father, also Robert, is listed as a silk weaver, aged fifty and his mother Elizabeth is forty-six. Robert junior is five and his sister Amelia is seven. Given the relatively advanced ages of Robert senior and Elizabeth, it is likely that Robert and Amelia were the youngest of a larger family, the older siblings having moved away. Elizabeth would have been forty-one when her son was born, but in an age of no effective contraception, late births were inevitable. Robert senior died in the summer of 1847. His death certificate gives no occupation, but he died in the newly-extended workhouse in Baker's Row, on 17 July. Henry Chapman was the registrar and the informant was Ann Meek, present at the death. It is likely that she was a workhouse nurse, and was illiterate in that she made her mark on the certificate. The cause of death was common enough in the disease-ridden 'hungry forties' – typhus fever.

The hungry forties in fact explains the collapse of the Mann family and it was all too common a story. From independent weaver in 1841 to death in the workhouse six years later is a reminder of how tough it was to make a living in competition with the factories and in a time of recession. Assuming that Mann senior had always been a silk weaver, he would have known the good times of the mid 1820s when there were thousands of weavers in the East End, but it would all have been downhill economically after that.

By 1851, Robert Mann, aged fifteen, is listed in the Whitechapel Workhouse records, but there is no mention of his mother or sister. This would have been his last year in the boys' ward – afterwards he would have mixed with the adult males, 'the broken workmen, the drunkards and dissolute, the inadequate and handicapped, the crippled and retarded'.[7] What had happened? There is no record of the deaths of Elizabeth or Amelia Mann so both must have left the workhouse by then. The most likely explanation is that Elizabeth remarried or at least found a new partner between 1847 and 1851. The workhouse was full of widows whose status in life had suddenly plummeted with the loss of a breadwinning husband and the way to avoid the hated 'Bastille' was to find another. But why leave Robert behind? Perhaps Elizabeth was ashamed of the fits her son had by now experienced or was unable to cope. Perhaps it was the choice of her new husband. Either way, it speaks volumes for motivation. Elizabeth Mann had found a new lover after Robert's father's death and had abandoned the boy to a sort of Hell-on-Earth. As Laurence Alison says, 'Research has shown that neglect and isolation are powerful disinhibitors to violence.' Once released, caged animals will often attack others because the 'normal prohibitions against aggression' are missing.

All Mann's victims, except Mary Kelly, were middle-aged and serial killers often fantasize about murdering their mothers. Some of them actually do it; others carry out their revenge killing on total strangers. Again, the comparisons with Robert Napper are staggering – 'From [Napper's] perspective [his mother] was a hypocrite and his dad was just a bastard who abandoned them.'[8]

In looking at pre- and post-offence behaviour, Douglas notes that the killer would have returned to an area 'where he could wash his hands of blood and remove his clothing'. This, of course, was the mortuary. He did not need to visit grave sites as many killers do because, in the case of four of his victims, he had the bodies all to himself for days before burial and in the case of Chapman, Eddowes and Kelly, had their body parts in his mortuary.

In my experience, profilers are as human as the rest of us. In 2000, John E Douglas plumped for David Cohen (Martin Fido's suspect) as plausible because it was presented, very ably by Fido, on a plate.[9] As we have seen, David Canter has done the same thing with James Maybrick.

What, then, is the case against Robert Mann? David Canter tells of a script he once offered to a film company in which the offender was as banal as his motive. It was turned down because, said the company, 'the audience would feel cheated by such a denouement. They would want to learn that it was all even more complicated than they could have imagined, not less so'.[10] And so it is with Jack. This does an appalling disservice to the truth. Murder is very rarely exotic and conspiratorial; the only thing that is bizarre about serial killers is the crimes they commit. Everything else *is* ordinary.

Who could be more ordinary than Robert Mann? Born to an impoverished weaving family in an area of impoverished weavers, he was left in the workhouse when his father died. Similar things happened to thousands of others. He would have been brought up in a harsh environment in a system that was deliberately designed to be ghastly. The Salvation Army Shelter for Women in Hanbury Street (one of the kinder institutions of its day) had rows of hard wooden beds, looking like coffins, and the 'uplifting' legend painted on the wall, 'Are you ready to die?' 'A child brought up in an institution,' warned 'General' William Booth of the Salvation Army, 'is too often only half-human.' When not in the workhouse picking oakum so that his hands bled, he would be out on the streets hours before dawn, waiting for a ship to arrive in the docks. Routinely, of 500 men at the dock gates, only twenty were taken on to work; the others shuffled away to find what 'tommy' they could by whatever means. They joined similar queues for the casual ward, the Spike, and those who failed here too, carried the banner in doorways and alleyways and Itchy Park. But this was the lot of thousands of the poor in nineteenth-century London and only one of them became Jack the Ripper. It would be fascinating to be able to note that the boy Robert Mann was abused, physically or even sexually by his mother; that she was a vicious drunk; that he exhibited signs commonly found in future serial killers, called the triad – bed-wetting, fire-starting and the torture of animals. The fact is that I cannot. The very reason that Mann was never caught is that we know so very little about him.

What we do know is that he lived and died in Whitechapel. And Robert Mann's death certificate contains a quiet bombshell. He died on 2 January 1896, in the Infirmary at Baker's Row, his home for years. The informant was the Assistant Medical Officer, A Strange and the Registrar, J E Brown. The cause of death as certified by S Moses LRCP was phthisis with chronic Bright's disease and bronchitis as secondaries. The bombshell lies in the occupation column which reads general labourer and gives a former address as 48 Wentworth Street.

By the time of Mann's death, there was no such number, the house having been demolished, but that indefatigable Ripper researcher John Bennett told me exactly what it was. 48 Wentworth Street was a doss-house, first opened in 1851. Between 6 April 1870 and 20 October 1888 (when it probably closed) it was owned by William Francis of Rochester Row, Westminster. It had three floors and was registered to hold twenty-five lodgers.

As Arthur Morrison wrote in 1889, Wentworth Street was:

> black and noisome, the road sticky with slime and palsied houses, rotten from chimney to cellar, leaning together, apparently by the mere coherence of their ingrained corruption. Dark, silent, uneasy shadows passing and crossing – human vermin in this reeking sink, like goblin exhalations... women with sunken, black-rimmed eyes, whose pallid faces appear and vanish by the light of an occasional gaslamp and look so like ill-covered skulls that we start at their stare. Horrible London? Yes.[11]

Look again at Spencer Chainey's geoprofile. Wentworth Street lies

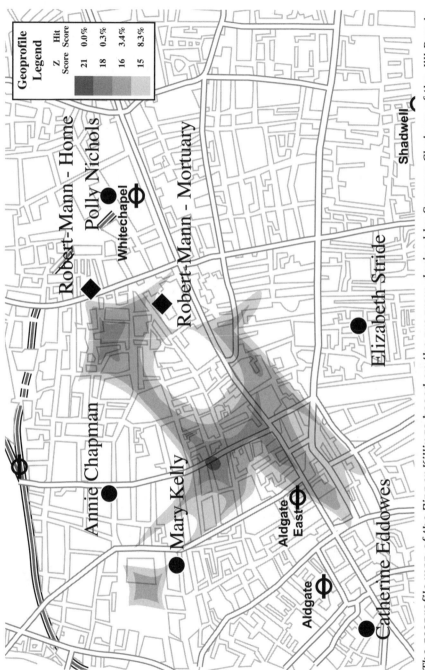

The geoprofile map of the Ripper Killings based on the program devised by Spencer Chainey of the Jill Dando Institute. The shaded area in the centre marks the pattern of Ripper murders, focusing on Wentworth Street, for some time the home of Robert Mann.

exactly in the epicentre of Jack's hunting ground, that tangle of the most wicked streets of the East End. Robert Mann knew those dingy courts like the back of his hand and he killed within the classic 'circle' pattern which today's geographical profilers recognize. The pattern of his kills is very telling, pointing to the lair that was so important to him – not who he killed, but where he killed was vital. Martha Tabram died on a landing on stairs in George Yard Buildings, an area perhaps four feet square. Polly Nichols was slaughtered on the pavement in Buck's Row, but her killer was trying to force her into the confined space of Brown's Stable Yard. Annie Chapman met her grisly end in the small yard behind No 29 Hanbury Street. Liz Stride's throat was slashed in the narrow entrance to Dutfield's Yard, just wide enough to allow a pony and trap through. Kate Eddowes was butchered in the darkest corner of claustrophobic Mitre Square. Mary Kelly's body was eviscerated in the room in Miller's Court that measured twelve feet by twelve. Alice McKenzie died in the narrow confines of Castle Alley, between two coster carts. Why? Of course the killer wanted somewhere private where he would not be disturbed, but much more than that, Robert Mann was trying to recreate his mortuary, that confined space in which he spent time alone with the dead.

It was here that he obtained his murder weapon, the sharp knife which various doctors described at inquests. Here he obtained the preservative for Annie Chapman's and Kate Eddowes' wombs, for Kate Eddowes' kidney and for Mary Kelly's heart. Here, he wallowed in his macabre fascination with the dead and was able to indulge whatever bizarre fantasies filled his mind. American serial killer Jeffrey Dahmer had a similar compulsion:

> 'He needed to enshrine his fascination with bodies,' writes David Canter, 'especially dead bodies and brought his victims into his apartment for the early stages of that ritualistic creation. He was planning to build a reliquary that would display the various reminders of his deadly sexual conquests. When asked what the purpose of this display was, he replied that it was "a place where I could feel at home".'

For Robert Mann, this was the function of the mortuary. And here, watching at doctors' elbows, he learned the rudiments of anatomy which litter his kills.

I cannot stress too much the importance of this building for Robert Mann. With the help of John Bennett's researches, I was able to stand on the site of the mortuary. It is very ordinary, like the man who worked there, merely a narrow alleyway between the gardens of modern houses on a small estate to the south of Old Montague Street. When serial killer Fred West was eventually arrested for murder, he was mortified to learn that the police had taken his house (lair and murder site) apart brick by brick. 'The foundations of his world had literally and symbolically been dug up,' writes David Canter. 'The web he had created had been destroyed.'[12]

I do not know when the mortuary was demolished. One account suggests the late 1880s, which had to be very soon after the murder of 'Clay Pipe' Alice. But we know from the events of Francis Coles' murder that it was still in use in February 1891. John Bennett believes it was not closed until 1894 or 1895 when the Davenant School was built close by.[13] This is crucial to Mann; the loss of this building and the privacy it afforded him, away from the bustle of the Infirmary, was devastating and explains as much as his physical illness why he was unable to continue his murderous work.

There is no doubt that Robert Mann was a huge risk-taker, the mark of a psychopath. He killed in the open, sometimes in near-daylight, always near to habitation. He walked past scores of people on the way to murder, his knife in his pocket. He walked back past them too, with blood on the blade and sometimes body parts in his pocket. Such was the unpredictability of his job as mortuary keeper that no one found his nocturnal wanderings unusual or worthy of question, but he could have been stopped at any moment.

One question remains unanswered. The coroner, Wynne Baxter, told the jury to disregard Mann's testimony, because he was subject to fits. We have no idea what sort of fits these were of course. If they were epileptic, of the minor type called petit mal, this *could* be a reference to a serial killer's aura phase, during which he would have seemed distant, not really aware of events around him. If more severe, of the grand mal type, then this is likely to be temporal lobe epilepsy. Only 10% of epileptics suffer from this type, but 79% of serial killers do. It is linked to a wide range of antisocial behaviours which includes anger, paranoia and regression.

'How could he have killed so many people without it being noticed?' David Canter asks, rhetorically, of the serial killer Fred West. 'This poorly educated, intellectually dull man...' We could ask the same of Robert Mann. 'People thought he was harmless,' Canter goes on, 'because he lacked fluency and was inarticulate.' And that was precisely the mistake Wynne Baxter made when he dismissed Mann as unreliable. He became, in that one sentence, a dribbling, senile village idiot as far as the Press of the day were concerned and the line has been followed by every writer on the Ripper ever since. In the graphic novel *From Hell* which has acquired iconic status, he is portrayed as ancient and actually has a falling-down fit in the mortuary in the presence of doctors and policemen.

David Canter is probably asking a lot when he says 'if only the original investigators had taken more notice of the geographical pattern of the crimes they might have got close to the culprit'. Serial killers were then called 'habitual murderers' if any such title was given to them. And they were so rare that no one in Britain at the time had any experience of them. But the facts speak for themselves. Not everything about Robert Mann fits the pattern we now expect of serial killers. We cannot tick all the boxes simply because we do not know enough about him. It may be that he fits our pattern of disturbed behaviour exactly, but the historical paper trail is simply not there. That is because of the social class from which he came and the social system into which he fitted. When I was researching this book, looking for the mortuary in Old Montague Street, I found a newly-painted phrase on a wall every bit as tantalizing as the Goulston Street graffito. It read 'Hitherto Pauper' which of course describes Robert Mann. Before this book he was just one of thousands; now he is the Whitechapel murderer.

Do I believe that Robert Mann was guilty? Yes, I do. Can I prove it? No – that was the job of the men of 1888 and they failed. There were all sorts of understandable reasons why they did, but the bottom line is that they let him get away with murder. Foremost among those reasons is the very ordinariness of Robert Mann, pauper inmate and mortuary keeper; and, just for a few weeks, Jack the Ripper.

Notes

Chapter 1

1. MEPO Docket No. 244.
2. Quoted in Marriner, Brian, *A Century of Sex Killers*, London, True Crime Library, 1992, p. 100.
3. Slaughterman – the East End was full of them.
4. A typical Victorian euphemism for menstruating.
5. Quoted in J W Robertson Scott, *The Life and Death of a Newspaper*, London, 1952, p. 40.
6. The older City Force patrolled the one square mile of the medieval City of London. The Metropolitan police, formed in 1829 by Robert Peel, then Home Secretary, was responsible for the much larger sprawl of expanding London.
7. Most Ripper experts today claim that locals were very willing to co-operate with the police. My contention is that 90% of Whitechapel's residents were recently arrived Eastern European Jews, with vivid memories of pogroms carried out on them by men in uniform paid by the government. I am not so sure that this group would be as helpful as all that.
8. And the Victorian Press were not unique in this. In the *Daily Mail* of 3 November 1952, a headline article on the shooting of PC Sidney Miles which would develop into the Craig and Bentley case contained twenty-five major errors.
9. R Anderson, *The Lighter Side of My Official Life*, London, 1910.
10. An anonymous booklet with a similar title – *Hvem Ar Jack Uppskararen?* was published in Sweden as early as 1889.
11. Eddlestone, John T, *Jack the Ripper, An encyclopaedia*, London, Metro, 2002, p. 237.
12. Quoted in Begg, Fido and Skinner, *The Jack the Ripper A-Z*, London, Headline, 1991.
13. Kraus also played the better-known hero in *The Cabinet of Dr Caligari*.

14. Sugden, Philip, *The Complete History of Jack the Ripper*, London, Robinson, 1994.
15. Quoted in Meikle, p. 137.

Chapter 2

1. *The Crimes of Jack the Ripper*, London, Capella Arcturus, 2007.
2. *Washington Post*, quoted in David Canter, *Mapping Murder*, London, Virgin, 2007.
3. Laurence Alison and Marie Eyre, *Killer in the Shadows*, London, Pennant Books, 2009,, p. 40.
4. David Canter, *Mapping Murder*, London, Virgin, 2007.
5. Laurence Alison and Marie Eyre, *Killer in the Shadows*, London, Pennant Books, 2009, p. 227.
6. Matters, p. 86.
7. *East London Observer*, July 1888.
8. R Holden, *A Facet Theory Approach to Homicide Crime Scene Analysis*, 1994 – unpublished M Phil dissertation, University of Surrey.
9. Canter, p. 291.
10. Canter, p. 179.

Chapter 3

1. As we have noted elsewhere, the police were not popular in the East End long before the Autumn of Terror. Arrests of locals often led to street fights and full scale riots.

Chapter 4

1. *ed.* Rosemary Herbert, *The Oxford Companion to Crime and Mystery Writing*.
2. Philip Sugden, *The Complete History of Jack the Ripper*, London, Robinson, 1995.
3. London, Metro, 2002.

Chapter 5

1. *An Account of Several Workhouses*, 1732.
2. Oakum was hemp fibre plucked by hand from rope and used to seal wooden-hulled ships and boats. Similar work was carried out in prisons and the oakum cut inmates' hands to pieces.
3. Some £8 million a year.

4. And was 'the fortress', home to the Kray brothers in the 1960s.
5. Jack London, *The People of the Abyss*, London, Thomas Nelson & Sons, 1903, p. 114–5.
6. John Law (Margaret Harkness), *Captain Lobe*, London, 1889.
7. Harold Schechter and David Everitt, *The A to Z Encyclopaedia of Serial Killers*, New York, Pocket Books (Simon and Schuster), 1996, p. 284.
8. Quoted in Tony Williams with Humphrey Price, *Uncle Jack*, London, Orion, 2005.
9. Joel Norris, *Serial Killers: The Growing Menace*, London, Arrow Books, 1990, p. 44.

Chapter 6

1. Joel Norris, *Serial Killers: The Growing Menace*, London, Arrow Books, 1990, p. 45.
2. Joel Norris, *Serial Killers: The Growing Menace*, London, Arrow Books, 1990, p. 55.
3. Joel Norris, *Serial Killers: The Growing Menace*, London, Arrow Books, 1990, p. 55.
4. The Stratton brothers, for armed robbery.
5. In researching for my recent book on crime during World War Two (*War Crimes*, Pen and Sword Books, 2008) I came across several examples of soldiers who covered for each other, lying about times and places as well as exchanging uniforms.

Chapter 7

1. Laurence Alison and Marie Eyre, *Killer in the Shadows*, London, Pennant Books, 2009, p. 92.
2. Quoted in Philip Sugden, *The Complete History of Jack the Ripper*, London, Robinson, 1994.
3. *The Daily Telegraph*, Tuesday 18 September 1888, p. 2.

Chapter 8

1. Inquest on September 24 1888, p. 3.
2. Joel Norris, *Serial Killers: The Growing Menace*, London, Arrow Books, 1990, p. 57–8.
3. Since the cause of his death was cirrhosis of the liver, we can assume that the drinking was a family thing!
4. Inquest on Thursday 20 September 1888.

Chapter 9

1. Spellings vary.
2. Although doctors carrying out her post mortem could find no deformity such as this.
3. According to other witnesses, the rain started about midnight.

Chapter 10

1. We only have the deputy's word for this conversation and it sounds a little too dramatic. At this stage, there was no reward available.

Chapter 11

1. Quoted in Michael Howell and Peter Ford, *The True History of the Elephant Man*, London, Penguin, 1980, p. 11.
2. Patricia Marne, *The Criminal Hand*, London, Sphere Books, 1991, p. 46–48.
3. Alison and Eyre, p. 149.
4. Melville Macnaghten, 1894.
5. Quoted in Alison and Eyre, p. 1.
6. This had been the notorious Ratcliffe Highway, the 'most dangerous street in London' and appalling mass murders had happened here in 1811.

Chapter 12

1. Some accounts say daughter.
2. Norris, Joel, *Serial Killers: the Growing Menace*, Arrow, London, 1990, p. 57.
3. Confusingly referred to as Pavilion Yard in some newspapers, as Eagle Place stood behind the Pavilion Theatre.

Chapter 13

1. Havelock Ellis, *The Criminal*, London, 1890.
2. Krafft-Ebing, *Psychopathia Sexualis* – this edition Creation Books, London, 2006.
3. John E Douglas, *The Cases That Haunt Us*, New York, Simon and Schuster, 2000, p. 32.
4. Alison and Eyre, p. 76.
5. John E Douglas, *The Cases That Haunt Us*, New York, Simon and Schuster, 2000, p. 64.

6. Alison and Eyre, p. 81.
7. Michael Howell and Peter Ford, *The True History of the Elephant Man*, London, Penguin, 1980, p. 40.
8. Alison and Eyre, p. 82.
9. Interestingly, Aaron Davis Cohen was admitted to the Whitechapel Workhouse Infirmary in December 1888, where he was examined by the medical superintendent, Dr Larder, and found to be violent and difficult to manage.
10. David Canter, p. 29.
11. Arthur G Morrison, *The Palace Journal*, London, April 1889.
12. David Canter, p. 79.
13. A photograph of the school with tennis courts in the foreground, taken about 1960, shows an external toilet block on the site of the former mortuary. Was it refurbished from the original building?

Bibliography

ALISON, Laurence & **EYRE**, Marie, *Killer in the Shadows*, London, Pennant, 2009

ANDERSON, Sir Robert, *Criminals and Crime*, London, James Nisbet, 1907

BALL, Pamela, *Jack the Ripper: A Psychic Investigation*, London, Arcturus, 1998

BEGG, Paul, *Jack the Ripper: The Facts*, London, Robson, 2004

BEGG, Paul, *Jack the Ripper: The Definitive History*, London, Pearson Education, 2005

BEGG, Paul, **FIDO**, Martin, **SKINNER**, Keith, *The Jack the Ripper A-Z*, London, Headline, 1991

BELLOC LOWNDES, Mrs, *The Lodger*, London, Readers' Library, 1927

BOOTH, William, *In Darkest England and the Way Out*, London, 1890

CANTER, David, *Mapping Murder*, London, Virgin, 2007

CLACK, Robert & **HUTCHINSON**, Philip, *The London of Jack the Ripper: Then and Now*, Derby, Breedon, 2007

CORNWELL, Patricia, *Portrait of a Killer: Jack the Ripper, Case Closed*, New York, Time Warner, 2002

CULLEN, Tom, *Autumn of Terror*, London, Fontana, 1966

DOUGLAS, John & **OLSHAKER**, Mark, *The Cases That Haunt Us*, London, Simon & Schuster, 2001

EDDLESTONE, John J, *Jack the Ripper: An Encyclopaedia*, London, Metro, 2002

EVANS, Stewart & **RUMBELOW**, Donald, *Jack the Ripper: Scotland Yard Investigates*, Stroud, Sutton, 2001

EVANS, Stewart & **SKINNER**, Keith, *Jack the Ripper: Letters From Hell*, Stroud, Sutton, 2001

FAIRCLOUGH, Melvyn, *The Ripper and the Royals*, London, Duckworth, 1991

FARSON, Daniel, *Jack the Ripper*, London, History Book Club, 1959

FIDO, Martin, *The Crimes, Detection and Death of Jack the Ripper*, London, Weidenfeld and Nicolson, 1987

HARRISON, Paul, *Jack the Ripper: The Mystery Solved*, London, Robert Hale, 1991

HARRISON, Shirley, *The Diary of Jack the Ripper*, London, Smith Gryphon, 1993

HAVELOCK ELLIS, Henry, *The Criminal*, London, Walter Scott, 1890

HOWELL, Michael & **FORD**, Peter, *The True History of the Elephant Man*, London, Penguin, 1980

JAKUBOWSKI, Maxim & **BRAUND**, Nathan, eds, *The Mammoth Book of Jack the Ripper*, London, Robinson, 1999

KEPPLE, Robert D with **BIRNES**, William J, *Signature Killers*, London, Arrow, 1998

KNIGHT, Stephen, *Jack the Ripper: The Final Solution*, London, Grafton, 1977

LEIGHTON, D J, *Ripper Suspect: The Secret Lives of Montague Druitt*, Stroud, Sutton, 2006

LINDER, Seth, **MORRIS**, Caroline & **SKINNER**, Keith, *Ripper Diary, the Inside Story*, Stroud, Sutton, 2003

LONDON, Jack, *The People of the Abyss*, London, Thomas Nelson, 1903

MACPHERSON, Euan, *The Trial of Jack the Ripper*, Edinburgh, Mainstream, 2005

MARNE, Patricia, *The Criminal Hand*, London, Sphere Books, 1991

MATTERS, Leonard, *Jack the Ripper*, London, WH Allen, 1929

McCORMICK, Donald, *The Identity of Jack the Ripper*, London, Jarrolds, 1959

MEIKLE, Dennis, *Jack the Ripper: The Murders and the Movies*, London, Reynolds and Hearne, 2002

MOORE, Alan & **CAMPBELL**, Eddie, *From Hell*, London, 2006

MOYLAN, J F, *Scotland Yard and the Metropolitan Police*, London, G P Putnam's Sons, 1929

NORRIS, Joel, *Serial Killers: The Growing Menace*, London, Arrow, 1990

ROLAND, Paul, *In the Minds of Murderers*, London, Arcturus, 2007

ROLAND, Paul, *The Crimes of Jack the Ripper*, London, Arcturus, 2007

RUMBELOW, Donald, *The Complete Jack the Ripper*, London, Penguin, 1987

SCHECHTER, Harold & **EVERITT**, David, *The A-Z Encyclopaedia of Serial Killers*, New York, Pocket Books, 1996

SUGDEN, Philip, *The Complete History of Jack the Ripper*, London, Robinson, 1994

TULLY, James, *The Secret of Prisoner 1167*, London, Robinson, 1997

VON KRAFFT-EBING, Richard, *Psychopathia Sexualis*. This edition, London, Wet Angel/Creation, 2006 (original edition Germany 1886)

WILLIAMS, Tony with **PRICE**, Humphrey, *Uncle Jack*, London, Orion, 2005

WILSON, Colin & **ODELL**, Robin, *Jack the Ripper: Summing Up and Verdict*, London, Corgi, 1988

WISE, Sarah, *The Blackest Streets: The Life And Death of a Victorian Slum*, London, Vintage, 2009

Contemporary Newspapers and Periodicals

East London Advertiser

East London Observer

Pall Mall Gazette

Police Illustrated News

Punch Vol XCV

Reynolds' News

Star

Suffolk Chronicle

Telegraph

The Times

Archives

HO 114220/221 (The National Archives, Kew)

St.B.G. (Stepney Board of Guardians) Wh/128/2 and Wh/147/4 (Metropolitan Archive, Islington)

Index